CAN YOU TELL WHAT IT IS YET?

To NED and Rozzie

ROLF HARRIS

MY AUTOBIOGRAPHY

CAN YOU TELL
WHAT IT IS YET?

from

Rolf

BANTAM PRESS

LONDON · NEW YORK · TORONTO · SYDNEY · AUCKLAND

TRANSWORLD PUBLISHERS
61–63 Uxbridge Road, London W5 5SA
a division of The Random House Group Ltd

RANDOM HOUSE AUSTRALIA (PTY) LTD
20 Alfred Street, Milsons Point, Sydney,
New South Wales 2061, Australia

RANDOM HOUSE NEW ZEALAND LTD
18 Poland Road, Glenfield, Auckland 10, New Zealand

RANDOM HOUSE SOUTH AFRICA (PTY) LTD
Endulini, 5a Jubilee Road, Parktown 2193, South Africa

Published 2001 by Bantam Press
a division of Transworld Publishers

Unless otherwise stated photographs are from the author's collection.

A catalogue record for this book is available from the British Library.
ISBN 0593 047427

Typeset in 12½/14¼ pt Ehrhardt by Falcon Oast Graphic Art Ltd

Printed in Great Britain
by Mackays of Chatham plc, Chatham, Kent

1 3 5 7 9 10 8 6 4 2

Dedicated to the memory of Marge and Crom,
my wonderful mum and dad

CONTENTS

Acknowledgements

M Y THANKS GO FIRST TO MY WONDERFUL WIFE, ALWEN, WHO has put up with me for all these years and is the rock on which everything has been built.

My thanks also to my Sydney-based brother, Bruce, who manages me worldwide (but much more of him in the text); and to my Sydney-based accountant, Tony Clune. I've known Tony for forty years. He has been and still is a marvellous friend and I only wish I'd asked for his worldwide financial advice a lot earlier. He has worked with Bruce to reorganize my finances on an upward path.

Jan Kennedy took over as my UK manager from the wonderful Billy Marsh. Working with my brother, she has been a major force in turning my career round and building it up over the last two decades. Thanks, Jan.

Pat Lake-Smith took over handling my public relations after Syd Gillingham retired. She has got to be one of the best, if not *the* best in the business.

Thanks to all the unsung backroom girls and boys who've helped me so much at every stage of my life.

And a particular thank you to Mike Rowbotham for all his hard work and his inspirational organization of the huge number of words involved in this story. He's marvellous. He speaks my language and understands how I talk and – a bit scary, this – how I think.

Chapter One

THE BOY FROM BASSENDEAN

IN THE SUMMER OF 1941, AT THE AGE OF ELEVEN, I HIT MY brother Bruce smack on the forehead with a clod of earth. It exploded on impact, covering his face in a fine powder of red dust. I could just see the whites of his eyes blinking back at me in shock.

Up until then my mate Teddy Merritt and I were getting pummelled from the trees by Bruce and his mate Cliff, who were using unripened gumnuts as ammunition. All of us were in shorts, bare feet and no shirts. Streaks of dusty perspiration looked like war paint on our chests.

I can still picture the lazy arc of that clod as it flew through the air. Everything went into slow motion. Bruce poked his head out from behind the smooth tree trunk, getting the lie of the land. At that precise moment, the clod landed like a small bomb.

Teddy let out a triumphant yell. Cliff was somewhere up in the branches. I was stunned. In my whole life I had never managed to hit anything I aimed at – not even a tin can on a fence post. Now I'd actually hit my *big brother*!

Bruce had an instant temper. His bellow of rage sent shivers up my spine. I set off running, knowing that I was going to die. It was just a matter of when and where. I figured that at least I had a head start because Bruce had to climb down the tree. That theory went straight down the drain. He took off from the branches and in mid-air his feet were already going round and round like bicycle wheels.

I scrambled up the bank on my hands and knees. Nico, our next-door neighbour, had a vineyard. I went tearing between the rows of grapevines, four feet high on either side of me. I could only go straight ahead, with death two paces behind me.

About two-thirds of the way along there was a break in the vines where Nico drove his tractor in from the road. I ducked through the break and saw the road ahead of me.

Nico had closed off the gap in the fence with wire netting. I hit the netting halfway up, scrambled upwards and rolled over the top. I heard Bruce hit the wire netting behind me. I was already running again, dodging the diesel drums and streaking down the narrow dirt track that led to our place. I wasn't game to look over my shoulder. Bruce was breathing down my neck.

I thought about going through the gate into our place, but the turn would have slowed me down. Instead I ran straight on. I did a stomach roll over the fence next door, landing on my feet. Bruce did the same, but his was an Olympic standard stomach roll and he closed the gap. We sprinted down the drive and raced round the neighbour's veranda. It must have sounded like a cavalry charge on the wooden floor. I leaped off the top of the steps and hared across their back garden, jumping rose bushes and out-pacing their old dog.

At the bottom of the garden they had a long sloping gum tree that grew parallel to the water. I went bounding up it and threw myself onto a rope that we'd tied across to a second tree back in our garden. Scrambling across the rope I hooked one leg over a branch and hauled myself upright. Turning, I saw Bruce grab the rope, ready to come across. Then for some reason he stopped. He dropped to his haunches and stared across at me. Both of us were sucking in huge gulps of air.

We looked at each other from opposing branches – a couple of yards apart.

He wiped his face with the back of his hand. The red dust had turned to mud during the chase. 'Don't you ever do that again or I'll kill ya,' he said.

'I know,' I replied meekly.

He leaned back against the trunk and closed his eyes. I waited.

After a while he climbed down and walked away. Not long after that he joined the army and was posted to Darwin during the war. It took me forty more years to really get to know him. And when I did, he turned my life around.

The house where we grew up was on the banks of a river, on the outskirts of a city, on the western edge of Australia. It was a magical place.

Dad built it himself. I can remember him sitting on top of the wooden frame, perched on a cross member, with the sun on his bare back. He needed more nails and I offered to bring them up. I put the bag of nails in my mouth and shimmied up the post like a monkey. I was three and a half years old.

From the top, I could see the Swan River. Wide, sluggish and brown, it meandered past the back garden like a giant snake searching for the sea. Nowadays, real estate like that is worth a fortune, but in the early 1930s Bassendean wasn't a very fashionable neighbourhood. Seven miles from the centre of Perth, it was a backwater caught between the bush and the big smoke.

When Mum and Dad bought the one and a quarter acre block it was covered in shoulder-high prickly bush and dotted with burrows. They bought the land on the 'never never' and were paying it off at a pound a week. Dad built the house out of second-hand materials and recycled nails. When he struck a problem, he'd pop next door to get advice from our neighbour, a retired builder.

For the first couple of years we lived in one room. The walls were overlapping weatherboard to about waist height, then fibro sheets, topped off with a red tile roof. Dad couldn't afford any lining or insulation so it was stinking hot in the summer and cold in the winter. I was never free of sniffles and sneezes in those first few years.

Like Topsy, the house just 'growed'. Dad added bits and pieces as he could afford it. One room became two and then three with an enclosed veranda. The latter (called a 'sleep-out') had fly wire screens all round, with big folding shutters, hinged at the top. These were propped up on support poles and could be lowered when it rained. I loved lying snug in bed as the rain pelted down, sending through the shutters a fine spray that settled on my nose and forehead.

The veranda was just long enough to fit two beds against the wall. These belonged to Bruce and me. We slept there all our childhood.

Our driveway was about eighty yards long. Dad planted NSW box trees down either side, interspersed with jacarandas. I was about eleven years old before those jacarandas blossomed. We had a huge fig tree up by the gate and six soft-shelled almond trees nearer the house. I used to go out with a length of bamboo and knock down the almonds, cracking open the shells with my fingers and thumb.

At the end of the drive you turned right and parked under a trellis of purple wisteria. The house was tucked neatly into a large square. The only windows were in the kitchen, overlooking Nico's vineyard and with a sideways view of the river. Dad had cut steps into the steep bank, leading down to the water's edge. He also built a small jetty using second-hand timber and off-cuts. The Swan was roughly sixty yards wide at that point. On the far side, stretching into the distance, were low-lying paddocks which flooded almost every year.

My dad, Cromwell Harris (everybody called him Crom), was a turbine driver at East Perth Power Station. For forty years he cycled to work every day on his pushbike – seven miles each way. He worked shift work – starting at either seven in the morning,

three in the afternoon or eleven at night. If his day off fell o.
Saturday, he would take us to the pictures at Bassendean.

It was a two-mile walk to the cinema, but I didn't mind. Once
there, I knew that I'd meet Johnny Weissmuller or Mickey Rooney,
or Judy Garland. And at intermission I'd get an ice cream for
threepence. Ice cream was an incredible luxury because nobody
had refrigerators in those days.

Coming home in the darkness, Dad would say, 'Here we go.'
And he'd let out a rooster crow that echoed through the night air.
Suddenly, all these poor bloody roosters would think, 'Hell's teeth,
I've slept in and I've missed it.' They would start crowing in a
chain reaction that came from every point of the compass. Bruce
and I would be in hysterics.

Dad also had a knee-jerk reaction to any loud noise. Hearing a
bang, thump or crash, he instantly went, '*Ky-yike*, *ki-yike*, ki-yike,
ki-yike . . .' like a dog who'd been shot and gone yelping off into
the distance. We laughed and laughed.

Mum convinced Dad to get dressed up one night to see a play
at His Majesty's Theatre in Perth. Dad never looked at ease in a
suit. He would iron his trousers by putting them under the
mattress and he hated ties. They went to see *Bitter Sweet*, a Noel
Coward play. At one point, this fellow says to the heroine, 'If you
won't marry me, you won't marry anybody.' He pulls a gun out
and shoots her. Bang!

Dad, from the middle of the audience, let loose, '*Ky-yike*,
ki-yike, ki-yike, ki-yike . . .' like a shot dog. Mum almost died of
embarrassment and Dad tried to hide under the seat. It stopped
the show. The heroine, lying dead on the stage, was shaking with
laughter.

My mother, Agnes Margaret Robbins as she was (everybody called
her Marge), was not a woman to be trifled with. She won gold
medals for mathematics and sport at Cardiff Girls' High School
and went on to become the first woman analytical chemist in
Wales.

Unfortunately, these talents were rather wasted in Bassendean, but she never let her frustration show. Instead she threw herself into amateur dramatics, tennis and raising a family.

It was a remarkable thing to see my mother playing tennis. She had been taught to serve underarm because it was considered the genteel thing to do when she was growing up. To raise the racket above one's head was regarded as unladylike.

She would bounce the ball and hit it underarm with such savage slice that the serve came across the net in a gigantic curve. When it hit the grass, the spin on the ball would make it dart off in the opposite direction. The damn thing was almost unplayable. It took four or five service games to work out where to put your racket. Even then, the ball would usually spin off the woodwork and go out.

Mum and Dad were childhood sweethearts. They met in 1906, at the age of ten, when Dad's family moved into a house opposite Mum's in Diana Street, Roath Park, Cardiff. Dad saved his Saturday halfpennies and bought her a small ring. I don't know if they plighted their troth, but it's a good story.

Marge was the daughter of a rent collector and lay preacher. Dad was the eldest of nine children of a struggling portrait painter called George F. Harris. George was regarded by the neighbours as being eccentric and flamboyant. He wore a brown velvet smoking jacket *in the middle of the day*, and had great pretensions to the life of a gentleman.

In reality, he barely had enough money to put food on the table. One of Dad's jobs was to visit the pawnbroker and hock his father's Freemason's cuffs and collar. Later, when George had sold a landscape or received a commission, Dad would go back and redeem the items.

George let his daughters study art but not the boys. 'Don't do what I do – you'll be permanently broke,' he told them. 'Go and learn a trade and get a steady job.'

Sadly this meant that Dad grew up as a frustrated artist. He kept a trunk full of art magazines and supplies in our living room, which was like a treasure trove that he could never truly unearth.

All families have skeletons in the closet, or stories they don't talk about. Dad would never speak of his father to me. They had a falling out and even now I have only a vague idea of what it was about. From what I can gather, when my father was about fifteen the family had moved to a small town in Wales called Sully, near Barry Island. Dad had taken a job as an apprentice in the local electrical supply company. He was left in charge one night and his brother Carl, two years younger, kept him company. As a bit of fun, probably egged on by Carl, Dad switched off the electricity to the town.

Unfortunately, the last train from Cardiff was due. In the darkness it shot straight past the station and stopped a mile down the track. In the pitch dark, people had to get off the train and stagger back up the line with their belongings. Ladies in fine dresses were ankle-deep in mud.

Of course, there was hell to pay. Next morning, the local policeman got word to the family that young Cromwell was to be arrested. My grandfather spirited Crom down to Cardiff docks and signed him up as a cabin boy on a cargo ship bound for South America.

This is where the story gets garbled. My Auntie Pixie always swore that Crom had been sexually abused by the crew on the journey. He came back from the four-month voyage absolutely hating his father and apparently never forgave him. He left for Australia on the first available boat, taking Carl with him. They spent six weeks at sea, living on bread and jam because the food was so terrible. Dad was only sixteen and Carl fourteen.

For the next two years they travelled the outback, doing all sorts of jobs from building shearing sheds to fixing bore pumps. When war broke out Dad lied about his age and said he was twenty-one. This meant he could vouch for Carl's being eighteen. They joined the Australian army and were sent to fight in Europe.

On their first English leave, the boys went straight to Cardiff to visit the rest of the family. My grandmother was horrified to see them as soldiers. She contacted the Australian military authorities and told them that Carl was under age. He was taken out of the service and had to wait until he turned eighteen before he could join up again.

Dad always felt that if they could have stayed together, the outcome might have been different. By the time Carl re-enlisted he was put into a different battalion. Unbeknown to each other, he and Dad were both sent to France and were wounded in the same battle.

A piece of shrapnel blew a two-inch-wide hole through Dad's helmet. Luckily, like most of the men, he wore the strap at the back of his neck and not beneath his chin, otherwise it would have taken his head off. Even so, a big piece of his skull had disappeared. Covered in blood, he was carted away to a military hospital. All his mates thought he was a goner.

The first thing he did when he regained consciousness was to ask after Carl. The doctors didn't know anything about his brother. Only afterwards did he discover that Carl had died in that very hospital earlier the same day.

For years afterwards Dad's helmet hung on the wall in our house in Bassendean – the two-inch hole flowering through the metal like some obscene spiky-petalled blossom. It was a reminder of Carl and of how appalling it had been in the trenches. Dad came away with a total horror of war and of violence of any sort. He would turn and walk away from any fight or argument.

Dad had met up with Marge Robbins on his first home leave in Cardiff. After the war their romance blossomed again. They wrote to each other when he went back to Australia and she'd taken a job in America as an analytical chemist. The rest of Dad's family migrated to Western Australia to join him there, but they found Perth to be too pedestrian and soon moved on to Sydney, a far more cosmopolitan city.

Three years after the war ended, Marge Robbins sailed to Australia and she and Dad were married. They set up home in Perth where Bruce was born in 1924 and I came along in March

1930. Mum chose short single names. She had grown to hate the long form of her own name when she had to write it on every page of every exam paper at school.

She chose 'Rolf' because she'd been reading *Robbery Under Arms* – a classic Australian novel by Rolf Boldrewood. If she'd known it was a pseudonym for Thomas Alexander Browne maybe she'd have called me Tom.

I must have been a real handful growing up, with permanently grazed knees, a sunburnt nose and boundless energy. It didn't dawn on me that we weren't rich, or poor. We just seemed to be the same as everyone else. At Christmas my stocking was full of stuff that Mum and Dad had collected over the year. I remember getting lots of coloured corks and burnt matchsticks one year. I used them to make little animals and figures by sharpening the matches at one end and sticking them into the corks to make legs and arms.

Bruce and I pulled the same trick on Dad every year. We'd get old carrots, potatoes and parsnips and wrap them very carefully using whatever paper we could find, usually newspaper. On Christmas morning, we'd give them to Dad and gather round him as he opened them up.

'Oh, it's just what I've always wanted,' he'd say, holding up a mouldy carrot. 'Isn't it marvellous.'

We loved playing tricks on Dad. If we had boiled eggs, we'd eat them quickly and then turn them upside down in the eggcup.

'Hey, Dad, there's another egg for you.'

'For me? Isn't that marvellous,' he'd say, putting on his actor's voice.

Then he'd knock the egg open and be absolutely astounded to find nothing inside. Bruce and I laughed every time and Dad never tired of playing along.

For Christmas dinner Mum would always make a pudding full of threepenny bits, sixpences and the odd shilling. She gave us all a helping, smothered in custard. Every year Dad would stumble to his feet, clutch his mouth and throw open the door as he ran out. We could hear him coughing and spluttering. He'd come back with his hands full of sixpences and shillings. Our eyes would open wide. Gosh, we were gonna be rich. We'd dig in and have another helping straight away.

When I was three and a half years old, I came home from kindergarten and found no one at the house. Mum had missed the bus from Perth where she was rehearsing a play.

I ran down to the river and out onto the jetty. You can guess what happened next. Reaching down to feel the water with my fingers, I tumbled in, fully clothed, and disappeared beneath the murky brown water. I knew just enough to hold my breath and bobbed back up to the surface. Then I dog-paddled to the ladder the way I had seen Bruce do it.

As I walked up to the house, soaking wet, I met Mum coming home from the later bus. She nearly died of fright. Apparently, she and Dad had a terrible row that night. He was furious that she hadn't been home to meet me. The next day Mum took me to the Education Department's holiday swimming classes at Crawley Baths. I was the youngest student they had ever had.

I started at Bassendean Primary School the following year. On my first day I cried before I reached the gates. I knew that you had to be at school before the bell went. Bruce had told me so. Unfortunately, Mum didn't seem to get the message. We were half a mile from the school gates and it was five minutes to nine.

'We gotta hurry. Come on,' I said, dragging at her hand.

'Just calm down. You're being enrolled today. It doesn't matter what time we get there.'

'No. Please, hurry,' I begged.

The bell rang and I burst into tears. I didn't want to get into trouble on my first day.

When I was finally enrolled, I sat on a long wooden bench next to a little girl called Betty Allen. She wanted to go to the lavatory but didn't know the protocol. Finally, she couldn't hold on any longer. A warm explosion of urine came running along the bench and soaked into my trousers. Betty burst into tears and I fell in love with her instantly.

Forty-five years later, sitting in an open-topped car in a cavalcade through the streets of Perth, I looked down to see a beautiful woman waving madly from the crowd.

'Do you remember me?' she called out.

'Betty Allen!'

Maybe it was a dose of sunstroke on a blazing hot day, but she still managed to make me feel dizzy.

Another kid in my class was Ray Noel. During playtime that first day, he pointed down at the dirt and said in a very excited voice, 'Look at the spider!'

'Where?'

'There.'

'I can't see anything.'

'There.'

I knelt down to get a closer look. He grabbed the back of my head and pushed my face into the dirt, grinding it down.

I looked up at him in stunned amazement. He acted as though nothing had happened. Then he pointed back to the same spot and said in the same excited voice, 'Look at the spider!'

I thought I must have missed it and looked down again.

Bang! My head slammed into the dirt.

At the risk of sounding like a complete idiot, I endured this six times before I decided that maybe there wasn't a spider there after all.

Ever since then, I've loathed all forms of 'humour' derived from 'con' tricks and making people look stupid or foolish. The most viciously unpleasant programmes on television, in my opinion, are those like *Candid Camera* or *Beadle's About* which play practical jokes on people, or make them look like idiots.

Bruce and I were forever fighting as kids. I guess he'd been the centre of attention for six years and then suddenly I came along and hogged the limelight. I was always showing off and looking for praise.

Bruce was very conscious about the clothes he wore and the way he parted his hair. He liked nice things and wanted to be seen as 'smart'. By comparison, I was loud, messy and embarrassing. I didn't care about my appearance, or whether I acted like a clown.

Having a little brother like me must have really cramped Bruce's style. He used to complain to Dad that I hung around him like a bad smell. I'd eavesdrop on him telling dirty jokes to his mates and then go and repeat them to Dad, getting the punchlines all wrong. Dad told Bruce that he had to be more careful about what he said in my hearing.

'Is he kidding?' Bruce told his mates, 'That pest of a kid has ears like radio antennae. He can pick up the spoken word at a hundred paces.'

Mum was forever trying to get us to speak correctly, with rounded vowels. 'How, now, brown cow,' we'd say, trying to lose the Aussie drawl.

When her father was turning seventy-five in Wales, she arranged to cut a special record to send to him. She wanted Bruce and me to each say a little poem. When it was my turn, I complained, 'I don't want to read it off the paper.' The words came out in the broadest Aussie drawl and of course couldn't be edited out. Mum was horrified.

It wasn't that she was a snob. Quite the opposite. But she knew how the world worked and what barriers were used to divide people.

Mum wasn't a social climber, or house-proud. That's one of the reasons kids loved coming to our place. Nobody cared if they walked into the house with wet feet, or went swimming in the nude. Every new kid was someone new for me to impress. I'd give them a guided tour of the house and then show them the river.

'Sling all your clothes off,' I'd say.

'What?'

'Yeah. Here's a towel. Wrap it round yourself. We're going down to have a swim in the nuddy.'

'In the nuddy?'

'Yeah.'

One particular kid, Brian Gillespie, nervously followed me down the steps. 'OK, I'm Tarzan and you're Boy,' I said, 'just like in the movies.'

He nodded.

'You fall in the river and you're drowning and I dive in and save you. Off you go.'

He fell very amateurishly off the end of the jetty. When he came up he began thrashing his arms about and going up and down. It was very convincing.

'Don't worry, Boy, I will save you,' I cried.

I took a running dive and surfaced in front of him. He grabbed my head with both hands and put all his weight on me. Down we went.

What's the matter with this kid? This wasn't in the script. He was climbing all over me and trying to stand on my head. I was four feet under the water with Brian on top of my shoulders. Luckily, my feet hit the mud and I started scrabbling towards the bank. My lungs were bursting.

I had stirred up so much mud that I couldn't see a thing. Finally my outstretched hands hit the ladder. I heaved our combined weights up the steps and my head finally broke the surface. I took a gasping breath.

'*What d'ya think you're doin'?*' I screamed. '*You nearly drowned me!*'

We were nose to nose.

In a tiny voice he said, 'I can't swim.'

My mouth dropped open in amazement. 'Why did you jump in?'

'You told me to.'

Through my sheer confidence, I had convinced someone who

couldn't swim to fall into the river. It could so easily have been a double disaster.

I started wearing glasses when I was eight. My teacher Mr Jackson (we called him Jacko) had noticed me squinting at the blackboard.

'Get your eyes tested, Harris.'

My first pair of specs was a revelation. Suddenly the world had sharp edges instead of being fuzzy.

Unfortunately, I lost so many pairs of glasses I must've nearly bankrupted Mum and Dad. My classic trick was to go sprinting down to the river with nothing on and dive off the jetty. Suddenly I'd remember my glasses and in mid-air do a twisting, convoluted U-turn but it was too late. The water swept them off never to be seen again.

My marks improved when I could see the blackboard, but I wasn't a particularly conscientious student. I spent too much time showing off. I used to entertain kids with cowboy fight scenes. I'd be shot and plunge off a table, or fall from a tree, crashing to the ground theatrically. The dying twitch was my best bit – that involuntary jerk of the legs with the last gurgling gasp.

I was mucking about in class one day, paying no attention to Jacko's maths lesson. Without warning, he gave us a lightning test of eight sums. I managed to get two of them right.

'Come up here, Harris.'

He bent me over the desk and gave me six cuts across the backside with a three-foot cane. I cried like mad.

Hero status is a strange thing in the schoolyard. Come playtime, news of my exploits had spread far and wide. People queued behind the boys' lavatory to examine the great weals on my backside. I had become a playground legend.

I went home proudly that afternoon and showed Mum my battle scars. She practically had an apoplectic fit. Next morning she marched me into the headmaster's office and almost demanded that Mr Jackson be executed immediately for attacking her son.

'How dare he do that to my boy? What possible reason is there for beating a child so savagely? What is this place – a school or a prison camp? No! Even prisoners get better treatment . . .'

Of course, I tried to stop her. I begged her not to kick up a fuss. It was awful. How would I ever live it down?

Mum always took an interest in my schooling. Every afternoon when I got home from school, she'd ambush me with all sorts of questions. 'How was your day? What did you learn? Who did you play with?'

I normally just shrugged or said, 'Nothing, Mum,' or, 'I can't remember,' or, 'I dunno.'

If Dad was home and doing some work outside, I'd seek him out and earbash him about everything that had happened since morning – acting out all the goings on, the secrets and the stories.

I don't know why I preferred telling Dad these things. Maybe because he let me tell it all in my own time. I loved my mum, but for some reason I really wanted to please Dad. It was *his* approval I sought.

He and Mum were very moral people. Neither of them would ever swear and I didn't tell them a naughty joke until I was nearly forty.

Once Mum knitted a bathing suit for herself which had all sorts of tassels attached. When she went into the water it doubled in size. Everything was hanging down.

'They look like pubic hairs,' I announced of the tassels.

She swung her hand round and slapped me across the face. I went scarlet. Mum didn't talk to me for two days. I was thirty years old when that happened.

The real sin, in Mum's eyes, was the demon drink. Her father had been a part-time lay preacher in a Welsh chapel and he lectured on the evils of alcohol. Mum took the view that anybody who drank was by definition a drunkard.

Again, it wasn't until my mid-thirties that I discovered Dad loved a beer. All those years of popping next door to get advice from the retired builder had been his excuse to have a quiet drink and a chat on the veranda.

On a holiday to Esperance, on the southern coast of Western Australia, we met a farming family who had a boy about my age. Colin 'Ginger' Herbert had bright orange hair and a face full of freckles.

From then on our parents arranged that during school holidays Ginger and I would take turns to stay at the other's home. That was fine. I loved the idea of being on a farm.

On my first morning there, Ginger and his brothers showed me their horse. 'She used to race,' said Ginger, as I backed away from this monster. 'She's a calm old thing. Wouldn't hurt a fly. Fancy having a ride?'

'Not just now.'

'Oh, come on. Just sit on her. You'll have no worries at all.'

They were all standing round me. It was a matter of honour. They led the horse over to a fence and waited for me to climb on board.

'Just keep hold of the reins,' said Ginger. 'And keep your knees pressed in.'

At the same time, he whacked the horse's rump with the flat of his hand and it took off at 700 miles an hour. I clung on for dear life as we galloped across the paddock and down the dirt road.

This racehorse was a born stayer. It ran for two and a half miles until it reached a fence. Then it went from full gallop to dead stop in the blink of an eye. I went straight over the top of the horse and the fence, landing in a heap on the other side. The horse turned round and casually trotted back to the stables, leaving me to walk.

Later in the milking shed, Ginger asked, 'Have you ever wondered how the milk stays up in the cow's udder and why it doesn't just pour out of the teats onto the ground?'

'No.'

'Well, it's really quite remarkable because each teat has a little valve inside. Have a look.'

I bent closer, peering beneath the placid cow. Ginger squirted milk straight into my eye. He and his brothers laughed like drains. I didn't blame them. I was this weird bespectacled kid from the city, who knew nothing about farming. To them I was fair game.

At breakfast I decided to impress them by playing our 'boiled egg' game with Ginger's dad. I finished my boiled egg and turned it over in the eggcup.

'Look, Mr Herbert, you've got another egg.'

He grabbed me by the scruff of the neck and forced my face down until my nose broke the surface of the eggshell.

'Don't play games with me, boy.'

I was shocked. It made me realize how lucky I was to have my dad. He would happily act the giddy goat and play along with our games without ever getting bored, or angry.

Mum and Dad were both singers, but neither could play the piano. They had high hopes for Bruce, but he didn't want to learn. The piano sat unplayed in the corner.

I was fooling around on it one day, when Mum asked if I'd like to learn.

'I'd love to.'

'You have to promise me that you'll practise. Lessons cost money.'

I promised her.

The following week I rode two miles to the convent on my push-bike. My piano teacher was Sister Mary Magdalene, a feisty little nun, who used to rap me across the knuckles with a ruler if I made a mistake.

She had a wonderful method of teaching the time values of the music and always insisted that I count as I played, 'One and two and three four, one two and three, rest.'

'You must make sure that boy counts . . . and counts out loud,' she'd say to Mum.

I don't think Mum had a clue why this was important, but from then on she would stand over me and say, 'Are you counting?'

'I am counting.'

'I can't hear you. Count out loud!'

'One and two, three . . .'

If my voice dropped, she'd shout from the other room, 'I can't hear you counting any more.'

And so it went on, day after day. It was a pain, yet miraculously the system worked. The strict time values were etched in my mind so deeply that even today it is like having a metronome going in my head.

Mary Magdalene's first commandment was, 'Thou shalt not play jazz or ragtime and especially not that dreaded boogie-woogie' (which she pronounced boojie-woojie). She also believed that playing by ear was a cheap trick. Whenever I tried to improvise she'd rap my knuckles and say, 'Chopin was a genius – you can't improve on his composition. Play what he's written.'

These rigid rules were like blinkers. I played classical music through all the grade exams and it took me another fifteen years to realize that all the chords and chord progressions were the same as those in the pop songs I heard on the radio. This revelation made me feel as though my formal music lessons had been wasted. Why don't music teachers tell you this? Music is music is music – one form isn't more or less legitimate than any other.

Despite Mary Magdalene's warnings, I secretly toyed with all sorts of music. When I heard Glenn Miller's 'In The Mood', the rhythm fascinated me because it was so different. I managed to get a copy of the sheet music and spent hours practising at home. It almost drove Mum mad.

Although I didn't realize it at the time, the sequence of bass notes for 'In The Mood' was exactly the same sequence as a favourite left hand line for boogie-woogie. I was hooked.

At about the same time I found a book called the *Art Shefte Piano Method* – a simple system of working out the chords for any song you'd heard. I had a great ear and this meant I could pick up tunes I heard on the wireless and work out a possible accompaniment. What freedom!

Soon I had a repertoire of comedy songs and sing-along tunes. I improvised shamelessly, making up lyrics and adding my own sound effects to cover any other shortcomings.

I didn't regard Bassendean as a backwater, yet slowly I became aware that it wasn't the centre of the universe. Partly this came from watching films and reading books. But mostly, my window to the world was the humble wireless that took pride of place in our living room.

If I pressed my eye up to the speaker, I could see the lights of the valves inside. And through some magic, beyond my comprehension at that age, I could hear voices coming through the static from Sydney, Melbourne and even from the BBC in London.

Of an evening, we'd gather round the wireless to hear our favourite shows. We only listened to the ABC. I think Mum considered commercial radio a bit 'common'.

We all loved *It's That Man Again* (ITMA), hosted by Tommy Handley, and *Take It From Here*, with Dick Bentley, Joy Nichols and Jimmy Edwards. Mum thought Mo McCacky (alias Roy Rene) was too crude and not a patch on the English comedians.

I was a proud member of the Argonauts Club and can still remember my number – Echo32. I'd lie on the floor, listening to the radio show, while doing artwork to send in. The best pictures would get discussed on air and the artist's name would be read out.

Ever since I can remember I had been drawing. Mum and Dad always had pencils and paper around the house. From early on, people talked about my drawings and paintings. I seemed to have been born with the ability to draw what I could see. When other kids were doing stick figures, I was doing complete pictures, with all the details of clothes, umbrellas and shoes.

I don't know if I had an artist's eye for beauty, or composition. Maybe these came later. In the beginning I just drew things that looked right and seemed to fit on the page.

My first-grade teacher at primary school used to collect all my drawings. 'You're going to be a really fine artist when you grow up,' she told me. More than forty years later, I tried to find her again on a visit to Perth. Sadly, she had died of cancer only a few months earlier. Her husband said that she had kept my drawings all her life. I hope I didn't disappoint her.

Chapter Two

SIXTEEN STROKES TO THE TURN

W HEN I WAS TEN YEARS OLD MUM AND DAD DECIDED THAT IT was time for me to meet the rest of the Harris clan, who had settled in Sydney. We took a train across the Nullabor Plain to Adelaide, then on to Melbourne, and went north-east by parlour car (bus) to Sydney. The journey took five days.

I learned to yodel early on during that trip. Some awful kid taught me. We were down the back of the train, leaning out the window, yodelling into the rushing air.

My grandmother lived at 24a Birrell Street, Waverley, and she was less than thrilled with me. I managed to blow up the gas water heater in the bathroom on the first day. I then sent her sprawling when I tied long clumps of grass together to form trip-wires under the clothesline.

In those days I climbed everything. I even had a trick where I could reach the ceiling of a room by wedging myself into a corner and using my heels and elbows to shimmy upwards like a human fly. When my grandmother came into the bathroom to run a bath, I yodelled to her from the corner of the ceiling and frightened the living daylights out of her. The poor woman didn't sleep for a week. She is on record as saying, 'I never heard that child make a pleasant sound.'

I don't know why I made so much noise. It was like a nervous reaction. Although I didn't lack confidence I often felt different from other kids – like an outsider who was trying to gain acceptance from the mob.

High school was the best example of this. At the age of twelve I sat a State-wide exam and won an entrance to Perth Modern School – a selective high school with a very good reputation. I just sneaked in because Mum had taught me how to solve problems using algebra.

A lot of famous people had gone there including entrepreneurs, economists, mining magnates and assorted politicians. Bob Hawke was a year ahead of me. Later he made the *Guinness Book of Records* for downing a yard of ale and also became Prime Minister. There's a wonderful symmetry to these two achievements. It could only happen in Australia.

From the very beginning I felt like an outsider. Partly I blame the uniform. 'Mod' had relaxed its dress code because of the war, but I was still supposed to have a grey blazer with a sphinx emblem embroidered on the pocket, and the same on the cap. These emblems cost a lot of money, so I painted mine with oil paints.

To make matters worse, I wore open-toed sandals that looked like landing barges on my feet. I might as well have had a sign round my neck saying, 'Look at me, my family can't afford proper shoes.'

All of this made me feel very self-conscious, but instead of retreating into my shell or avoiding attention, I did completely the opposite. If people were going to look at me when I walked into the room, then I might as well give them a good reason.

In a big loud voice I'd say, 'Hey, how ya going?' I jumped straight in and grabbed the spotlight. This didn't stop me feeling self-conscious, but at least I'd given them a different reason for looking at me.

*

In my first year at 'Mod' I was the best swimmer. I entered every event for every age group at the annual swimming carnival. The sports master took me aside and said, 'It's not a joke, Harris.' I convinced him that I was serious and went on to win every event but one.

In my second year a classmate, Garrick Agnew, doubled in size. He had a five o'clock shadow and towered over everyone. I was still skin and bone. From then on, right through school, I was the second best swimmer.

At the selection trials for the Australian National Swimming Championships in 1946 Garrick was amazing. He won almost every event. By then he had such a psychological edge on me that the merest glance from him and I was lost.

On a stormy night at Claremont Baths in Perth, we stood alongside each other waiting for the 110-yards backstroke trial. The baths were built on the river and open to the elements. Waves were sloshing through the wooden slats between the pylons.

Halfway through the race a wave lifted Garrick and dumped him onto the turning board. His arm hooked over the edge and he turned badly. I found myself two yards ahead and held on to win.

It meant that I was eligible to go to Melbourne for the national championships. Garrick had obviously been selected and he said to me afterwards, 'Oh, well, you'll be company for me. I can always beat you when we get over there.' He wasn't bragging, he was stating a fact.

Being the star performer, Garrick had his airfare paid by the State swimming organizers, but I had to find £65 – a lot of money in those days. One of Dad's mates from the Bassendean Roads Board, an enthusiastic communist, organized two special fundraising nights at the local pictures.

During the intermission, he got up on the stage and said, 'Now this young lad he's a marvellous swimmer. He's got a chance to go to Melbourne for the Australian Championships, but we need to raise the money for his airfare. Now he's going to entertain you and then we're gonna pass the hat round. So here he is, Rolf Harris.'

My stomach did a complete loop. There must have been 120 people in the cinema – all focused on me. I was used to playing for a handful of people standing round the piano at home.

I started mumbling about getting to Melbourne but had to swallow in the middle of a word. Someone yelled, 'Sing us a song.'

I had some music with me, growing damp in my sweaty hands. I played a piano solo called 'In a Persian Market' which seemed to go on for about an hour. People must have been bored witless. Then I sang 'The Legion of the Lost' – a rousing tune that Dad and I often sang together at home. The choice of song was ridiculous. Here was a fifteen-year-old singing about a guy trapped in the French Foreign Legion? My voice had only just broken.

I didn't take my eyes off the sheet music to look at the audience. Normally I didn't need any encouragement to show off, but this was different. These people were being asked to dip into their pockets for me and I didn't know any of them.

Over two nights we raised enough for my airfare. I flew to Melbourne with six other swimmers on a huge adventure. Mum and Dad made the trip in their little car, crossing the vast expanse of the Nullabor on the longest straightest stretch of road in the world.

My swimming coach Percy Oliver had been the Australian backstroke champion and represented Australia at the 1936 Berlin Olympics. Just before I flew to Melbourne he gave me his Olympic silk full-length bathers. They were worn and patched, but I treasured them. We had a week of training in Melbourne before the championships. I concentrated on practising my turn. As I swam down the first lap, I noticed a large doorway to the left. I counted my strokes from that door. It was sixteen flat out and then into the turn.

I rehearsed this over and over. Sixteen strokes, then turn. It meant that I didn't have to look behind me to spot the wall. I knew exactly when to spin and push off for the final fifty-five yards.

On the night of the junior backstroke final, I glanced across to see Garrick a few lanes away. He looked supremely confident. That was OK. I had Percy's Olympic bathing suit. I was going to win.

'On your marks . . . Get set . . . BANG!'

I did a great start and tried to keep my stroke even as the crowd roared. Ignoring everything else, I came down the pool and turned my head slightly, looking for the door. Because the stands were packed with people, I couldn't see it!

I hadn't banked on this. I kept stroking and desperately searching for it. Suddenly I glimpsed the top of the door. I'd passed it. By how many strokes? I guessed three. I counted thirteen more, going flat out, and then turned. My hand hit the wall and I spun perfectly. It was a wonderful feeling.

Everybody else in the field had slowed down for the turn. I came out of my turn two yards ahead and could see them all. Nobody was taking that race from me. In those final few yards I knew that I had it won. Garrick came nowhere. I swam that race in my dreams every night for six months. I won it each time and woke, sweating like mad with my heart pounding.

The world turns on details like that. Winning the championship changed my life. I came home to Perth as the junior backstroke champion of Australia and a hometown hero. Garrick had failed to win a race.

Of course, I revelled in my fame. I strode through the playground, with my shirt open to the waist and my sleeves rolled right up to the shoulders. I slouched at my desk, looking cool and incomparable.

One of the teachers eventually brought me down to earth. 'Now listen, Harris,' he said politely. 'I know you're the Australian junior backstroke champion. Congratulations. But can you try to be a bit more normal. Button up that shirt and sit up straight. Nobody likes a show-off.'

My success in Melbourne prompted the people of Bassendean to form their own swimming club. I was elected captain. The townsfolk donated their time and the local Roads Board provided the heavy machinery. We gathered at the Point Reserve one Saturday morning, where the Helena River joins the Swan River. Sinking long pylons into the mud, we built two jetties fifty-five yards apart and created our own pool.

Swimming was the only sport that ever really interested me. It didn't cost any money and I had a river in my back garden. Frankly, I couldn't see the point of body contact sports like Aussie Rules Football. I was also hopeless at them. In the only Aussie Rules game I ever played, I got the ball and was suddenly jumped on by six guys.

Garrick, a brilliant footballer, screamed for the ball. 'Pass it! Pass it!'

My eyes shining with hero-worship, I handed it to him. 'Here you go.'

He threw it down in disgust. 'Jeez! You're supposed to *punch* the ball!'

Apart from my swimming triumph, being a good artist gained me notoriety at school. By the time I reached third year I had every glamorous fifth-year girl begging me to do posters for the school dance. Normally they wouldn't have been seen dead talking to a lowly third year.

I was pretty shy with girls, which must have been very evident to Hazel Allen, my first girlfriend. I wanted to ask her to the school dance, but didn't have the courage. Firstly I had John Hall (the school matinée idol) find out if she was going with anyone else. The answer was no. Then I asked Ron Gray, who was supposed to be a bit sweet on her, if he was going to ask her. He said no. Then I asked John to ask Hazel if she'd go with me. What a palaver!

'How are you gonna get home?' John asked me.

'I don't know.'

'Why don't you ask Hazel if you can stay the night at her place?'

The idea terrified me. 'Do you think I should?'

'I'll ask her for you.'

So he did.

I wasn't very worldly about matters of the heart. Mum had taken me aside when I was about eleven and given me a book – *What All Young Men Should Know* by the very Reverend Sir Giles Something-or-other. Mum stood over me while I read it from cover to cover.

'Anything you don't understand?' she asked.

'No.'

'Are you sure there's nothing you want to ask me?'

'Absolutely.' I just wanted to get out of there!

In truth the book gave me no specifics at all – just lots of innuendo and skating round the edges of the subject. The message seemed to be: 'Now you wouldn't want anyone doing that to your sister, would you?'

Of course, I knew all about sex already from behind the bike shed. Somebody had told me that you had to have a needle shoved up your penis before you could get a girl pregnant. Then Colin Gardiner came rushing up one day and said, 'I've found out what it's called. I looked it up in the dictionary – sectional intercourse.'

Dad was far more taciturn on the subject. The only warning he ever gave me came before I headed off on a cycling trip to the south-west of the State with a bunch of mates. Dad took me aside and started talking about the teacher who was going with us.

'He's not like other blokes.'

'Yes, Dad.'

'He doesn't like girls.'

'Yes, yes . . . OK . . .' I turned away and wouldn't let him finish the conversation. We all knew about this teacher and what he was like. It didn't worry us. I just hated hearing that sort of thing from my father.

Hazel and I were together until I left high school and started university. It all fell to shreds then because I was so scruffy and dishevelled away from the strict dress code of 'Mod'. I had never been very interested in clothes or dressing nicely.

The crowning insult came when I arrived to pick her up from

her Saturday job at a chemist's shop. It was drizzling with rain and I wore a pair of green shorts, a shirt made from curtain material, army boots and no socks. Over the top I was wearing Dad's Home Guard greatcoat.

Hazel caught sight of me and walked back inside. She couldn't believe I had arrived to collect her looking like a tramp.

I was sad that it finished. I thought it was love. But physical love and compatibility aren't the same thing. We had very little in common. Hazel wasn't artistic or interested in music. I was forever wanting her to wear bright colours, but she preferred muted tones.

Looking back it was the best thing for both of us. Hazel stayed in Perth and worked in chemists all her life. She married and had four lovely kids. We're still great friends and I see her every time I go home.

In my final year at Perth Modern I'd been elected a prefect. The headmaster called me into his office.

'Harris, your name has been put forward as a prefect. I'm very much in two minds about it. I don't know how I should put this, but if we make you a prefect you have to give me certain guarantees.'

I swallowed hard. 'Like what, sir?'

'Well, you have to promise me that you'll get your hair cut on a regular basis and that you'll try to look presentable. Wear a tie and a decent suit. Look the part. Can you give me that assurance?'

'Yes, sir.'

I went racing home and said to Dad, 'They're going to make me a prefect next year. The headmaster says I've got to promise to have my hair cut and look presentable.'

Dad said, 'You didn't *promise* him, did you?'

'Yeah.'

'Hmph!' He gave me a disgusted look and stomped out of the room. Secretly I think he was thrilled, but he hated seeing authority figures pushing people around or making them conform. Dad was quite anti-establishment, and working class to his bootstraps.

My interest in art had never waned. It was another example of how I focused on something I was good at and dismissed the rest. I was fortunate to find at Perth Modern School a marvellously enthusiastic art master called Frank E. Mills and another enthusiast, Jock Campbell, from the Education Department, who organized Saturday morning art classes.

When the weekend art group had its first exhibition, it was opened by the Lieutenant Governor of Western Australia, Sir James Mitchell – a great political figure in the west. Knowing he was coming, I painted his portrait from a newspaper photograph.

On the day of the opening, Mum made a beeline for Sir James.

'My son would very much like to paint you in the flesh,' she said, proudly showing him the portrait.

Sir James politely told her that I should talk to his secretary. Nervously, I approached the secretary who gave me his office phone number.

Next morning, with Mum prodding me, I made the phone call. We didn't have a telephone, so I rode my bike down the street and put two pennies in the public phone. My hands were trembling.

'Sir James can give you an hour on Saturday, from ten to eleven,' said his secretary.

I thought the time was quite odd. Why would he want to start at ten minutes to eleven?

I arrived too early and hung around until twenty minutes to eleven before ringing the bell. The door opened and a stony-faced underling peered down at me. I was informed very tersely that Sir James had been waiting for more than forty minutes. The secretary had meant from 10 a.m. to 11 a.m. – not from ten minutes to eleven until ten to twelve.

'You must learn to be more punctual, young man,' said Sir James, as I tried to explain. With my hands trembling, I frantically started to paint him sitting in his study. The finished portrait was eventually bought by the Northam Art Gallery in WA and still hangs in Northam today.

Forty-five years later, I thought about the painting again as I watched a play about Sir James Mitchell. Called *No Sugar*, it was written by a sixty-year-old Aborigine who had grown up in WA. It told the story of when Sir James had been the ambitious local MP for Northam, fighting a close election campaign. The local Aboriginal community was seen as an eyesore by many voters, who didn't want to look at black faces, or see their ramshackle collections of scattered belongings.

Sir James solved the problem by having the Aborigines moved. They were herded onto trains with only what they could carry and taken 300 miles away. Dumped in what was virtually a concentration camp, they were given rations of tea and flour but no sugar.

I sat there in the theatre, watching this play, with tears running down my cheeks. All of this had gone on only an hour or so up the track from Bassendean. While I was growing up in my carefree, happy life, Aborigines were being shunted out of their homelands by the very man I had revered and whose portrait I'd painted. I felt angry and betrayed.

At the age of sixteen I held my first solo exhibition – mainly land-scapes done in watercolour and a few in oils. I had been pretty much self-taught, with lots of encouragement from Mum and Dad. I didn't ever deconstruct my paintings and ask myself why I had made particular decisions about the composition or colours I used. I suppose I was a realist, because I painted what I saw and tried to capture a moment in time as accurately as I could.

I loved the feeling of standing in front of a blank piece of paper, or canvas. At that moment, anything seemed possible. I could redraw the world afresh.

I would start by sketching the scene in pencil and then creating a wash for the sky. Slowly I would fill in the scene.

Frank Mills, the art master at 'Mod', had taught me that you have to plan a watercolour like a campaign. And he kept reminding me that colours dried much paler than they appeared when wet, so I should paint them bolder than they looked.

Coupled with my ability to draw things as I saw them, his advice started to get me some wonderful results.

All of the paintings in my first exhibition sold. I banked the money. After a second exhibition the following year, I had enough to buy a car.

Dad did the choosing – I didn't have a clue. He bought me an old 1928 Singer – made by the same company that produced the sewing machines. I called her Chloe and painted her in two tones of brown, with a portrait of a naked woman on the back. When I say she was naked, it only showed as far as her bare shoulders. The rest was all suggestion.

I taught myself to drive by sitting on the school bus behind the driver and copying all the gear changes and foot movements on the clutch and accelerator. People must have thought I was mad.

A high school student with his own car was unheard of in those days. Yet while other students were envying me, I felt the same way about them. All the kids in my year had their futures already mapped out. They were going to be doctors, journalists, mining engineers or politicians.

For the most part, it came true. Garrick Agnew became a mining entrepreneur and gained a knighthood. Max Newton was the first editor of the *Australian Financial Review*. Lloyd Zampatti became an industrialist. John Stone was the Federal Treasurer. All of these guys were at school with me and they knew exactly what they wanted to be. I used to stand back and admire their certainty. I couldn't think of anything that I could do that would make me a living.

During my last year at high school I went across to Sydney for the Australian Swimming Championships. By then I had graduated to the senior ranks and found the competition too strong.

Bruce had settled in Sydney after the war. He tried to get a job in radio, but was told he'd have to wait five months for an interview. Auntie Pat, Dad's youngest sister, was an artist in Sydney and had done some work in advertising. She suggested the idea to Bruce and he went along to Lintas, a big city firm.

The interviewer told him that if he proved himself to be any good at selling they might be interested. So Bruce walked out and got a job in a department store selling shirts. He topped the sales figures two months in a row and went back to Lintas.

'You really ought to be married,' the interviewer said, 'otherwise you don't know what the ordinary public want to buy. Most of them are married. They're the ones spending the money.'

'You want me to get married?'

'Well, it would certainly help your chances. Yes.'

So Bruce proposed to his sweetheart and set off to Adelaide where she lived. He came back to Lintas as a newly married man and they took him on as a copywriter. He went on to become the company's top executive.

Seeing him so certain about his future made me feel even more lost. What was I going to do? Swimming wasn't a meal ticket and I'd never worked hard enough on my music to become a real pianist. I quite liked the idea of being an artist, although it seemed rather precarious.

While staying with Aunt Pixie in Vaucluse, I decided to try to find an artist called Hayward Veal, who had been a childhood hero of mine. I first saw one of his paintings at the State Art Gallery in Perth – a wonderful impressionist scene of a misty early-morning Sydney Harbour.

Hayward Veal, known to his friends as Bill, had a studio in the narrow streets of the inner city. Following Aunt Pixie's directions, I found the place and discovered a sign on the door saying 'Back in ten minutes'.

With visions of being taken on as an art student and becoming a painter, I waited on the doorstep for an hour and a half, tossing bits of gravel at a tin can in the gutter.

I went back the next day and the day after. The same sign still hung on the door. Eventually, I gave it away.

A few months later, in my school leaving exam, I passed seven subjects with three distinctions – in art, music and physics. The result in physics amazed everyone, but I had a good teacher, Vin Serventy. On the strength of these results, I won a Hackett bursary, which meant that university became an option. The bursary would pay my fees as long as I worked hard enough to warrant it.

Leaving school came as an enormous shock to me. I felt as though I had been cast adrift. On my first day at university, I wandered around in a daze, waiting for somebody to tell me where I should be and what books I should have. I couldn't get used to the idea of optional tutorials and flexible timetables. I needed the structure of nine to three, with desks in neat rows and a roll call every morning, just like high school.

In the meantime, I was still painting every spare minute when I wasn't swim-training. Quite a few of the club members would train at our place each day. Afterwards, we'd troop up from the river into the house and sit round the piano in our wet bathers, singing songs we'd heard on the radio. One of them was 'Seven Beers with the Wrong Woman' – a comic song that had become my party piece. I chopped and changed the lyrics and did my own sound effects – mostly to cover my crummy piano playing.

> *One night I walked into a beer joint*
> *Where lonely souls abide,*
> *And standing there before me* (wolf whistle)
> *A lovely blonde I spied* (huff puff).
> *She seemed to be looking right at me* (pant, pant)
> *So I whispered in her little pink ear* (pssst, hey, pssst)
> *'Oh please Ma'am, lovely lady, won't you join me in a beer'*
> (fffffttpppt, duh duh duh, glug, glug, glug, glug).
> *Seven beers with the wrong woman . . .*

I figured that I didn't have a good enough voice or play the piano well enough to sing serious songs, so I made them funny. I did several Danny Kaye numbers and a song called 'Cocktails for Two' by Spike Jones and the City Slickers.

Australia's Amateur Hour was a popular radio show of the time. Normally it was broadcast from Sydney or Melbourne, but the show had gone on the road and was coming to Perth. Basically, it was a talent show, with eight contestants each week. Listeners would send in postal votes for their favourite.

Unbeknown to me, the kids from the swimming club put my name forward. They wanted me to sing 'Seven Beers with the Wrong Woman'.

I wasn't sure at first, but thought it might be a laugh to go to the audition. I breezed through, showing off like mad. I was more surprised than anyone when they gave me a spot on the first show.

Amateur Hour went to air from His Majesty's Theatre in Perth. I wore a brightly coloured open-necked tartan shirt and all the kids from the swimming club were in the audience with Mum and Dad.

Terry Dear, the master of ceremonies, introduced me as a very promising eighteen-year-old. 'That's a rather loud shirt you're wearing,' he said in his cultured accent.

'Yes, it's the McHarris tartan,' I said, getting a laugh.

'He's a character, this one. Let's hear a big round of applause for No. 4 from Perth, Rolf Harris.'

I was so nervous that I wondered if my mouth would work. The first sound effect of a wolf whistle got a laugh from the audience. I began to relax, but I didn't look at them. I just imagined that I was sitting at home, playing the piano for the kids.

When the postal votes were counted I won with a record 2,004. A reply paid telegram arrived two days later from the *Amateur Hour* people.

'Please confirm no previous stage appearance since broadcast. If so, two to three week booking with Edgely and Dawe [a touring theatrical company] commencing 24 April at His Majesty's Theatre, Perth. £12 a week.'

The whole scenario had been so unexpected that I couldn't take it seriously. It was almost surreal. I was just an eighteen-year-old kid, showing off and making my mates laugh. I had no thoughts of a career in show business.

I sang two songs on the show – 'Seven Beers' and the Hoagy Carmichael classic, 'The Old Music Master'. I added my own bit of virtuoso boogie-woogie at the end. It was a wonderful fortnight and then it was back to university. Neither seemed to be long term.

On my first holiday from uni, I got a job at an asbestos mine up in the Hammersley Ranges. It was Mum's idea. She'd read an article in the *Australian Women's Weekly* about Wittemoon Gorge and its fantastic scenery.

'You could do some marvellous paintings,' she said.

I signed on for the six weeks and took my paints along. I managed to do only two canvases in all that time. It was 121°F in the shade. For the first forty-eight hours I was sick from drinking too much water, trying to cope with the heat.

When it came to mining, I was totally useless. We were underground, shovelling rock into trucks that were dragged along railway lines by a small diesel engine. The drives were only five feet high which meant I couldn't stand up straight. Bent double all the time, I soon had a backache.

The blast teams would come in at the end of the drilling shift and set charges, blowing up the rock face. Then the shovel gangs in sweat-soaked singlets and hard hats would go back into the drive and clear all the rubble by the end of their shift. I was lucky to fill one truck in that time.

I was so useless that after three days they took me off the shovelling. Instead I was assigned to help lay down the water pipes that were needed to cool the drills. Every few days we had to add new pipe to reach the end of the shaft.

Lofty was in charge. He was a great old guy, about sixty-odd with a bad leg. To me he seemed ancient. Together, we'd jump in a jeep and collect pipe from abandoned trial mineshafts up on the surface, take them back, lag them and join them up.

Lofty used to say, 'When you have a job the first thing you do is sit down and have a smoke and think about it. You work out exactly what you have to do, then you'll only have to do it once.'

It's the same philosophy as 'measure twice and cut once'.

I didn't smoke, but I used to love sitting and listening to Lofty's pearls of wisdom. It was marvellous to have someone who was so much older, talking to me man to man, as an equal.

He gave me the benefit of all his knowledge about sex and women, and mentioned various things I might care to experiment with.

I must have been sitting there with my mouth open in disbelief and amazement.

'Honestly,' he said, 'they love it. Ya gotta try it all next time.'

Outwardly I was shocked, but inwardly this was wonderful information for a young bloke who didn't have a clue.

For all his humour, Lofty had a great sadness about him, which bordered on bitterness. During the First World War, he'd joined the Australian Light Horse Brigade, enlisting with his own horse, as all the men did. They were sent across to North Africa and were involved in terrible fighting.

'That horse of mine, we bloody near starved together,' said Lofty. 'We bloody near died of thirst, but I shared my water with him. I used to get my hat, punch it open and fill it from my canteen. He'd have the first drink and I'd have the rest. We went through all that shit together and came out the other side. We looked after each other and we survived.

'But when the war was over, the bloody powers that be said they couldn't afford to take our horses back to Australia. They took them to a huge cliff and galloped 'em over the edge into the sea. Killed 'em all. They were *our* bloody horses. How could they do that?' He had tears in his eyes. 'After that I said, "Fuck Australia." This country broke my bloody heart. I don't give a shit about patriotism. This country can go and get stuffed.'

Back at university, I struggled on, still feeling like a fish out of water. I lasted two years before losing my bursary. I failed psychology twice and was asked to leave.

What now? I wondered. Mum and Dad had always talked about my becoming a schoolteacher. It seemed like as good an idea as any. I enrolled at teachers' college in Claremont and discovered that it was just like being back at high school again. I knew what lectures I had to go to and what assignments were due. Somebody was telling me exactly what I needed to do. I felt right at home.

By then I'd joined a dance band made up of some local guys. We had a sax player, a drummer and a pianist, while I played the piano accordion . . . not very well.

I had inherited the accordion from Bruce. Mum and Dad had bought him a little eight-bass, but he wanted a bigger, flashier model. That was Bruce all over. He always wanted to look cool and impress people. The eight-bass accordion was beneath his dignity so he never bothered learning. Instead I picked it up when I was about twelve, and started playing. I loved the freedom it gave me to carry my music around. I even played it while riding my bike no hands down Bassendean Parade.

With the money I'd made from my exhibitions, I finally splashed out and bought a 48-bass accordion. It weighed a ton, but it gave me all the chords and bass notes to play a whole new range of songs.

Our band played gigs across the city every weekend, doing dances, parties and weddings. After a while the piano player, Bruce Marshall, moved interstate. We turned into a three-piece, with Eddie Burnie on sax, Bill Allen on drums and me playing the piano. Musically, I was the weakest link. Sister Mary Magdalene would have been horrified at the songs we played, and even more so at my technique.

I loved performing. It was a logical extension of showing off as a kid, only now I had more people to impress. It still didn't enter my head to make it a career. The band made barely twenty quid a gig.

After two years at teachers' college, I graduated and was given my first job. Under the bond system, I had to give the State three years of service as a teacher because the Education Department had funded my training and paid me a weekly wage during those two years.

My first job was tailor-made for me. I taught swimming to schoolchildren at various pools around Perth, our club pool in Bassendean being one of them. I spent all day outdoors and played music at night. It was the sort of routine that can make months and years disappear in the blink of an eye.

The summer of 1951 was long, dry and hot. The river fell to a record low. Even the sandy beach at the Point Reserve was left high and dry, as the river shrank. I was in and out of the muddy churned-up water, teaching kids how to float and how not to panic. I never thought twice about pollution even though I knew the abattoir upstream was always flushing rubbish into the Helena River, which joined the Swan River right where I was teaching.

Mum and Dad had gone on a holiday. It was the first time they had been away together that any of us could remember. They'd fixed for me to stay with family friends, Mr and Mrs Devenish, who lived in South Perth.

After finishing the swimming lessons, I washed the mud off my feet and tossed my wet gear on the back seat of the car. I drove towards South Perth. Stopping at an intersection, I tried to look right to see if any traffic was coming but couldn't move my head. I had to swing my whole body round.

Then I tried to look left and the same thing happened. My head seemed to be locked onto my shoulders and wouldn't swivel. With great difficulty, I kept driving, but I felt stiffer by the minute. By the time I reached the Devenishes' house, I could barely get out of the car. I had to slide down the seat and ease out sideways.

Mrs Devenish told me to take a couple of aspirin and lie down. Some time later she called me for dinner. I tried to get up but couldn't lift my head from the pillow. I couldn't put my chin down to my chest or bend my knees. Nothing worked. Staring straight at the ceiling, I felt an icy fear grip me. One word kept hammering away in my head – 'polio'.

Strapped to a stretcher, I was taken by ambulance to Perth

General Hospital. The doctors gathered round and scraped the soles of my feet and asked me to move my limbs. I felt absolutely nothing. I could see the puzzled looks on their faces.

Although terrified of being paralysed, I insisted that nobody contact Mum and Dad. I didn't want them to panic or cut short their holiday. Instead I did a lot of praying and staring at the ceiling. Lying there, in a body that didn't respond and seemed foreign to me, I began thinking about my life. What if I never walked again? What if I couldn't swim, or paint, or play the accordion? I'd rather be dead.

A guy in the bed next to me was given a lumbar puncture to take fluid from his spine. I could hear him grunting and then screaming from behind the curtain and imagined him bent double.

Later that day a specialist came to see me. He had a stethoscope draped over his shoulders, in the same way as I carried my towel when I went swimming.

'The good news is that it's not polio,' he said. 'Apart from that, I can't tell you anything. We really don't know what's wrong with you.'

'So what are you going to do?' I asked, unable to turn my head to look at him.

'Well, we could take a lumbar puncture and study the fluid.'

'Will that help?'

'I don't know. There's not much we can do, so I'll leave it up to you.'

I thought about the bloke in the next bed. 'No thanks.'

After a week in hospital, I slowly began getting better. The paralysis wasn't permanent. Although nobody knew for sure, I seemed to have caught some form of virus that created very similar symptoms to polio, without the long-term effects.

For a month I was scratched, pinched, poked and prodded, as doctors monitored my recovery. Mum and Dad came home just as I started getting the feeling back in my feet. They were shocked, but relieved.

Lying in a hospital bed, unable to move, I had a lot of time to think. I began to question what I was doing with my life. I was twenty-one years old and still living at home with Mum and Dad. I had my meals cooked for me and my washing done. If I needed to write a letter, Mum would draft it for me and check the spelling.

Did I really want to be a teacher? It was comfortable as careers go, but it didn't inspire me in the same way as painting did. I only had to visit an art gallery to know that. I knew that if I stayed a teacher, I'd become a Sunday painter, which is like being a weekend driver.

Lying in bed one day, staring at the patterns of light on the ceiling thrown by the venetian blinds, I made a decision. If I managed to walk out of that hospital, I wanted to be a painter. Perhaps I could be a portrait painter like my grandfather. It was something genuine, honest and respected. I could do that.

I told Mum and Dad that I was going to study art and keep myself at art school by entertaining people at night. Then I dropped the bombshell about doing all this in London.

'Why not Sydney?' asked Mum. 'There are perfectly good art schools in Sydney.'

I tried to explain that London was the hub of the universe. I had grown up listening to stories about Britain. Mum and Dad still called it 'home'. I had also grown up listening to BBC radio shows and watching English films at the cinema. I imagined a place full of umbrellas, warm beer, flat caps and bowler hats.

It was a magical, bustling, unexplored new world for me. That's what I wanted. In Sydney I had all my aunts and uncles, as well as a big brother. I knew what would happen. I'd stay with Auntie Pixie, or Auntie Jo. They'd just take over Mum's role of making decisions for me, as well as cooking, washing and ironing. It was too easy.

I wanted to stand on my own two feet. I wanted to be the smallish fish in the biggest pond. How else would I know if the boy from Bassendean was good enough?

Chapter Three

A PASSAGE TO ENGLAND

FREMANTLE DOCKS WERE SO PACKED WITH PEOPLE IT LOOKED as though they'd been sprinkled with hundreds and thousands. The Italian liner *Oceania* rose above the colourful throng and gleamed so white that she hurt the eyes.

My parents and friends had come down to wave me off. Mum was crying and Dad was close to tears. I tried to cheer them up.

'It's only for a year,' I said to Mum and gave her a hug. She dabbed at her eyes and started fussing with my collar.

I had a year's leave without pay from the Education Department. Dad had signed a guarantee for my £1,500 bond. If I didn't return he would have to pay the money to the State.

Dad shook my hand and wished me luck. Australian men don't hug. He put his arm round Mum's shoulders.

I waved to them from the gangway and again from the ship's deck. Streamers fluttered from the railings in the Fremantle Doctor – the legendary breeze that arrives most afternoons in Perth to cool things down.

It took ages for the ship to leave. I dragged out my accordion and began playing songs. Everybody on deck and on the dock

41

joined in. We sang 'Waltzing Matilda', 'Irene Goodnight', 'Throw a Silver Dollar', 'Green Grow the Rushes-O' – all the songs I knew. Afterwards, I stayed on deck to see the coast of Western Australia disappear. Then I began to look forward. Would all the stories about England be true? Would there be street barrows and flower-sellers on every corner? Could you hear Big Ben chiming from across London? Was the flag above Buckingham Palace raised and lowered to signal if the monarch was at home or not?

Heady with excitement, I went down to the bar and discovered my first mistake. I had no money for extras or incidentals. When I paid for my fare, all the meals and transfers were included. I assumed that I wouldn't need any money until I arrived in England, so I had put all my savings (£297) in a bank account.

Other passengers were buying orange juice and beers, but I couldn't return a shout, or even buy *myself* a drink. It wasn't about alcohol. I didn't drink the stuff. I remember having a beer one afternoon after teachers' college – just the one – and I felt very blurry and woke the next morning with a shocking hangover. From then on I stuck to soft drinks.

Perhaps, subconsciously, all of Mum's lectures about the evils of alcohol had rubbed off on me. As a teenager we either take on board our parents' attitudes and prejudices, or we rebel against them. I took them on board. Bruce, however, has always been totally at ease with having a few drinks.

That evening on the *Oceania* I pulled out my piano accordion and began playing when the ship's band took a break. Luigi, the lead fiddle player, quite liked me hanging around, but I don't think the other members of the band appreciated my horning in on their act.

Luigi was a lovable rogue with an eye for the ladies. He was in his mid-fifties, with languid eyes and greying hair at the temples. He had a trick where he could make his fiddle sound as though it was actually talking. Whenever I walked into the lounge, he would start playing. 'Hello, Rolfo, have you been getting any today?'

I shook my head.

'Oh, well, the night is still young.'

Two days out of Perth, I had my twenty-second birthday. Luigi and the band struck up happy birthday and all the passengers began singing. Then they presented me with a big round tin of Capstan cigarettes.

'I don't smoke,' I said.

'Open it.'

It was stuffed full of rolled up lire, dollars and pounds. They had taken a whip-round amongst the passengers and crew because they knew I had no money. I was overwhelmed by their generosity. They barely knew me.

During the voyage I fell madly in love with a broken-hearted German girl called Dita Voelkner. She was thirty-two years old, with a straight up and down figure, a waif-like face and dramatic half-closed dreamy eyes that made her look like Marlene Dietrich – mysterious and lovely.

Dita had married an Australian serviceman straight after the war and migrated Down Under. Unfortunately, away from the glamour of the Occupation forces, he turned out to be a regular Aussie bloke, who drank and gambled. She also discovered that her new surroundings were harsh and alien compared to Europe. She walked out and caught the first boat for home.

Dita cried a lot and I followed her around like a lovesick puppy.

'I can't stand Australia,' she complained. 'Nobody has any time for anything except drinking and gambling. And Australian men are barbarians.'

'I don't drink or gamble,' I said, hopefully.

'Hmmmmph!'

Then she gave me a sickly smile through her tears. My heart pounded.

One evening, standing up on deck, Dita and I were chatting with a young German couple, who were laughing and joking with each other. Dita wore a boob tube and her bare shoulders looked pale and lovely.

As a joke, the German chap slipped behind her and whipped the boob tube down to her waist. Dita spun round and slapped me across the face. Bang! I went reeling across the deck, my eyes watering, as she stormed off. The German was laughing himself stupid.

I tried to clear my name with Dita but it was too late. All her worst fears about Australian men had been substantiated. From then on I was forced to look at her from a distance, unable to mend her broken heart.

The *Oceania* sailed across the Indian Ocean, up through the Suez Canal into the Mediterranean. At Genoa in Italy we disembarked. All the train fares had been included in the original package I bought in Perth. I caught the train north into Switzerland, reaching Zurich in the middle of the night.

I made one last attempt to woo Dita. She was on the same train, but I was in first class and she was in a third-class compartment. I asked the guard it if was OK for me to go back and see her.

'Why you want to go to cattle truck?' he said.

'To see a lady.'

'Ah,' he said, giving me a knowing wink.

I sat and talked to Dita for a while, but it was too late. She had seen enough of Australian men.

After the day in Zurich, I took the onward train to France. On board I met a bunch of young South African dentists who were on their way to London. Les Lazarus and Barry Cohen were two of them. We spent all night singing songs, as the train rattled through the French countryside.

'Stop off and see Paris with us,' said Les.

'I don't have any money.'

'We'll lend you some.'

I didn't take much convincing. We went everywhere together in Paris, laughing and singing. Every pretty girl would get serenaded in the middle of the street.

That's my girl, take a look at her, she belongs to me.
That's my girl, hands off, don't touch.
She looks just like an angel,
But she's human just the same.
And I ain't takin' chances,
I won't tell her address or even her name.
'Cause that's my girl. Take a look at her, she belongs to me.
That's my girl . . .

The Moulin Rouge was a real eye-opener. I had never heard of it, but all those flashes of thigh and gusset seemed positively shocking. I didn't know where to look, or not to look.

Afterwards, we wandered along the cobblestoned streets in Montmartre.

'Hey, look at this,' said Barry.

The poster showed several semi-clad women. 'What does it say?'

Les started flicking through his French phrase book. 'It's a museum,' he said.

'What sort of museum?'

'A bloody interesting one, by the look of it.'

We paid the entrance fee and walked through a heavy curtain. My eyes shot out on stalks. Two semi-clad young women cavorted on a bed. One of them wore a strap-on device around her hips and they were showing dozens of different positions of sexual congress. The room was so small it was like standing in someone's bedroom.

'Would you like to stay and make some love with the young ladies?' said the old French woman from the front desk. She wore a velvet dress and vivid red lipstick. The guys ummed and ahhed.

I was so embarrassed that I began glancing about for something to do. I picked up the thing the girls had been using and looked at it gingerly.

'Don't touch that,' whispered Barry. 'You could get some disease!'

I dropped it as though I'd been bitten and furiously rubbed my hands on my trousers.

Some of the fellows were keen to stay, but I just wanted to get out of there. I'd never actually seen a prostitute, but I knew they existed. In Perth the brothels in Roe Street were famous, or should I say infamous. They had wire netting round them and little hinged wooden hatches on the doors to let those inside suss out any visitors. I heard guys talking about what happened, but I wouldn't drive down the street for quids. I'd be too frightened of being seen there.

After two days in Paris, I caught the train for London with my new friends. My first glimpse of England came from the ferry. The white cliffs of Dover didn't look particularly white in the murky morning light. Mist clung to the tops of waves and the seagulls sounded far more shrill and raucous than the Australian variety.

It was April 1952. Springtime. The ship ground to a halt and swayed gently as the huge ramps were moved into place. The rails were connected and the train eased onto the mainline track. By mid-morning the sun had burned off the mist. My eyes were glued to the countryside. I marvelled at the brilliant colours. I had never seen such bright greens and so many trees in blossom.

Everything was so ordered and neat – the fields in perfect squares, divided by hedgerows, fences and lichen-covered stone. There was none of the chaos of the Australian bush.

At Waterloo Station I looked up to see Gwenny Burton waiting on the platform. Gwenny had been my arts and crafts tutor at teachers' college. She had come to London on a two-year course.

Gwenny and I jumped into a black cab and she took me on a guided tour. We crossed over Waterloo Bridge and I looked along the Thames at the historic skyline, from the stately dome of St Paul's Cathedral to the towers of Westminster. By the time we reached Trafalgar Square I was hanging out the window of the cab, trying to take it all in.

'Look! Look!' I said, pointing at Nelson's Column and Admiralty Arch.

Gwenny laughed. 'I know. I know.'

We swung under the arch and the bustling city gave way to countryside. Right there, in the middle of the city, was a huge park, with a lake and ducks. Nannies were pushing prams and office girls were heading to work in Whitehall, with faces the colour of white porcelain and fulsome skirts cinched at the waist.

Grey, battered old London was preening itself on a beautiful morning. It was hard to believe that the war had ended only seven years earlier. I loved the way that the lichen clung to the slate roofs and the stone steps were worn down in the middle. I doubt if there was a building in Bassendean that was over a hundred years old, yet now I was looking at places that had been around centuries before Captain James Cook set foot in Australia.

Gwenny pointed out Buckingham Palace and I was the first to see the Houses of Parliament. Here were all the images I had grown up seeing in books and on newsreels – the black cabs, double-decker buses, flower barrows and Thames barges. All of them were *real*.

I wanted to paint every second streetscape and fasten the images in my mind. I wanted to ask people questions just to hear their accents and their stories.

As we drove up Fleet Street, I spied a bloke wearing a bowler hat. 'Will you look at that!' I said. Someone else wore a top hat, grey tailcoat and black-striped trousers. I thought those sorts of clothes were only worn in films.

Gwenny had booked me into the YMCA for a couple of days until I found proper digs. She helped me carry my cases to my room. As the lift rattled and clanked, I started telling her all about my plans to go to art college and make money by performing at night. 'I've got some great songs. I'll play you some. There must be a piano around here.'

A young man who was sharing the lift apologized for interrupting. 'I know where there's a piano,' he said, sounding very self-assured. He said his name was Stuart Madrell. 'Would you mind if I came along? I'm very interested in talented people.'

He showed us to a piano in the basement and I sang a few Danny Kaye numbers. Stuart lavished praise on me – which only confirmed what I already suspected about my talents.

'You've got a bright future,' he said, with a note of caution.

'Is something wrong?'

'Well, of course you can't work in the entertainment field unless you're a member of Actors' Equity or the Variety Artists' Federation.'

'Oh,' I said, getting worried.

'Yes, they're very strict about that.'

'How do you become a member?'

'Well, it just so happens that the secretary of the VAF is a great chum of mine. I could have a word with him. Maybe I could even get you in without having to bother with an audition.'

'Could you!' Gwenny exclaimed.

'Be delighted. Do you have any coppers?'

I gave him some spare change and followed him to a phone box. I waited outside while he had a long, animated conversation. I could just hear his voice through the glass. 'Yes, I've met this young chap . . . He's absolutely top notch, no doubt about it.' (He pronounced it no dight abight it.) . . . Do you think we can bypass the audition and get him straight in? . . . Oh, great . . . Marvellous. Thanks awfully. I'll tell him.'

Stuart gave me the thumbs up. I beamed. What luck!

He explained the details. All I had to do was give him the three pounds ten membership fee and he would pass it on to his friend. My membership card would arrive in the post.

My entire savings of £297 had been lodged with the Australian Commonwealth Bank at Australia House at the top of the Strand. Stuart came with me to get the three pounds ten. On the way we stopped for coffee and a sandwich. I also bought him a packet of cigarettes because he didn't have any money on him.

For the next two days we kicked around London together. Stuart showed me how to use the Underground and the red

London buses. It struck me as odd that he never had any money with him. I was always paying for everything.

After two days he disappeared and I finally woke up to the fact that I'd been conned. I always imagined that I'd beat the living daylights out of Stuart if I ever saw him again, but years later I spotted him on the other side of Tottenham Court Road.

'G'day, Stuart,' I yelled. He saw me and went belting off down the road. I wasn't going to hit him, or make a fuss. In truth, I'm very grateful that he taught me such an important lesson so early and so cheaply. If he'd played his cards right he could quite easily have had *all* my savings.

After two days at the YMCA I had to find somewhere else to live. I remembered the South African dentists, who had a flat in Earl's Court. Turning up on their doorstep unannounced, I spent the next few days sleeping on the floor, wrapped in my overcoat.

Before leaving Perth I'd made a point of collecting names and addresses of relatives and possible showbiz contacts. A band leader in Perth had given me the name of Ray Hartley, a successful piano player and composer, who had come from the wheat belt in WA.

When I looked at the address it was just around the corner in Earl's Court Square. With nothing to lose, I went straight over and rang the doorbell. A stocky cleaning lady, with a mop in her hand, answered. She pushed a loose strand of hair from her eyes.

'What d'ye want?' she asked in a lilting Irish accent.

'I was looking for Ray Hartley.'

She motioned down the hall and stepped to one side.

Ray was tall and patrician-looking, in his early thirties. He had a single room on the ground floor of the boarding house.

'Where are you staying?' he asked.

'I'm sleeping on the floor at a place round the corner.'

'I'm pretty sure there are some rooms here,' he said, 'I could talk to Mrs Squirrel.'

We went in search of the landlady.

'She doesn't stand for any cheek,' Ray whispered. 'Her husband is an engineer or something like that. He's away working in Saudi Arabia.'

We found Mrs Squirrel in the kitchen and she went away to get the keys. It never occurred to me to ask if there were any single rooms. I was used to being told what to do.

'There's a bathroom at the end of the corridor,' she said, as we reached the third floor. 'You'll have to share with Malcolm. He's a music student. He's not here at the moment . . .'

She fumbled with the key in the lock. 'It's three pounds ten a week, including breakfast and evening meals.'

The door opened. The room had two beds, two wardrobes, a gas ring, a mantelpiece and a washbasin in the corner. My heart leaped when I saw the brand new upright piano in the corner. I had visions of me practising my cabaret right there in the room.

'It's great,' I said. 'Can I move in today?'

She looked me up and down. 'That'll be two weeks' rent in advance. It's extra for laundry.'

I was settled and unpacked by the time my room-mate Malcolm Lipkin arrived home.

'G'day, how's it going?' I said, thrusting out my hand. I started telling him about my musical background. He looked decidedly underwhelmed. Malcolm was studying at the Royal College of Music and regarded himself as a 'serious' musician.

Any hope of using his piano quickly evaporated. The first time he caught me playing a bit of boogie-woogie, he slammed the cover shut and turned the key. From then on it remained locked whenever he left the room – even to go to the bathroom.

We had nothing in common. In truth, we were like oil and water. We each had habits which infuriated the other. I hated the way he washed his face and upper body in the washbasin every morning and never remembered to bring a towel. He would grope his way across the room, bumping into my bed and spraying me with a cascade of ice-cold water.

For my part, I snored. Shoes would land on me in the middle of the night, hurled from the other side of the room. I also drove

Malcolm mad by doing oil paintings in the room. The smell of turpentine and oil paint was so overpowering I had to keep the windows wide open, which meant the room was freezing.

After a while Malcolm and I barely spoke to each other. We lived together in armed neutrality, each hoping the other would be the first to move out.

There were sixteen residents at the boarding house – mostly music students, with the odd businessman and a couple of foreign students trying to improve their English.

On the first evening I met Alex Haussmann from Stuttgart in Germany. He was a year or two older than me and had come to England to pass the British Chartered Accountancy exam. Unfortunately, he couldn't get into college unless he first passed exams in a range of subjects – all of them to be taken in English. Not surprisingly, he spent every spare moment swotting in his room.

It was quite strange to meet a German in London. Although the war had been over for nearly seven years, rationing continued and there were other reminders everywhere. The mountains of rubble had been cleared away, but there were still great gaps in the streets where buildings had been destroyed. Flowers and weeds grew from the cracks and crevices.

I don't know if Alex struck any problems. He didn't say anything. We didn't talk about the Nazis, or Hitler, or the concentration camps. Instead I told him of my carefree childhood in Australia, swimming in the river and picking fruit off the trees.

For his part, Alex told me of being forced into uniform at fourteen years old in the last desperate years of the war. Scared out of their wits, he and his brother had to man an anti-aircraft gun in a blacked-out city, hugging each other to stay warm.

Alex and I had both been just kids during the war. It wasn't *our* conflict. To me he was just an ordinary bloke with a fascinating accent. Even so, I was very thankful to have grown up in Australia and not Germany.

I began helping Alex with his English, picking him up on his pronunciation and explaining the grammatical rules. At the same time, he started to teach me German, which I had once tried unsuccessfully to learn at high school. In his tiny room, poring over books together, we started a friendship that is still solid today.

Mrs Squirrel served up typically English fare – roast lamb, roast beef, mashed potato, peas and gravy. We all had ration books, which came as a shock to me. Each month we handed them over to Mrs Squirrel and she cut out the coupons to get butter, eggs and meat.

There was an air of genteel silence about the dining room, especially at breakfast. Most people were fully dressed ready for business or college. Hardly a word was ever spoken. I bounded into this mausoleum atmosphere wearing only a pair of shorts, with bare feet flapping on the lino.

'How's it going?' I bellowed. My voice echoed round the room. 'Come on, give us a big smile!'

Nobody knew what to say, so nobody said anything. This happened every morning and I naively imagined that I was going to break down their British reserve. It didn't happen.

Normally, Mrs Squirrel would arrive with a serving dish full of porridge. 'You really should wear some shoes,' she scolded. 'You'll catch your death of cold.'

What she really meant to say was, 'Go upstairs and put some clothes on. You're a bloody disgrace.'

One of the music students, Hugh Beaumont, conned me into believing he was French and offered to give me lessons. For weeks he kept the charade going.

'What you 'ave to get right eez your accent,' he said. 'Put your lips together like this.'

I puckered up.

'Now roll your rs like this,' he said. 'The French language it came from the French court. The French nobleman was, how you say, effeminate . . . like a lady. This is why you must push ze lips forward . . . like this . . .'

I did these facial contortions while the other music students were laughing themselves silly behind my back. When I finally twigged, I couldn't believe they could have kept the joke going for so long.

Alex and I hung out together. He loved my devil-may-care casualness and I liked his formal charm. He was a smartly dressed European man about town while I was the raw colonial boy.

My dress sense was appalling and Alex gave me his hand-me-down shirts. They were nylon – a real novelty. It was wonderful being able to wash them, hang them up and have them ready to wear next morning with no ironing.

At a party in Battersea one night, Alex got into a disagreement with a well-spoken English chap, who was immaculately dressed. He was holding forth about how appalling nylon shirts were. 'You wash them a few times and they turn yellow.'

'Rubbish,' said Alex. 'Look at this!' He turned and grabbed me by the collar. 'I had this shirt for three years, washed it every day, and it has never gone yellow.'

I went hot and cold with embarrassment. Everybody in the room looked at me. From that moment on I have never worn anybody else's hand-me-downs. Alex never realized I was upset.

Teaching him about English foibles and customs was almost as hard as teaching him how to pronounce particular words. Jokes were especially difficult because punch lines rarely translate exactly.

'Why is zis funny?' he would say. 'I don't get zat.'

Sometimes Alex's mistakes were wonderfully apt. He would translate straight from German into English – slightly messing up the syntax. One day he meant to say to me 'How shall we leave it?' but it came out as 'How shall we remain?'

'Friends, I hope,' I replied.

We laughed. This became our catchphrase whenever we said goodbye to each other. It was nice to always part with a smile.

Having settled into Earl's Court Square, it was time to become a famous painter. First, I had to find an art school. I went straight to the British Council, an organization that was supposed to look after anyone who came from the colonies. Ushered into a plush-looking office, I said no to a cup of tea and got down to business.

'I want to go to art school.'

The middle-aged public servant looked rather bemused. 'Any particular art school?'

'No. Which one do you think?'

His brow creased.

'I want a good one. I want to learn about portrait painting.'

'Mmmm, let me see . . . which art school did you previously attend?'

'None.'

'Do you have a portfolio?'

'A what?' (What was a portfolio?)

He tried again. 'Do you have any paintings?'

'Oh, loads of them. I did them on the boat coming over. I've got cartoon sketches and a portrait of Luigi. He was one of the musicians on the boat—'

'Yes, well, you'll have to leave it with me,' he said, stopping me in mid-sentence. He made a note of my name and then ushered me out the door. I went back to the boarding house feeling very confident.

A week later, I was back at the British Council to find out what progress had been made. From then on, I turned up every week, driving the poor fellow mad. I'm sure he finally did something out of pure desperation.

He gave me the name and address of the City & Guilds Art School in Kennington. 'You've been accepted for the foundation course,' he said, relieved to get me off his back.

I had no idea what a foundation course entailed but was supremely confident that I would wow them with my outrageous talent.

On my first week at art college, I started to learn how to do etchings. I fidgeted and fumbled through the theory and practical workshops. It seemed like such a waste of time. I wanted to be a portrait painter. Why couldn't I go straight to doing that?

It turned out that a foundation course was designed to give students experience of a range of artistic disciplines, such as etching, poster-making, sculpture, life drawing, etc. ... The theory is that this allows them to make up their minds about where to specialize.

I was useless at life drawing, which came as a real shock. I thought I was brilliant at everything to do with art. Up until that moment, I had always been the best artist in my class, or my school, or at Saturday morning art lessons. Now, for the first time, I couldn't do things that other students took for granted. I didn't have a clue.

Life drawing and anatomy involve learning how the body is put together – how muscle, sinew and bone work together. What happens when we bend an arm, or turn a hand from palm up to palm down? How do we draw these things?

To my eternal shame, I thought these classes were boring and pointless. Only years later did I realize their importance. There are some artists, like cartoonist Bill Tidy, who can draw the most beautiful outline of a human leg with a single line, apparently without even thinking, because they know exactly how that leg works – inside and out. Even now when I do a life drawing, I try to capture a 'likeness' rather than trying to learn how the body is shaped by different poses.

I found it boring at art school because I wasn't any good at it. That's the ugly truth. All of the things I did well had come naturally to me. I had never had to work hard at drawing or being a good swimmer, I was just having fun. Playing the piano was the same, although it was a hard slog at first. At the same time, I had always avoided things that I wasn't very good at.

In a funny sort of way, I feel that self-confidence is enormously important in life. If we lose that conceit that makes us feel we are pretty good, we lose a major part of what makes us tick and who we are.

The English girls at college thought I was a loud, brash Aussie, with appalling dress sense and no alarm clock. I always arrived late for class, breezing in, loudly making my apologies and then borrowing stuff that I'd forgotten. They had no idea of what made me tick . . . nor did they want to find out.

Among the students was a stunning blonde, with delicate features and a dynamite figure beneath her paint and plaster-splattered jeans. Her name was Alwen Hughes and I used to watch her sometimes in class. She would get a look of concentration on her face, pursing her lips and occasionally brushing strands of hair out of her eyes. So intense and yet so beautiful.

Each morning, I poked my head around her easel and said, 'How's it going? Give us a big smile?'

She would shoot backwards in horror, struck dumb. I'm sure she thought I was mad. At the same time I thought she was incredibly stuck up. At the end of our foundation year Alwen moved to the Royal College of Art to study sculpture. I thought I'd never see her again.

'When are we going to paint portraits?' I'd ask the lecturers, as they wandered back and forth behind our easels, making strange noises that we later had to decipher as art criticism.

The answer was always the same. 'First things first.'

In the meantime, my impossible fortune of £297 was rapidly disappearing. It was time to find a job. My idea of performing in cabaret struck a major hurdle. Most of my repertoire consisted of Danny Kaye songs or American records that I'd copied or parodied. In England, I discovered, this material was at least ten years out of date.

The music coming out of America had a feel-good flavour with people like Pat Boone, Rosemary Clooney and Perry Como dominating the pop charts. Noel Coward was playing in the West End, singing wonderfully clever parodies about current events and the changing times.

By comparison, my comedy was raw and unsubtle. I can't be blamed. Australia was like that. What was regarded as being hysterically funny Down Under was old hat in the UK.

Delving into my address book, I called a radio producer whose name I'd been given. I spent five minutes singing my own praises until finally he said, 'Have you your book handy?'

'My book?'

'Your dates . . . diary.'

'Oh . . . er . . . no. I don't have a diary. But don't worry, I'll remember the appointment.'

'Right. How does July the twenty-second look?'

I laughed. I thought he was joking. It was early May.

'Are you serious?' I said. 'I don't know what I'll be doing in July. I may not even be in the country. Don't you have any free time before then?'

'I'm afraid not, old boy.'

I lamely ended the phone call. This wasn't going to be as easy as I thought.

Chapter Four

'LOSE THAT ATROCIOUS ACCENT, OLD BOY'

M Y FIRST JOB WAS AT A MUSIC HALL CALLED THE PLAYERS'
Theatre down by the Embankment. I had to sit in front of
a fake campfire, wearing a hat with bobbing corks around the
brim, and sing 'Waltzing Matilda'. Talk about being typecast! But
having exhausted every contact in my book, I wasn't in a position
to be choosy.

Ray Hartley gave me the name of an Australian producer,
Trafford Whitelock, who worked for the BBC's *Midday Music
Hall*. I wrote a letter and waited anxiously for a reply.

In the meantime, I spent a week visiting all my mum's relatives
in Cardiff. One of my South African dentist mates was doing a
locum stint in Wales, in a little town called Porth, so I also paid
him a visit for a night.

The bus from Cardiff to Porth twisted and turned through
the valleys, where the tiny villages clustered round the coal
mines and were surrounded by slagheaps. A guy got on the bus
who was so drunk he kept falling sideways every time we rounded
a corner. He would keel over into the aisle, hit his head on the seat

opposite and send a spray of sparks from the cigarette in his mouth.

The bus stopped and I thought, 'It's about time! Surely they're going to throw him off.'

But instead, he stood up unsteadily and began singing 'Sospan Fach' (The Little Saucepan), a famous Welsh song. He started softly, in a quiet rumbling voice, and built up steam. Then he stopped and turned to face the passengers.

'Call yourselves bloody Welshmen?' he shouted. 'What's the matter with you? Sing!'

Now they're definitely going to sling him off, I thought. Not a bit of it. Everyone in the bus turned in their seats to face him and on cue they joined him in one of the most spine-tingling four-part harmonies I'd ever heard.

I've listened to many Welsh songs since then and learned quite a few of them, but 'Sospan Fach' has a special place in my heart.

On the bus trip to Wales I'd met a nice-looking girl from Whitchurch in Shropshire, who invited me to stay over at her parents' farm on the way back to London, which I happily did. Sarah lived with her mum and her sister. I don't know what happened to their father. In the morning, bright and early, she appeared at breakfast in riding breeches, scarlet jacket and hard hat.

'Fancy coming on a hunt?'

Me? The boy from Bassendean – on a real British hunt! I couldn't believe it. Mind you, she explained that she only had one horse.

'You could ride my bicycle,' she suggested.

What a relief. Ever since my runaway ride on Ginger's race-horse, I'd been distinctly nervous around horses.

We headed off along the narrow country lanes, with me pedalling idly alongside Sarah, who sat six feet above me in the saddle, looking marvellous in her jacket and breeches.

The hunt gathered in the forecourt of a large local estate. The air filled with the baying of the hounds and the clink of glasses as the 'hunt cup' was passed round. These were the true landed gentry, with their brilliantly polished leather boots and stable girls running errands for them.

Being on horseback, they couldn't help but talk down to me. Yet what most intimidated me was their posh accents. I could feel the bike getting smaller and smaller until I imagined I was riding a child's tricycle and dressed in a clown's outfit.

The horns sounded and the hunt began. Riders galloped off across the field, jumping hedges and ditches. I bumped along after them and soon realized this was impossible. Dragging the bike over a gate in the hedge, I tried to head off along the lane in the same general direction. Soon I was hopelessly lost.

It was a warm sunny day and I ended up walking with the bike. I feasted on fat ripe blackberries from the roadside hedges. It was lovely. After a while I tucked myself into the corner of a field on a bed of dry leaves and drifted off into a delicious sleep.

I woke and shivered. The sun had gone behind scudding clouds. It took me a few minutes to recapture the thread of what I was doing there lying on a pile of leaves in the middle of the countryside.

I went in search of the hunt. After a while I met a man walking two very hangdog-looking hounds that had obviously lost touch with the pack and were in disgrace. From his directions, I finally fetched up in the right field but discovered that Sarah had headed home half an hour earlier. Talk about lost. I had no idea where she lived and didn't know her surname. All the farms looked the same. I ended up having to walk backwards every now and then, to see if I recognized the view from when we headed out in the morning. It was dark by the time I fetched up at Sarah's farm exhausted and dishevelled.

'Oh, there you are,' she said as she opened the door, totally unconcerned.

The family had a huge Pyrenean mountain hound that terrified them. I was so at ease with dogs that I began fooling around with it, ruffling its head and rolling over on the ground in a mock fight, while they stood back nervously, warning me all the time.

The next afternoon, I strolled past the dog and it made a lightning lunge for me. Thank goodness it was on a strong chain that jerked it backwards. Even so, it still managed to get a glancing grip on my left arm, sinking its teeth through my shirt and into the muscle. I instinctively jerked back, ripping my sleeve to shreds. The dog was going berserk, growling ferociously.

The three women stood back, white-faced, with a look that said, 'I told you so.'

It taught me a lesson about dogs that I carry with me to this day. Never get between one of them and its food.

Waiting for me when I got back to the boarding house in Earl's Court was a letter from the BBC. To avoid the embarrassment of an audition, Trafford Whitelock suggested that I make a recording and send it to him. He recommended a recording studio near Bond Street Station.

It cost two pounds ten shillings to cut a record. I put down two songs on a small shiny black disc and then decided to also make a recording for Mum and Dad. I planned it carefully. Starting at the far side of the studio, I began whistling and walking towards the microphone. I wanted it to sound as though it was me, whistling as I walked down the long driveway at home.

Then I created a sound effect of my footsteps up on the veranda, opening the fly wire screen door. There could be no re-takes. I had to get it right the first time.

It worked like a dream. When I played it back you would have sworn it was me strolling down through the trees, up the steps and through the door.

'Anyone home?' I shouted.

Then I sat next to the microphone and chatted about my adventures in Wales and what I'd been doing in London and finished with a song. I posted the record to Australia and hand-delivered my audition disc to the BBC at Aeolian Hall in Bond Street.

I had no idea of the emotional impact my voice would have on Mum and Dad. They told me years later that they were only able to play the first few minutes of the record. My poor little dog, Buster Fleabags, went mad with excitement. He kept scratching and yelping, trying to get into the speaker to find me, thinking I was home again after all these months. Mum and Dad were in tears. They took the needle off the record and never played it again.

Thankfully, I had more success with *Midday Music Hall*. Trafford Whitelock liked my audition disc and asked me to sing one of my Danny Kaye impersonations. When the contract arrived I rushed in to Ray Hartley.

'Doing one show is fine,' he said, 'but it won't pay your rent for very long. A contract for a whole series, *that* would be worth getting excited about.'

I came away feeling strangely subdued.

Summer had arrived and the window boxes were brimming with flowers, hanging baskets decorated the street lamps and people went walking through the parks in the long twilight.

Although austerity measures were still widespread, there seemed to be a real sense of optimism in the air. Having struggled through the war years and aftermath, young people were now having fun again, going to dances, listening to music. New buildings were going up everywhere, covering the scars left by the Blitz. It was a wonderful time to be in London.

Early in the summer Bob and Shelda Wrightson arrived from Western Australia. My first romance with Hazel had blossomed at Bob and Shelda's dance school in Perth and now they had come to England to compete in the World Ballroom Dancing Championships in Blackpool.

The timing was perfect. All the top acts performed at the seaside resorts during July and August as part of the 'summer season'. Here was my chance to be 'discovered', while at the same time giving moral support to Bob and Shelda in their quest for the championship.

I caught a bus from Victoria Coach Station and soon dragged

out my piano accordion to keep everyone entertained. I told them all how I was going to lay them in the aisles up in Blackpool. They said I was brilliant, but of course, I knew that already.

At the end of that exhausting trip, I found a boarding house and flirted outrageously with the landlady's pretty daughter. 'Enough of that,' said her mum, with a stony look. I was treading on dangerous ground.

Well rested and ready to take on the world, I set off next morning lugging my great heavy accordion case. I turned up at the stage door of a theatre on Blackpool Pier. The stage doorman looked bored to tears.

'I've come to audition,' I said.

'What for?' He stubbed out his cigarette on the sole of his shoe.

'For this show.' I showed him my accordion and started telling him all about my act.

'No point in telling me, son,' he said. 'You've had a wasted journey.'

He explained that all of the theatres were booked up for the whole season. Most of the acts had been signed up as long ago as the end of the previous summer.

'Couldn't I just wait and run through my stuff for the star of the show?' I asked hopefully.

'No point, son. Get yourself an agent and he'll arrange auditions for you.'

So I turned round and lugged my great heavy accordion case back to the boarding house. The trip wasn't entirely wasted. I got to watch Bob and Shelda become the world ballroom dancing champions. I was their only supporter.

Television was still in its infancy in the early 1950s. TV sets were expensive and the closest a lot of people came to seeing one was in a shop window. The BBC *was* television – there were no other stations. Most of the programmes were light entertainment and variety shows, with stars who had come from radio or the stage.

I read an advertisement which announced that open auditions

were being held in Shepherd's Bush so I went along and waited my turn.

Sitting at the piano, I did an impersonation of Danny Kaye singing 'Fairy Pipers on the Hill', in what I fondly imagined was a refined English accent. A camera filmed the proceedings and beamed the pictures and sound throughout the building. Producers could sit in their offices and watch the young hopefuls do their stuff.

A week later, I was asked to come in again. This time they wanted me to go through my music in detail so they could arrange it for a big TV orchestra. I was amazed.

'Do you mean that you're going to put me on television?' I asked, still a bit slow on the uptake.

'Yes.'

'Singing and playing?'

'Yes.'

I must have looked like a stunned mullet. The spot I'd been given was on *Benny Hill's Variety Showcase*. I'd never seen the show and knew nothing of Benny Hill. He was yet to become famous as a comedian and was simply the front man for the show.

A week later I sat in the stalls of the BBC Television Theatre on Shepherd's Bush Green waiting my turn to rehearse. The orchestra had been warming up. I'd never done any singing except with my own accompaniment, or at most a three-piece band. Now I had thirty musicians – an instant audience of experts. I felt sick.

Sitting on the other side of the stalls was another young man. He saw me looking nervously in his direction and made his way across the empty rows of seats. He held out his hand and gave me a big confident smile.

'Let me introduce myself,' he said. 'My name's Des O'Connor. Remember that name. You're going to hear a lot more of me.'

I couldn't think of anything to say in the face of so much confidence. He was about my age, but I looked at him in awe. Des wasn't singing in those days. He told jokes and had a very funny line of patter.

When my turn came to rehearse, I was so nervous that my lips kept sticking to my teeth. The musical director, Harry Rabinowitz, had to stop the orchestra and keep saying to me, 'You're rushing. Let's try it again.'

I grew more and more panicky. The orchestra was half the width of the theatre away which meant that the sound seemed to reach me late. This threw out my timing and I compensated by too little or too much.

All television was 'live' in those days. There were no second chances. On the night of the show, I waited backstage dressed in my dinner jacket and bow tie. When my turn came, I was so nervous that everything seemed to pass in a blur.

The audience was in darkness and I could just see the first few rows. I didn't look at anyone. I kept staring straight ahead into the darkness just above their heads. The cameras were at the front of the stage. I wasn't sure if I should look directly at them, or not.

For most of the song I was in and out of time with the orchestra. At least by the final notes we were together. I heard the applause and Benny Hill emerged into the spotlight. I then had to get off stage quickly before the next act. I must have been fairly dreadful because there was no mention of my name in the newspaper notices next day.

My abiding memory of the show is of a dancer with a pretty face and dark shadows under her eyes. Two days later she committed suicide and the newspapers published a sad little photo of her in the single-column piece. It sent a chill up my spine.

One Sunday morning at about seven o'clock, I woke to a strange silence in the street below. Then I heard excited voices. A couple of Aussie girls were staying in the room below me. Something must be happening outside.

Opening the curtains I saw snowflakes the size of two bob bits floating silently down. Pulling on a pair of shorts I dashed down the corridor to Alex's room.

'It's snowing! It's snowing!' I yelled, banging on his door.

'So vot!' came his grumpy reply. Then I realized that Alex had seen snow all his life. For me it was the first time. I made a miniature snowman on my window ledge, and later went out and threw snowballs at parked cars.

Alex passed his exams in every subject, which thrilled us both. We celebrated by cooking up a feast in my room. Mum had packed me a huge hamper of food before I left Australia. There were tins of corned beef, ham, baked beans and sausages. We buttered slabs of bread and had stewed steak on top. What luxury!

Alex invited me to spend Christmas in Germany with his family. The Haussmanns paid for the trip as a way of thanking me for all the help I'd given Alex.

Although Alex had mentioned that his father was the Justice Minister in the South German parliament, I had no idea how important this was until I saw their house. It was impossibly grand, with a sweeping staircase and dozens of rooms. At dinner, I was suddenly confronted with six pieces of exquisite cutlery on either side of gleaming white bone-china plates. Four crystal goblets were arranged in front of me.

To my horror, I discovered that houseguests were served first. A serving girl in an antique lace pinafore over a black dress stood at my right side with a silver plate of salad held about two inches from my right ear. I managed to get a healthy portion of salad halfway to my plate when the salad servers disengaged. Sloppy wet leaves, covered in oil and vinegar, sprayed in every direction.

I didn't know enough German to apologize or make any sort of joke. The silence seemed to last for ever.

On Christmas Eve they handed out presents. Everybody was dressed up to the nines sitting round the tree. I hadn't brought any decent clothes. (Well, I didn't *have* any decent clothes.) There were 'oohs' and 'aahs' as wrapping paper was torn away.

Sitting in this home, unable to speak to anyone except Alex, I felt like a lost soul. Then I heard my name called. Alex's father handed me a present. I unwrapped it. It was a simple white cup with the word 'Rolf' in blue glazed lettering on the side. I burst into tears in front of everyone.

Lonely and far from home, I was overwhelmed by home-sickness. Mr Haussmann was suddenly also in tears. He gave me a huge hug. Neither of us knew the words, but both of us understood the emotion. The warmth I was shown by that family was quite extraordinary. They made me feel very welcome and very special.

Alex had a little stepbrother and stepsister. I used to tell them stories, inventing characters and doing little drawings. In particular they loved a story about an octopus and a shark. Octopus was *Seepolyp* in German, so he became Herr Polyp. As I came up with new adventures and drawings, the kids would help me learn new German words and correct my pronunciation.

I began to realize that drawing is like a universal language that crosses all borders and cultures, captivating children and adults alike. It could even be called the ultimate form of magic. Starting from the blank page, the options are infinite, and nobody knows what will emerge except the artist.

Back in London I finally acted on the advice of Trafford Whitelock and the stage doorman at Blackpool. I went looking for an agent. Trafford had suggested I try International Artists Representation (IAR), which had a good reputation.

I made an appointment and found myself in the office of Phyllis Rounce, one of the partners. I put on the relaxed air of someone who was used to this sort of thing.

'Take a seat,' she said.

'I'm not that interested in chairs,' I said, trying to sound laid back. Instead, I sat on the floor, propped against the wall, and began telling her how good I was. Phyl must have wondered what on earth she'd struck, as she peered at this weird Australian who was just visible over the edge of her desk. I found out later that they had another Aussie on their books, Bill Kerr, so she must have had some idea of what to expect.

Having spent twenty minutes waxing lyrical about my prowess, I finally drew breath. Phyl took the opportunity to interrupt and ask a few questions. She would start looking for openings for me, she said, as I was ushered outside.

That went well, I thought.

I hopped on a train back to Earl's Court and was amazed to find a phone message waiting when I arrived. Phyl had arranged an audition for the next day. How impressive!

The Gargoyle was a tiny cabaret room, just off Curzon Street near Hyde Park. Sitting at a piano, I ran through all my Danny Kaye stuff, while the manager, Bertie Meadows, and Phyl sat up the back out of sight in the darkness.

I finished everything I knew and stopped playing. I could hear muffled whispers in the dark. It was the first time Phyl had heard my stuff and I was quite nervous. As they carried on chatting I began to fidget, growing embarrassed by the delay.

I toyed with some boogie-woogie on the piano to keep myself occupied. The muttering stopped. After a while Bertie Meadows called out. 'Now that's the sort of thing my patrons would love. Can you do any more?'

'Yeah!'

I proceeded to play him loads more. Sister Mary Magdalene would have been horrified.

The upshot was a four-week engagement starting on Monday night. I say 'night' but in reality my half-hour spot didn't start until two in the morning.

Phyl Rounce told me afterwards that Bertie had been reluctant to sign me when he heard my Danny Kaye impressions. He took the attitude, 'Who wants to hear an imitation of Danny Kaye when you can see the real thing at the London Palladium?'

It was amazing to think that my musical hero was so close. I had seen him in all those wonderful films and listened to his songs on the radio. And now he was performing just round the corner.

Did I rush out to buy a ticket?

No I did not.

Why?

Because, in my own estimation, people like me didn't go to the theatre. I thought the London Palladium was for toffs in dinner suits and bow ties; well-to-do people with rounded accents and houses in Bayswater and Belgravia.

The theatre had always been beyond my aspirations. It was like the opera and symphony concerts. These things belonged to different people. As a result, I never went to see Danny Kaye live, and I regret it to this day.

My first week of cabaret was a disaster. The clientele was mostly made up of young Guards officers who all sounded like Terry-Thomas and had pretty debutantes on their arms. I tried to sound English – remembering all those elocution lessons from Mum – but these people could spot the phoney accent a mile off.

Colonel Bill Alexander, the other partner at IAR, had told me that I sounded like some sort of second-rate cockney. 'Lose that atrocious accent, old boy, otherwise you'll never work at all, do you see.'

He was at least twice my age and spoke in a wonderful plummy voice, so I figured he knew what he was talking about.

The really upper-crust English accent had always made me feel incredibly small (just look at the fox-hunting fiasco). It was the sort of voice that had me wanting to tug my forelock and duck my head. I felt like a stunted pimply-faced youth among real adults.

I don't know where this came from. Dad had always railed against the idea of class making someone better. At the same time I knew that the only Australians who spoke like that had gone to expensive private schools to learn just that – to speak 'properly'. And it seemed as though the only reason for them to speak 'properly' was to put other people in their place.

Hard as I tried to remember the lessons Dad taught me about all of us being equal, I forgot them completely whenever someone finished a sentence with 'old boy' and peered down their nose at me. No matter what Dad said, the *real* world was divided by class and I came from the bottom one.

Despite all my best efforts to sound English during my cabaret performance, it made no difference. The audience ignored me and talked constantly. I died a thousand deaths in the space of only half an hour.

Most nights when I finished my allotted spot, nobody even noticed. I slipped out of the club and set off walking home from the West End to Earl's Court. The tube had stopped running and a cab would cost me my wages for the night.

It was around four by the time I reached the boarding house. By 10 a.m. next day I'd be fast asleep across my desk at art college.

One night I was walking home and I came across a long low brick wall which I remembered seeing from the number 30 bus heading into town. I used to love walking on brick walls as a kid. In a split second I was up there, my tiredness forgotten.

Balancing with my arms outspread, I walked for about fifty yards along this wall giggling to myself. Suddenly, a voice echoed from below. 'What are you doing, sir?'

I looked down to see two London bobbies staring up at me from the pavement.

'Er . . . I was . . . er . . . walking on this wall.'

'Why, sir?'

'Er . . . well . . . when I was a kid I used to . . . you know . . .'

'Would you come down here please, sir?'

Feeling rather sheepish, I hopped down and landed with a thump in front of them.

'Where are you going, sir?'

'Home. I'm heading home . . . I live just up the road.' I waved my arm vaguely in the direction of Earl's Court.

'Where exactly?'

'What?'

'Where exactly do you live, sir?'

At that moment someone wiped a wet cloth across the slate of my mind. I couldn't remember. The policemen waited.

'This is going to sound stupid, but I've forgotten where I live. It's just up there . . .' I laughed . . . alone.

'Would you know the way, sir?'

'Of course. I live there!'

'We'll come along with you, sir.'

I tried to explain that it wasn't really necessary, but they insisted. The three of us trooped off. I led the way, trying to bridge the silence by making polite, cheerful conversation. It wasn't easy because I was the only one talking.

Finally we reached my street. I read the name off the signpost and it all came flooding back. 'Of course, 35 Earl's Court Square. That's where I live.'

'We'll just come right home with you, sir.'

'There's really no need. I'll be alright from here.'

They wouldn't take no for an answer. Similarly, when I reached the front door they insisted on seeing me safely inside.

I fumbled in my pocket for the keys. My embarrassed laugh seemed rather high-pitched and desperate. 'You're not going to believe this, but I've left my front door key in my other trousers.'

Even in the darkness, I could see their eyebrows lift.

'Sir, is there anyone in the house who could vouch for you?'

I didn't know what 'vouch for' meant, but I spluttered, 'The landlady knows me . . . Mrs Squirrel.'

A few weeks earlier I'd forgotten my key and spent a filthy and miserable night in the coal cellar trying to keep warm because I didn't want to wake anybody up. Next morning Mrs Squirrel told me very firmly, 'Don't be so stupid. I'll always answer the door.'

While contemplating this, the more senior of the policemen interrupted my thoughts and said, 'Would you care to ring the bell, sir?'

After about five minutes Mrs Squirrel appeared at the door in her dressing gown. In a moment of blind panic I thought she might deny knowing me. Instead, she said, 'Of course I know him – he lives here.'

The policemen apologized to Mrs Squirrel and bade her good night. At the same time they looked at me suspiciously and didn't say a thing. I'm sure they thought I was a dangerous lunatic.

*

At least once a week I made a trip to Savoy House on the Strand, where I could read all the papers from home and catch up with other West Aussies. Among them was Max Dimmitt, the son of the West Australian Agent General in London. Max was going out with Aussie actress Anne Haddy, who years later would star in *Neighbours*.

'There's a new club opening in Fulham,' he said excitedly. 'It's called the Down Under Club. Thursday night is the big opening. Why don't you bring your squeeze box down and we'll have some fun?'

The Down Under Club was in a row of terraces. The basements had been knocked through to create one big open room. It had sawdust on the floor and fishing nets strung from the ceiling. By the time I arrived a couple of hundred people had packed the place and the bar was doing a roaring trade.

The owner, Ted Falcon Barker, was an Aussie with a glamorous-looking wife called Belle. He was happy to let me play a few songs and didn't bother with any introduction. Three hours later I was exhausted and still singing myself stupid.

The audience was so noisy and raucous I was amazed that none of the neighbours complained. At closing time punters spilled onto the street, singing loudly and weaving along the footpaths. Years later I discovered that Ted had foreseen the problem and invited the local police bigwig down to the club.

'Now look, we're going to get complaints, but I'm sure we can come to some sort of arrangement,' he said, as he slipped an envelope across the table. Ted also took the precaution of having the entire conversation secretly tape-recorded. This was his insurance policy, just in case the policeman ever tried to renege on the deal. After that money changed hands regularly and no raids ever took place.

At the end of that opening night Ted asked me to come back the following week, but I said it was too exhausting.

A couple of weeks later he phoned me. 'Well look. I can't pay you anything at the moment, but what if I advertise that you're coming next week? If you pull in a decent crowd, we'll talk about what I could afford.'

I agreed.

The place was absolutely jumping when I arrived. After I'd played for three solid hours Ted offered to pay me thirty bob a night – ridiculous money. I should have done something about it then, but I'd never been a businessman. Instead I told myself it was money for jam because I enjoyed it so much.

My reputation with finances had never been very good. As a teenager when I started doing commissions for portraits and landscapes I didn't discuss the payment until after the event. Not surprisingly, this tended to seriously diminish my bargaining power.

The same was true of my gigs with the band. I agreed with the first figure anyone suggested just to get over the awkward business of talking about money as quickly as possible.

Dad had always said, 'Money is the last thing you worry about. The important thing is to be doing what you want to do.' That seemed a reasonable philosophy to me. Unfortunately, it was never likely to make me rich.

Dad's attitude was that you didn't discuss money. It wasn't a polite subject. I must have taken this on board because I was lousy at raising the topic.

I played at the Down Under Club every Thursday night from eight to eleven. I arrived early and hung around, watching the clock tick down. Even though I knew quite a few people in the crowd, I still felt nervous.

There was no introduction or drum roll or dimming of the lights. Instead I just wandered out into the centre of the crowd with the accordion strapped to my shoulders. Shuffling in the sawdust, I stared at my feet for the first twenty minutes. I normally started with an instrumental – 'Swingin' Shepherd Blues', 'Baby Elephant Walk' or 'Swingin' Safari'.

By eight thirty I'd managed to get my eyes up from the floor to waist height and by nine o'clock I was actually looking at people.

The microphone hung from the ceiling between the fishing nets. If by chance I was foolish enough to hit the net above my head, a shower of dust would descend and I couldn't see for half an hour, let alone sing properly.

As my confidence grew I started belting out the songs they wanted to hear with choruses they all knew. They loved the well-known Aussie songs like 'Waltzing Matilda' and raucous numbers with naughty verses that were subtle rather than crude.

One of the songs was about a Welsh engine driver called Crawshaw Bailey, although I called him Cosher Bailey because it was easier to sing. It had to be sung in a Welsh accent, of course. Here's just a taste of it.

> *Oh he's got a sister Grace*
> *And she's got us in disgrace.*
> *It's alright in Piccadilly*
> *But she tried it in Caerphilly.*

Everyone joined in the chorus:

> *Have you ever saw, have you ever saw,*
> *Have you ever saw such a funny thing before.*
>
> *He's got a brother Matthew,*
> *He do love to climb up statues.*
> *Once he climbed right up on Venus*
> *But he fell and broke his elbow.*
> *Have you ever saw, have you ever saw,*
> *Have you ever saw such a funny thing before.*

At the end of all the verses I'd stop and say, 'Look, there's one final bit, and honestly, the chap who wrote this should have been given the poet laureateship for sheer poetical construction of a verse.' Slightly *colla voce*, I sang:

Little Willy's much improved
Since he had them both removed.
No incentive, no desire
Sings falsetto in the choir.

One of the biggest laughs was for a parody of an old Edwardian melodrama. I did both voices – a gin-sodden upper-crust lecher, Sir Jasper, and the quavering falsetto pleas of the heroine.

Sir Jasper: 'The whip!'

Our heroine: 'No, no.'

'The whip!'

'No, no, anything but the whip!'

'Anything?'

'The whip.'

'Where are you?'

'I won't tell you.'

'Where *are* you?'

'I will not tell you.'

'By God, woman, when I find you I'm going to brutally ravish you.'

'I'm in the cupboard under the stairs.'

And more in that vein ... very juvenile stuff really, but the crowd at the Down Under Club loved it.

Very early on I decided that I wouldn't do jokes that were crude or relied on filth alone for laughs. Most of the time inferences worked better than direct references and subtlety got bigger laughs than whacking people in the face.

One of my favourite routines was delivered in the haughty tones of a Church of England vicar.

'I must ask the young gentlemen in the congregation to refrain from writing their racing tips in the back of the prayer books. We find this practice most irreligious and the information ... unreliable.'

Then the crowd joined in for the chorus:

Come and join us, come and join us,
Come and join our happy army,
Come and join us, come and join us,
Come and join our happy throng.

Other verses included: 'I must ask the young gentlemen of the congregation to refrain from throwing their cigarette butts in the toilets as this practice blocks the drains and makes the butts so difficult to re-roll,' and 'Miss Johnson, well-known spinster of this parish, passed away last week and was laid to rest with the simple inscription on her tomb, "Returned unopened."'

My savings had well and truly run out and I'd become the archetypal struggling art student. Mum and Dad would send me twenty quid when they could afford it, along with food parcels packed with enough tins to last me six months. At least I was never going to starve.

The late nights were playing hell with my art college lectures and my time-keeping had become even more erratic. A lot of the other students were far more dedicated. One mate, Clive Gunnell, worked all night on the telephone exchange and went to college during the day. He lived entirely on onions and vitamin pills and I don't know how he kept going (or how anyone could sit next to him).

In my second year I moved from City & Guilds to the Central School of Arts and Crafts in Tottenham Court Road. I found it even worse. Again there was no suggestion of painting portraits. Instead the lectures were about how to plan murals, which didn't interest me at all.

After a while I started missing classes and concentrating on getting work. Apart from the Down Under Club and occasional cabaret spots, I painted portraits for five quid a time. Unfortunately, most of my friends were equally broke and couldn't afford to pay me.

Phyl Rounce managed to get me a spot in a review called *One Under the Eight* produced by Josephine Douglas, a hot-shot radio producer, best known later for her TV production *What's My Line?*

There were seven of us in this review, doing specially written material at a little upstairs theatre in Wilton Place, near Hyde Park Corner.

I sang a song called 'Down Below' with a guy called Arthur Bentley. We were supposed to be sewermen working underneath St James's Park. We came up out of a hole in the stage, dressed in filthy overalls, singing:

> *It's amazing what yer finds, dahn below,*
> *Many fings of diff'rent kinds, dahn below,*
> *There's a wristwatch all entwined, in a lengf of bacon rind,*
> *Mind yer . . . that ain't all yer find . . . dahn below.*

The manager of the theatre, Oliver Moxam, was soon to open a larger refurbished nightclub on the ground floor. After one of the review shows, I suggested that I could do the cabaret for him when the new club opened. He agreed and on the opening night I did twenty minutes at the piano singing Danny Kaye songs and anything else that I considered posh enough for this sort of up-market audience.

When I finished Oliver came on stage to introduce 'a very special friend who has just come from entertaining at the Savoy Hotel'.

Hermione Gingold was one of the top cabaret entertainers in London at the time and later she appeared in many films. She's probably best remembered for playing Maurice Chevalier's old flame in *Gigi*. They sang the duet 'Ah, Yes, I Remember It Well'.

Hermione electrified the place. The big news story of that week was the first ever sex-change operation. Chris Jorgenson had just become Christine Jorgenson.

Accompanied by a pianist, Hermione sat on the edge of the grand piano, tucked up her hair under a cloth cap, stuck a pipe in her mouth and sang, 'I changed my sex a week ago today . . .'

It was a comic masterpiece, dealing with every aspect you could think of surrounding the subject. All the delicate pauses, asides and raised eyebrows were perfectly timed. I sat totally mesmerized, hanging on her every word.

Afterwards Oliver came across to me and asked if I'd like to meet Miss Gingold.

Ushered into her presence, I shook her hand.

'Can I tell you something about your performance?' she said.

I nodded. I thought she was going to say how good I was. What she actually said was, 'You never looked at me once.'

'Sorry . . . What?'

'You never looked at me once in your entire performance.'

'But I didn't know who you were then. I've only just met you.'

'You misunderstand me. You didn't look at *anyone* in the audience. You worked to a spot on the wall above our heads. You effectively gave us all permission to talk among ourselves or do whatever we liked – light a cigarette, get up and go to the bar . . . If you're not looking at us, we don't feel we have to pay attention.'

My first impulse was to defend myself, but I sort of knew that she was right.

'It doesn't matter how good your songs are or how well you play the piano or how clever you are at telling a joke,' she carried on, 'you will never achieve your potential unless you have the courage to meet people's eyes. If you look at one person in the audience and talk and sing directly to that one individual, by some indefinable magic everybody else in the room believes you are talking to them personally.'

Hermione also told me to be aware of everything happening in the audience.

'If somebody sneezes, don't ignore it. Everybody else in the place has heard it, so you might as well say, "Bless you." And if a waiter drops a tray of glasses, it's no use acting as though it hasn't happened. Acknowledge it. Make it part of the act. It shows that you're on the ball.'

I hated admitting it, but she had read me like a book. Whenever

I performed, whether at the Down Under Club or the Gargoyle Room, I didn't have the nerve to make eye contact with the audience. It was so much easier to look at the wall behind them and hope everything was OK.

Hermione had just given me the most valuable piece of advice I would ever receive in my whole career. It became like a mantra and I passed it on to every young wannabe I met along the way.

She made me realize that performing was like war. If you don't win, you lose. There is no honourable draw. Entertaining people means taking charge. They appreciate being told what to do. They want to forget their troubles for a few hours and let someone else make the decisions.

Clement Freud, the grandson of Sigmund Freud, gave a lot of young hopefuls their start in the cabaret field. I was one of them. He was a wonderful bon vivant and raconteur, with a flamboyant sense of style. His Royal Court Theatre Club in Sloane Square was another one of those swanky places full of Guards officers in uniform, or men in immaculate dinner jackets. The women looked as if they had stepped straight from the society pages of *Tatler*.

Some nights the place was pretty empty but I always felt I had to do my full hour spot. One particular evening, the staff out-numbered patrons by about three to one. I soldiered on bravely through the silence, my mouth dry as dust.

I came off stage and Clement said in his typically deep throaty voice, 'You're such a masochist, old boy. If you're dying out there, get off.' He had raised an eyebrow and tilted his head to one side.

'But you're paying me for the cabaret.'

'Look, old boy, you don't have to put up with that. If they're not interested, just finish the song you're doing and get off.'

I should have taken his advice. I died out there on more nights than I care to remember. Sometimes I felt suffocated by the silence and at other times drowned out by the chatter from the tables, as people totally ignored the show.

There were lots of little corners and alcoves with tables where people could sit in relative privacy. I came off stage one night and said to Clement, 'Did you see the couple in the alcove on my right? He was all over her like a rash.'

'Yes,' replied Clement dryly. 'I very nearly sent him over a finger bowl.'

My jaw dropped.

All through the fifties I laboured under the mistaken idea that there were two distinct sorts of entertainment. On the one hand there was the refined, upper-crust sort that involved dinner jackets, polite applause and Guards officers and their 'debs'. On the other hand there were the rollicking, madcap, boisterous nights at the Down Under Club. The two were totally different and unconnected in my mind. The piano was a refined cabaret instrument and the accordion was for rough, scruff sing-alongs. The Royal Court Theatre Club was the 'real world' of entertainment, while the Down Under Club was just a bit of fun.

The material I sang at each venue was also totally different. I thought the rollicking naughty lyrics of 'Cosher Bailey' would horrify the ladies and gentlemen at the Royal Court Theatre Club.

This was rubbish, of course. I was so paranoid about class that I thought only 'sophisticated' comedy would work for Clement's patrons. For them I wore a dinner jacket, put on what I assumed was an English accent and sang whimsical little ditties full of wordplay and banter.

One of the songs I wrote for the club was called 'Maximilian Mouse'.

> *I am a mouse called Maximilian mouse,*
> *And I live in my Maximilian . . . mouse house.*
> *I'm very well bred, I'm pure Castilian mouse,*
> *And I come from a long, long, long, long, long,*
> *   long line of . . . Castilian mouses. Ole!*

At this point I would leap to my feet, whack the piano 'one two' with my hands and then strike a bullfighter's pose with one arm wrapped around my body and the other raised, with the hand drooping over my head.

The audience, thinking the remarkably short song was over, lurched into applause. Then I sat down and carried on with the rest of the song. It told the story of a tiny mouse who is accidentally forced into fighting a huge bull.

It was a whimsical piece of fun, very Noel Coward in style. I would never have dreamed of doing that at the Down Under Club. They'd have killed me, I thought.

Another 'sophisticated' song started off as a poem I read in *Punch*. Women's fashion at the time seemed fixated with A-line and H-line dresses. I set the poem to music.

> *What will your line be next, my love?*
> *Will it be 'H' or 'A'?*
> *What letter, my pet, of the alphabet*
> *Are you going to be today?*

It went on in a similar vein. This to me was a perfect song for the Royal Court Theatre crowd.

I kept both sides of my work totally separate and would never let them meet. Phyl Rounce and Clement Freud had no idea that I led rowdy sing-alongs in a basement in Fulham every Thursday night.

Of course, this created problems when I had to do both gigs on the one night. After finishing at the Down Under Club I would tear across to Sloane Square and do a quick change into my dinner jacket and bow tie in the toilet. Always slightly late, I arrived just as Clement was doing his little routine of telling a few jokes before giving me a big cabaret introduction.

Doing two shows on the one night wrecked my voice and often I couldn't croak afterwards until Saturday morning. Living a secret life is never easy.

Chapter Five

'AUSTRALIAN ARE WE, SIR?'

IN JUNE 1953, ALL OF LONDON WAS PREPARING FOR THE Coronation of Queen Elizabeth. Loads of Aussie troops were in England as part of the celebrations. I looked out of my third-floor window one Sunday morning and saw soldiers marching down the street, wearing their familiar slouch hats.

Grabbing my accordion, I opened the window and sat on the ledge with my legs dangling outside, playing 'Waltzing Matilda'. The drill sergeant gave an 'eyes left' command as they passed. They all looked up at me as they swung along. I hope I gave them as big a lift as they gave me.

The night before the Coronation, Alex and I took a blanket each and set off on the last tube for Hyde Park Corner. I lugged my accordion the whole way because I figured it would help pass the time. We chose our spot on the route of the royal procession and settled down for the night. It was bloody freezing. There were people all round us wrapped in blankets and sipping mugs of tea from Thermos flasks.

An hour or so later a lady with a tape recorder came wandering along doing interviews with visitors from all parts of the world.

She was thrilled to hear me playing 'Waltzing Matilda'. As I finished the chorus, she asked me about the Coronation and I told her how exciting it was.

Even though it drizzled with rain, nothing could dampen Coronation Day. The young Elizabeth looked beautiful as she waved from a golden carriage.

A month later, I had an ecstatic letter from Mum. She and Dad had been listening to the BBC reporting from London on the Coronation. In the background they could hear someone playing 'Waltzing Matilda' on the accordion and singing along with it.

'It's Rolf,' shouted Mum.

'Rubbish, woman,' Dad said. 'There must be a million Australians in England.'

'Don't you think I know my own son's voice?'

They argued for an hour. I think Dad was trying to protect her from the sense of loneliness and loss.

When my letter arrived giving them all my latest news, Mum was able to say, 'I told you so.'

My original plan of spending a year away had quickly been forgotten. Twelve months wasn't long enough. I had too many things I wanted to do.

Whatever happened, I knew that I wasn't going back to teaching. As soon as I could afford it, I planned to repay my bond to the Education Department.

I missed Australia, particularly Mum and Dad and Buster Fleabags. Certain things made me feel homesick. In bed one morning, in that half-world between sleep and waking, I heard Dad in the kitchen scraping the toast into the sink. He always burned the toast. I knew at that moment if I opened my eyes I would see him through the curtain separating the sleep–out from the kitchen. He'd be sitting at the table with a cup of tea and his toast.

But when my eyes opened, I saw nothing except a wall a few inches away. The noise had been Malcolm doing something on the other side of the room. Instead of being back in Bassendean, I was on the other side of the world.

Another time, I was showing Alex a book that Mum had sent me. It had photographs of Perth and I began explaining each scene and the memories they held for me. Suddenly, I found myself crying. I was embarrassed to be sobbing in front of another bloke, but Alex put his arm round my shoulders and told me not to worry.

A lot of Aussies make it through the first winter, but the second drives them home. The low dark skies seem to weigh them down and they miss the sunshine. Instead, I found the starkness of winter in England to be quite beautiful. I was forever painting scenes in my mind as the bus moved me through the mist and fog.

Aesthetically and artistically, the northern winter is fascinating. I love the way the misty atmosphere can create a sense of comparative distance. You can determine how far away objects are by their different tones. Something half a mile away, for example, can be a very pale grey and objects that are closer appear darker. By mixing four or five blue-greys on a palette, you can create a scene with the most amazing depth just by positioning things in their different tones.

I found it much harder to paint the English countryside in the summer. The trees are just big green blobs. Gum trees, no matter how full of leaves they are, still show the skeleton of branches underneath. I missed that.

Disillusioned with art school, I didn't bother going back after my second year. Although still interested in being a portrait painter, I thought there had to be a better way.

Fate stepped in when I read an article in the newspaper about an Australian Artists' Association being formed in London. Any interested parties were invited to come along to the first meeting at Australia House on the Strand.

I turned up and took a seat. Among those on stage was a man I recognized as Hayward ('Bill') Veal, the hero of my teenage aspirations to be a painter. He was living in London and helping launch the new association.

Hoping to meet him, I put my name up for one of the committees, but he was surrounded by people and I couldn't get close to him that night.

A week later, totally by chance, I bumped into Bill Veal and his wife, Minka, on the platform at Earl's Court Station. I told him the story of spending three days waiting for him outside his Sydney studio. The notice on the door had said, 'Back in ten minutes.'

'Oh, that,' he laughed. 'I never took that down.'

We caught the same train and chatted all the way to the West End like old friends.

'What sort of things do you want to do with your art?' he asked.

'I want to paint like you.'

He laughed and seemed embarrassed. He was a very modest man.

As he and Minka stepped off the tube, he turned to me. 'Listen. I'm running a two-week course at Heatherley's Art School during their holidays. It starts next week. Why don't you come along?'

'I haven't got any money.'

'Don't worry about that. You may not even want to stay.'

I couldn't believe my luck. The following Monday I turned up at Heatherley's Art School, near Victoria Station. I had my box of oil paints, brushes and some canvas paper. I couldn't afford proper canvas.

Bill had organized bits and pieces of still life for the students to paint. I chose a bunch of flowers and began slathering down thick paint. I really wanted to impress him. When I tried to put bright yellow on top of a dark brown background, the colours mixed and turned to mud. It was dreadful.

Bill looked over my shoulder.

'Well, ah, it's not quite what I meant to do,' I stammered, feeling embarrassed.

'Leave that and come with me,' he said.

He took me to a different corner of the studio and handed me a proper canvas.

'I can't afford it.'

'Don't worry about that. You can't go painting on a bit of paper.' He pointed to a table. 'Now I want you to set up something that interests you. It doesn't matter what it is. Just something you think you'd like to paint.'

I set up a vase and some bottles of different shapes and sizes. Bill handed me a single tube of Burnt Sienna. 'Now look. Here's a brush, some turpentine and a rag. I want you to use as little paint as you can. Nothing thick. And I want you to do the whole picture at once. Don't start at the edge, or in the middle. Do everything at once as a blur. You can try half closing your eyes when you look at it. Paint the blur, with the darks and lights roughly in the right places. Forget the fine detail.'

'All in monochrome?' I asked incredulously.

'Yes. Kill the whole white canvas. Once you've done that, I'll come back.'

I did as he asked, trying to paint the complete picture at once, using as little paint as possible.

Bill came back and said, 'Now look at your picture. Then look at the subject. Find me three big differences between the painting and the scene. Just the big differences.'

'Well, the shape of that dark bit isn't right. It should be rounder.'

'OK. Think of another one.'

'Well, you see where the light reflects off the biggest bottle? I'm not happy with that.'

'Which one do you think is the most important?'

'Probably the dark bit.'

'Right. Fix that first.'

He watched me work with a paintbrush and rag. 'Now what's the biggest difference?'

'Definitely the light.'

'OK, fix that.'

Bruce and me: we were forever fighting as kids, but Bruce finally rescued me.

THE HARRIS CLAN

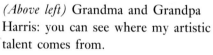

(*Above left*) Grandma and Grandpa Harris: you can see where my artistic talent comes from.

(*Above right*) Brothers in arms: Crom and Carl in uniform.

(*Below*) Dad in his Aussie slouch hat…and (*left*) in civvies – a true working-class hero.

(Above left) Two little boys: baby me supported by Bruce.

(Above right) Bruce, Mum, me and our menagerie.

(Left) Me as Tarzan up a tree.

SWIMMING YEARS

OPPOSITE

(Above left) My painting of our wonderful river bank in Bassendean.

(Above right) Bruce playing Huck Finn. Mum and me on the jetty.

(Below) Our house from the river.

(Top) Part fish, part 15-year-old.

(Centre) On my way to the Aussie swimming championships in Melbourne.

(Right) A home-town hero (check the glasses!).

PAINTING AND PERFORMING

(Above) My first music teacher, Sister Mary Magdalene, taught me to read music.

(Right) The dog whisperer.

(Below) Auditioning for *Australia's Amateur Hour*, a national radio show.

(*Right*) My portrait of Sir James Mitchell, who turned from hero to villain in my eyes.

(*Far right*) Entertaining with my new squeeze box.

(*Above*) Chloe was my first car. My art exhibitions paid for her.

(*Right*) My portrait of Mum and two-colour linocut of Dad.

OFF TO ENGLAND

(Left) Dad made the same voyage (by sail, in the opposite direction) when he was a young man.

(Centre left) Saying goodbye to Mum and Dad on the quay, hoping Mum wouldn't cry.

(Below left) Keeping up on-board morale with a song.

(Above) A cut-out of Mum and Dad to remind me of home.

I got a bit of turps on the rag and wiped that away.

'Now what's the biggest difference?'

'The shadow is too dark in this corner.'

'Fix that up.'

Bit by bit, I slowly refined the painting. It was a revelation. I had hardly used any paint at all, but finished with a marvellous impressionist still life of the table and three bottles.

Bill clapped me on the shoulder. 'Paint what you see, don't paint what you know. If you can't see the edge of the bottle because it's transparent, then don't paint the edge. Everyone knows it's there, but if you can't see it, don't paint it.'

From that day onwards, Bill took me under his wing. He and his wife, Minka, were wonderful, feeding me at their flat in Earl's Court and taking me to galleries. Bill and I went painting together, setting up our easels beside the Thames, on Hampstead Heath or Barnes Common. We talked about art and he told me about life.

'How's the bank account?' he'd say. 'Are the spiders still in there?' He knew I was scared to look at my finances because I was always broke.

I told him the sorry tale.

'Bloody hell, we'll have to do something about that,' he said. 'I might have something for you.'

Bill was forever putting money-making schemes my way. For my sins I began designing paint-by-number pictures which I hated. I also managed to convince the editor of *London Mystery Magazine* to take several illustrations from me on a regular basis.

In the meantime, I kept doing portraits for a fiver a time. I did a wonderful one of Charlie Cave, a Londoner who worked at Savoy House, where the West Australian Government had its office. I'd tried Bill's technique and painted Charlie over several evenings. The likeness was wonderful.

Not long afterwards, I was walking along the Embankment to the Underground with Charlie's portrait under my arm when I came across a big open-air exhibition of paintings. Hundreds of visitors were wandering along, stopping to look at the work. What a brilliant idea!

I had visions of exhibiting Charlie's portrait and being flooded with commissions. I'd be rich! All I had to do was get to the Embankment early, claim my six feet of space on the wire netting and let my lone painting sell my skills.

Next morning I arrived at nine thirty. Every space was taken. I couldn't believe it.

Not to be deterred, I set my alarm clock and dragged myself out of bed the next day in time to catch the first train. I arrived at 7 a.m. bleary-eyed and clutching the portrait. Again, every space was taken. This was ridiculous.

There was only one thing for it. I caught the last train that evening, equipped with my tartan travelling rug and plans to sleep on a park bench all night. Come what may, I was going to be the first person there in the morning. The warden had let me put my painting in his lock-up shed, so I didn't have to keep lugging it back and forth.

That evening, I wandered sheepishly about the Embankment, trying to pluck up the courage to lie down on one of the benches. I had a bonus box of food that had just arrived that day from Mum. She had crystallized some of the wonderful figs from our tree in Bassendean and topped them with a layer of shelled almonds. It smelled and tasted of home.

As it grew later, the number of people on the Embankment dwindled. I finally picked out a bench that wasn't too close to a street lamp and lay down to sleep.

A torch shining in my eyes woke me. 'What are you doing, sir?' said a gruff voice.

I croaked, 'Er . . . well . . . ah.'

As I tried to get my head together, the voice said, 'Australian are you, sir?'

How could he have possibly known that?

'Er . . . yes.'

'What are you doing?'

I explained, very logically, that I needed to be up early to get a spot in the open-air art exhibition. All my previous attempts had failed, hence the all-night vigil.

'Right, carry on, sir,' said the policeman, strolling off alongside his colleague with his hands behind his back.

I closed my eyes and marvelled at how polite London bobbies were.

Drifting back into a deep sleep, I was woken some time later by another torch shining in my eyes.

'What are we doing, sir?'

'Ar . . . er . . .'

'Australian are we, sir?'

I was getting annoyed. How on earth did he know I was Australian? Did I talk in my sleep? Was it plastered on my forehead? Or perhaps the local bobbies were swapping notes with each other: 'Hey, there's an Aussie sleeping on a park bench down there. He's good for a laugh.'

Again I explained my rationale for being on the bench. These two policemen wished me goodnight and moved on. I imagined them looking for another couple of bobbies to send my way.

Unfortunately, by now sleep was beyond me. I sat up, opened the box and had some sticky figs and almonds. As I contemplated what to do with myself, a young chap came wandering along the path and gave me a look that said, 'Alright if I sit down?'

'Missed my last train,' he volunteered, taking a seat next to me on the bench.

'Like some figs or almonds?'

'No thanks.'

We sat in silence for a few moments.

'I don't quite know what to do,' he said, as he dropped his head gently on my shoulder.

What a shock! I stood up so quickly that his head snapped back with a jolt. 'I've, ah . . . just got to . . . find somewhere for a leak,' I mumbled. 'Can you keep an eye on my stuff for me?'

'Sure.'

I set off in search of some shrubbery, feeling rather nervous about my newfound bench companion. Having relieved myself, I came back and sat on the far end of the bench, keeping the blanket and box between us.

We made some pointless small talk and he introduced himself as Toby. Eventually he asked, 'Do you fancy a cup of tea?'

I laughed. 'Fat chance of that. Where would you get a cup of tea at this time of night?'

'Lyons' Corner House,' he said. 'Come on, I'll show you.'

He was already up and walking so I gathered my stuff and set off at a trot after him. We left the little bit of greenery down by the Thames, passed the Players' Theatre under the arches of Charing Cross railway station and came to Lyons' Corner House where Villiers Street meets the Strand.

To my amazement a side door was open and the two of us were soon climbing the wide staircase to the first floor.

Toby explained, 'This place is open all night. Most of the staff from the West End clubs come here when they've finished work. You can get a cup of tea and wait until the first buses and trains start running.'

I stood at the top of the stairs open-mouthed. The place was jumping. Quite a few people in the crowd were beautifully dressed in dinner jackets, evening gowns and cocktail dresses. There were chefs, waiters, cigarette girls, musicians, showgirls, and blokes who looked to me like gangsters. Everybody seemed to know everybody else.

I looked a total scruff in my oldest pair of trousers and a rain-coat that I used when I went out painting with Bill Veal. The dirt and paint splodges were ingrained in the fabric. I also had my strange-looking package wrapped in a blanket.

Toby had disappeared into the crowd. I could just see him with his back to me at the far side of the room, chatting away to some-one. I felt deserted and totally out of place.

Picking my way through the crowd, I bought a cup of tea and tried to find a space to sit down. Eventually, I fetched up on a table right by the central aisle. It was the only seat left in the place.

As I sat sipping my tea, I looked up. On the far side of the room, a fellow stood up and locked eyes with mine. I stopped with the cup halfway to my mouth, mesmerized by this figure. He wore black trousers, a gleaming white tuxedo jacket and an emerald green silk shirt and white bow tie.

He slowly began walking towards me, very deliberately and with intent. Never once did he take his eyes from mine. My gaze faltered every now and then, but when I looked back up, he was still looking straight at me. I felt like a mouse with a friendly snake coming to eat me.

The room fell silent, as people switched their attention to the pageant unfolding before them. Still frozen, with my cup in mid-air, I realized that this man was wearing make-up! He had blue eye shadow and faint lipstick, as well as a definite base of powder. The crowd seemed to part as he glided across the room and then stopped directly in front of me. He tucked his chin to his chest and contrived to look down at me under lowered brows.

'Hello,' he whispered in a throaty voice.

He blinked dreamily and ran the limp fingers of his right hand languidly up the front of my grubby fawn raincoat.

Not a teaspoon stirred in any cup. We were surrounded by silence.

Madly, I tried to think of something to say . . . anything.

'Er . . . ah . . . I . . . just came up for a cup of tea.' Brilliant, Rolf!

I searched desperately for Toby. I finally spotted him on the far side of the room.

'Him . . . yes . . I came with him . . .' I pointed across the crowd, hoping it would establish my bona fides, or better still, rescue me.

'Hmmmph,' said the painted man in the white tuxedo. He puffed up in disgust and tossed back his curls. Spinning on a brilliantly polished heel, he minced back through the crowd. I had never been so relieved in my life.

Conversation resumed at normal levels and I gulped down my

tea. Tucking my blanket-covered box under my arm, I headed for the door. As I turned to go down the stairs a huge Jamaican wearing a thick woollen hip-length jacket grabbed my bundle from behind me and boomed, 'How much fo' de blanket, man?'

I gave a slight yelp of fright as I wrenched the package free from his grip and flew down the stairs three at a time. Out on the street, I half ran and half walked down Villiers Street, with my heart thumping like mad. Every so often I looked over my shoulder.

Just as my heartbeat began returning to normal, I noticed a long piece of knotted string in the gutter. I realized I had nothing with me to use to hang my portrait up on the netting. As I bent down to pick up the string, two long shadows fell across me.

I straightened up. Two beat bobbies were silhouetted against a street lamp at the top end of the street. Both had their hands behind their backs and were watching my every move.

Self-consciously, I began walking away. The shadows followed me. It's amazing how guilty you feel in strange surroundings when confronted by the law. I was totally innocent of any wrongdoing, yet I felt nervous. I could just imagine them saying to each other, 'What's that suspicious-looking package he's carrying under his arm?'

I started giggling. I imagined telling them, 'A box of crystallized figs and almonds from my mum in Australia.' I wouldn't believe it myself.

Their footsteps were getting closer and I started to slow down. The older of the two bobbies spoke first. 'What have you got there, sir?' he asked.

I burst into hysterical laughter.

'What are you laughing at, sir?'

'Well (giggle, giggle) you'll never believe me.' Tears of panic were starting to trickle down my cheeks.

'Try us.'

'Honestly, you won't believe it.' By now I was clutching my stomach and snorting, I was laughing so hard.

'Just try me,' said the older policeman, who was still amazingly polite.

I straightened my face, looked at them both and was about to say something when I shrieked with laughter again. I simply couldn't stop. The two of them stood unmoved. After several false starts, I somehow managed to gain control.

'I just got it today . . . from my mum in Australia. You're gonna find this hard to believe . . . it's a box of figs and almonds.' I exploded in laughter again.

With icy calm, the older policeman said, 'Open it up, if you would, sir.'

'I told you that you wouldn't believe me.'

'Just open it up.'

I unwrapped the blanket, untied the box and opened the lid to reveal the sticky mass of figs and almonds. 'Would you like some?' I offered.

Both of them looked at the box and back at me. I'm fairly sure they were both convinced they were dealing with a demented idiot. Fortunately for me they could do nothing about it. I wished them good evening as they walked away. My stomach hurt from laughing so hard.

I carried on down to the bench in the Embankment park. Once again, I lay down and composed myself for sleep. Some time later I was woken by two people talking rather loudly as they walked past. How inconsiderate, I thought.

I opened my eyes and daylight flooded in. The sun was high in the sky. It was 10.45 a.m. and yet again I had missed my spot at the open-air gallery. People gave me funny looks as I staggered to my feet and made my way to the warden's lock-up. I didn't care any more. I just wanted to get my painting and go home. I never did exhibit Charlie's portrait.

Another of my attempts at money-making involved songwriting. My first one had been an autobiographical song called 'I've Lost My Mummy', about a small boy lost in a shop. I took it down to Ray Hartley to get his professional opinion and expected a torrent of praise.

Ray shrugged. 'Look, it doesn't matter what *I* think. There are at least sixty top music publishers in London. Take it round to them. They're the people who count. I'm flat out getting my *own* songs published.'

'Couldn't you just tell me what *you* think?'

'No.'

I was really disappointed. I only wanted his approval. The idea of taking it to publishers was too much like stepping out into the *real* world and putting my work on the line. I wasn't ready for that.

As a result, I didn't take a single song of the dozen I wrote in London to any of the publishers in Tin Pan Alley. For all my bravado and big talk, I didn't have the courage to risk rejection.

For two years I had been playing the Down Under Club and I was still earning peanuts. I told Ted that I wanted to quit because it just wasn't worth it.

'Well, how about three pounds ten?'

'OK, then.'

It was still ridiculously little, but as was typical of me, I accepted the first offer to avoid having to talk any more about money. I spent another three years playing at the club.

It might not have been the 'real world' of entertainment, but Thursday night at the Down Under Club was a tremendous safety valve for me. I could be unashamedly Australian after a week of wearing collars and playing the 'piarno'.

Phyl Rounce never discovered this side of my life. In the meantime she kept finding me 'proper' work, which included all the latest auditions for films and stage shows.

I made the last call back for the chorus of *Paint Your Wagon* and turned up on spec for crowd work in B-movies. I even managed to get a few minor roles. In the 1955 Tommy Trinder film *You Lucky People* I played a bearded soldier and had three lines of dialogue.

For years afterwards whenever I ran into Tommy (a big music hall star in his day) he'd shout, 'How's the old kangaroo?' He was letting me know that he remembered me. Nice.

Chapter Six

IT'S CALLED TELEVISION

M Y GRAND DREAMS OF BECOMING A PORTRAIT PAINTER HAD taken a few knocks. Nothing had panned out as easily as I'd hoped. At the same time, I had drifted into show business almost effortlessly, doing gigs for a week here and a week there.

I can't remember making a conscious decision to concentrate on one thing and not the other. Perhaps being an entertainer held the promise of a steadier income – though only just.

One of the watershed moments came on a Sunday afternoon at a big posh house in Roehampton, London. My mum's relatives, the Hagens, regularly invited me to Sunday lunch, where I would eat enough food to last until mid-afternoon Tuesday.

The family had two children, Liza aged eight and Rick, four, and after lunch we sat in the lounge while I told them stories and did drawings. Rick always wanted a bloodthirsty plot, with lots of swordplay and people being run through, while Liza preferred me to draw fairies in silken gowns. It was quite a challenge keeping both of them happy.

One of the stories I told them had the same character that I'd invented in Germany for Alex Haussmann's stepbrother and stepsister. I changed the hero's name to Oliver Polip the Octopus and added a sea fairy for Liza and some bloodthirsty pirate action for Rick.

Later that day I sat down with the kids to watch television. The show was called *Bengo the Boxer Dog*. A presenter with a thick middle-European accent told a story about Bengo and drew the same immaculate picture of this dog over and over again. He was clearly a terrific artist, but he drew too slowly, with no vitality or energy. Every drawing was identical and they bore no relation to the story.

Soon I noticed that Liza and Rick had gone out into the garden to play. They were clearly as bored as I was. Television was such a gripping medium and this show was losing the very youngsters it was designed to entertain. If I couldn't do better than that I'd want my head examined.

That evening I wrote a letter to the BBC. Part of my pitch was my ability to draw quickly. I didn't waste time on drawing perfect hands with exactly the right number of fingers. A bunch of bananas did the trick. My approach was to get on with the action and encourage the kids to use their imagination.

Drawing is the ultimate magic. From a blank piece of paper and an idea in your head, you create something from nothing. Try watching a child doing a drawing. It's mesmerizing. Only they know what's coming next and there is no limit to what they can draw.

A week after posting the letter, I had a reply from Michael Westmore, the head producer of children's programmes at the BBC. He invited me to come in and see him.

I decided to sell him the idea of Oliver Polip. Like an idiot, I spent the evening beforehand drawing a series of pictures in a little feint-lined notebook. I failed to realize, of course, that by drawing the pictures in advance, I was throwing away my main selling point – my ability to draw quickly while telling a story.

When I arrived at Michael Westmore's office, he was busy dictating letters to his secretary. Another assistant was sorting files in a filing cabinet and a young chap was running through differ-ent tunes on an upright piano in the corner.

'Right, show us what you can do, old boy,' said Westmore, with-out bothering to look up from his desk. I found myself a chair and began telling the story of the octopus and the shark. I was so ner-vous that perspiration leaked down my back and I kept tugging at my collar and tie. Meanwhile, he carried on dictating a letter. 'Dear sir, with reference to your correspondence of the fif-teenth—' He broke off to say, 'No, Muriel, the pink folder goes in the bottom drawer.' He glanced at the piano player. 'That's nice, Joe. Can you marry that short phrase with the thing you played earlier? . . . Yes, that's better.' He waved a hand towards me, 'Carry on, old boy, I'm with you.'

How was I supposed to sell myself to a man who was doing three other things at once?

I found myself talking faster and faster. I was trying to remem-ber Colonel Alexander's advice about sounding English, but that soon fell by the wayside. In the end, I was gabbling so quickly I couldn't even understand myself.

Eventually I ran out of steam and stuttered to a halt.

'Finished, old boy?'

I nodded miserably.

'Jolly good. We'll give you a ring.'

That's it, I thought. My one and only chance . . . gone. I took my miserable little book of pencil drawings and slunk out feeling in total despair.

It was Friday afternoon and I moped all weekend. On Monday morning, I set about finishing a portrait in my room. Somebody yelled from the ground floor that I had a phone call.

'Who's it from?'

'The BBC.'

I came down the stairs three at a time. A beautifully modulated Oxford English voice asked after my well-being. It was Michael Westmore.

'That story about the octopus and the shark, old boy. Very good, very good. We won't use that. Got another idea. Wondered if you'd care to come and see us.'

(Would I?) 'When?'

'Today.'

I was on a bus within five minutes. Less than an hour later I walked into the reception at BBC Lime Grove and was shunted along to a room on the ground floor. Michael Westmore introduced me to Robert Tronson, a BBC producer/director, and Bob Harbin, a puppeteer and magician.

'We've commissioned a new series,' said Michael. 'Bob here has created a puppet which he operates himself. What's he called again?'

'Fuzz,' said Bob, holding up his handiwork. The puppet had a round striped body, a tennis ball sized head with a bowler hat, and two little inflatable arms made of party squeakers that unrolled and rolled back in again when the puppeteer blew them.

Michael explained that the main presenter of the show, Richard Warner, was embarrassed about working with Fuzz. 'He says it's ridiculous for an actor of his stature to be talking to a puppet. He can't relate to it. Just thought of you, old boy. Wondered if you could draw some pictures of Fuzz and tell some stories?'

I didn't have a doubt in my mind.

'Yeah, how are you going, Fuzz?' I said, sitting down next to him. 'You what? . . . And is it hurting when you do that? . . . Let me try to help you . . . Is that better now? . . . Great. OK, let me show you something . . .'

I started sketching Fuzz on the big piece of cardboard provided, drawing him from different angles. I was in my element. All three adults in the room were captivated by the magic of watching the drawings develop.

Finally Michael asked me if I could come up with a five-minute story with half a dozen drawings for the following Saturday. 'Maybe you can be telling Fuzz about his ancestor King Fuzz climbing up an oak tree to hide from the Roundheads. What do you think? Bob will help you.'

'So Saturday is another audition?' I asked.

'Oh no, dear boy. We go to air. First show of a new series.'

My stomach lurched. I wanted to say, 'No, you've got it wrong. I only do auditions, I don't do the real thing.'

Still in shock, I had coffee with Bob Harbin and we worked out the details of the story. Bob was a South African who had come to England twenty years earlier to make his name as a magician and illusionist. He was a fantastic performer and many of the big illusions that you imagine have existed for ever were invented by him. Things like the 'Zigzag Woman', where you put an assistant in a box, close the panels and then cut the box in three, using metal blades. These smaller boxes are then shuffled around so the head might appear in the middle and the hands at the bottom and the feet where the head should be.

Bob had been very successful for a lot of years until his career seemed to reach a plateau. Tommy Cooper came along, to all intents and purposes a bumbling amateur magician who never quite got anything right. That was his selling point. He told terrible jokes, looked like a sack of potatoes and had a wonderful hangdog face, yet his comic timing was impeccable.

By comparison, Bob was a classic illusionist, not a comedian. And I think it disappointed him that he didn't have the success or status that Tommy Cooper enjoyed. Ultimately, he became another jobbing magician and had found himself on children's television operating a puppet.

We arranged to meet up at his house for a rehearsal. In the meantime I prepared a script and plotted out the drawings. Because Fuzz communicated with squeaks and whistles, it made for very one-sided dialogue.

Bob warned me in advance about his wife, Dolly. 'She loves Australians, but just be careful what you say and do.'

Dolly had once been Bob's assistant when they toured doing magic shows. And then one night in the dressing room before a performance, her costume caught alight on the gas fire. She was horribly burned and left with scars covering a third of her body.

Now she lived in constant pain, confined to a wheelchair. Despite her scars, I could see that she'd once been a beautiful woman. She treated me very warily. I think she regarded any new face as someone who wanted to steal her husband's ideas or get something for nothing. Bob was such a gentle soul that people sometimes took advantage of him.

I felt tremendously sorry for him. He clearly felt enormous guilt for what had happened to Dolly. That's probably why they were still together. He lived with a woman consumed by bitterness, who rarely had a pleasant word to say about anybody.

'Poor stupid Bob,' she called him, even in his presence. 'He'll never make any money. He'll never be famous.'

In truth, Bob Harbin was one of the finest men I have ever met. Along with Bill Veal he became a father figure to me, telling me about life, sharing his wisdom and fuelling my dreams. I think Bob saw a bit of himself in me. We had both arrived in the UK seeking adventure and fame.

For that first show I came up with six drawings to illustrate a story about King Fuzz and the Roundheads. We rehearsed the segment a few times at the Sulgrave Boys' Club, down the road from Shepherd's Bush.

I was a pain in the backside because I knew it all – when to turn to the camera, when to talk, when to draw. I was even advising other people how to do their bits. My over-confidence came from hours of practising in my room at Earl's Court, pretending the doorknob was a TV camera. This, in turn, stemmed from an article that I'd read years earlier in the *Sunday Times* in Perth.

The story was about this square box in the corner of the living room that was taking over America. People were shunning the cinemas in their thousands to stay at home and watch something called 'television'. What I remembered most about the article was that various people who had been very successful on radio had failed to make the transition to TV because they didn't know how to look at the camera.

Up until then their careers had revolved around standing in

front of a microphone, reading scripts. Nobody ever saw them. Now they were on show and every mannerism made a difference. If their eyes moved away from the screen to read a script they looked shifty. If they fidgeted too much, they looked nervous.

The presenters who had made the transition successfully, the article said, were those who had been able to discard the script altogether and live off their wits. They could also look at the camera lens and not be overwhelmed by the knowledge that they were addressing thousands of people. Instead they imagined they were speaking to one single person, or just one family in their living room.

This didn't mean looking fixedly at the camera like a snake mesmerizing its prey. That would have made people uncomfortable. It meant treating the camera the way you would treat another person – looking away now and then, smiling, nodding and occasionally asking questions as if expecting an answer.

I was only sixteen years old when I read this and yet I remember saying to myself, 'I could do that.' It wasn't a case of *wanting* to do it – I simply knew that I could.

Now I had the opportunity. I sat in my room on the edge of the bed with my doorknob 'camera', chatting away as though talking to an old friend. I told it stories, asked questions and sometimes dropped to a whisper as I leaned forward, taking the imagined viewer into my confidence. This was just like acting to an unseen audience of one. Most of my life I'd been acting out roles – doing cowboy death scenes at playtime, or pretending to be Tarzan.

Feeling supremely confident, I arrived at the studio for the first broadcast of the new series. The hour-long show was called *Jigsaw* and my ten-minute segment with Fuzz was forty minutes into the hour.

The floor manager, a big bluff Irishman called Desmond O'Donovan, boomed, 'One minute to go, all quiet in the studio.'

I felt myself go hot and cold and my stomach did a complete somersault. My confidence was suddenly undermined by nerves.

Could I really do this? Or was I about to make a complete fool of myself on TV?

I had forty minutes to wait before my segment of the show. I contemplated going quietly out of the soundproof door so that I could walk up and down the corridor to calm my nerves. I got as far as the door and then panicked. What if I lost track of time? What if I missed my segment? Too scared to leave, I sweated it out in the studio.

Finally it was my turn. I had the piano in front of me and a big board to my left holding sheets of grey cardboard for the drawings. Fuzz was on the far side of the board with Bob Harbin crouched down out of sight. Fuzz had the easy job of buzzing and squeaking, while I had to keep up a constant patter and draw at the same time. Stumbling over the first few words, I kept telling myself not to speak too quickly.

I told the story of King Fuzz and the Roundheads using six drawings, which were done in black chalk. Then I sang a song with Fuzz squeaking approval. The ten minutes seemed to last an hour.

When the show finished, Bob Tronson came down from the control room.

'Very good. You were nervous. I could see that. But it's going to be fine,' he told me.

'So what happens now?'

'We'll book you for the next six shows.'

Wonderful! Bob Harbin and I shook hands in congratulation. The rest of the weekend passed in a blur. I wanted to stop people in the street and tell them my good news.

This euphoria lasted until Monday when Robert Tronson phoned. 'Sorry, old boy, you're out.'

'What do you mean?'

'The head of Children's TV, Freda Lingstrom, has never been known to actually watch children's television, but she saw this because it's a new show. She said that we couldn't have two people with a beard and glasses doing drawings on children's television. It will "confuse the kiddywinkies", she said.'

'You're joking.'

'Sorry.'

'Who's the other one?'

'Reginald Jeffryes.'

'The guy who does "Mr and Mrs Mumbo"? But he's nothing like me. He's sixty if he's a day. He's got wire-framed glasses. He's balding with a grey goatee. I'm twenty-three with dark hair and horn-rimmed glasses.'

'I know, I know. But she's the boss, what can I do?'

'But you liked the show. Isn't there any way round it?'

Maybe the fact that I was an Australian gave me the courage to suggest 'getting round' the problem. After all, I had nothing to lose. I couldn't go running home to Mum in Eastbourne if I failed – she was 9,000 miles away.

Bob said, 'What on earth do you mean, old boy?'

'Well, just that. You're the producer. If *you* thought I was good . . . if *you* saw the potential . . . surely there must be some way to get round this woman's objections.'

There was a long pause. 'What an extraordinary suggestion.' He thought for a little longer. 'I'll tell you what I'm prepared to do. As head of Children's Television she has to sign all the contracts for the next six programmes for everyone working on the show. That's a lot of contracts and I doubt if she even reads them. I'll write one out for you and leave it in the middle of the pile. If she questions the contract I'll have to say it was a mistake. But if she signs it, then you're in.'

She signed the contract. For the next seven years I worked regularly on BBC children's shows and never once did I meet up with Freda Lingstrom.

The first three shows of the series didn't mention my name in the credits or in the *Radio Times*. Then my relatives in Wales wrote a letter to the BBC asking why the young man doing drawings on *Jigsaw* was never mentioned. After that my name began appearing.

We did a show every fortnight and I was paid £30 for each of them. Only paying three and a half quid for food and lodging, it meant I no longer had to write back to Mum and Dad for money. Before long I could even splash out on a car – a Morris Traveller, bought on the 'never never'.

We did three six-part series of *Jigsaw* during the year. Bob Harbin became my mentor. Apart from knowing a lot about show business, he set me right on any problems I had with girls, or relationships.

When I think back now I wonder how I could have reached twenty-three years of age with so little idea about how the female of the species thinks and acts. Maybe it's because I didn't have any sisters. More than likely, I just wasn't very observant.

My first serious girlfriend in London was a Melbourne girl, Barbara Karmel. I met her at the Australian Artists' Association meeting in the Strand. At first I was more interested in her sister, but realized right away that she was totally indifferent to me.

Barbara and I went out together for about two years, off and on. She put up with a lot from me. I was prone to taking up with someone else and then expecting to bounce back to Barbara if things didn't work out. I tried to be honest right from the beginning when I told her that I wasn't interested in marriage or long-term commitment. I think maybe she thought she could change that.

Barbara felt I was frittering away my talents on too many different things. She thought I should concentrate on being either a serious artist, or a cabaret star. She didn't see any future at all in children's television.

What infuriated her most of all was my inability to discuss anything serious. I was quite content to just waltz along, cracking jokes and making funny sound effects. Whenever I thought any situation was getting too deep, I tried to lighten things up, or change the subject.

Although she was a lovely girl, Barbara was so earnest and proper that I didn't once take her to the Down Under Club because I thought she would have disapproved. I also failed to win over her mother, who, like Barbara, felt I couldn't be serious. In particular, she disliked the way I was always seeking praise for any painting or drawing. It was a sign of immaturity, she said, which was probably right. I once turned up on her doorstep mid-afternoon with a pastel drawing of the Victoria and Albert Museum I'd just done. As she opened the door, my first words were, 'What do you think of this?'

She slammed the door.

At the end of the third series of *Jigsaw*, the floor manager Desmond O'Donovan took me to one side during the cast party.

'I'm being promoted to full producer next year,' he said. 'I'd love to use you in a new series but I don't think Fuzz works. He's too static. He doesn't talk.'

I thought I was about to be fired.

'Can you come up with another idea?' he said. 'We really need something that talks.'

'OK. But what about Bob?'

'We'll think of something for him.'

It was a bit daunting having to come up with a new idea. I was very comfortable doing the segments with Fuzz.

During the break, I took Barbara for a holiday to Spain along with a friend from Queensland called Marie Warnes. We took the Morris Traveller across on the ferry and drove down through France. Eventually, we stopped at a small town called San Feliú de Guixols on the Costa Brava. It was a wonderful two weeks swimming and lying on the sand.

With plenty of time to think, I came up with a new idea for the show. The character was a really cheeky schoolboy called Willoughby that I could draw afresh every week. I wanted to create a sort of instant animation so the character would come to life the moment I finished drawing him.

Rather than run the idea past Desmond, I decided to go for broke. Back in London I bought a large drawing board and a thin flat sheet of aluminium. Using all sorts of cutting knives, fretsaws, chisels, hammers, screws and springs, I made a piece of equipment that could bring my idea to life.

It needed a person to crouch behind the board to operate the eyes and mouth as well as becoming the 'voice' of Willoughby. When I showed the finished product to Desmond he was thrilled. He suggested Peter Hawkins as the voice behind the scenes.

The new one-hour show was called *Whirligig* and Willoughby had a ten-minute slot. True to his word, Desmond found a spot for Bob Harbin, who did a segment on origami (Japanese paper folding) which was one of his passions.

In the opening show I began telling a story and drawing a picture of a young boy. As I added freckles to his face, his eyes began moving restlessly back and forth as if by magic. Willoughby appeared to come to life. Next thing his mouth opened and he complained that I was taking too long.

From the beginning Peter Hawkins and I were on the same wavelength. Working together we altered and perfected the scripts I wrote – polishing the jokes and one-liners.

In an age when television only showed perfectly behaved and well-spoken children called Nigel or Rodney, Willoughby came as a heck of a shock. He was an out-and-out cockney, with a cheeky line of patter, who was always prepared to flout authority. His manners, or rather his lack of them, upset a lot of parents.

Eventually the complaints became so numerous that I was asked by the BBC to do something about it. During one episode, I slapped a piece of sticking plaster on Willoughby's mouth to shut him up. He kept muttering while I gave him a lecture on his manners. The parents were appeased.

At the same time, I came up with increasingly elaborate graphics to complement the story lines. Using split pins and cardboard cut to shape and painted, I created sunken galleons and haunted houses for Willoughby to explore, with moving bits such as quivering knives that suddenly appeared in tree trunks as if thrown.

We had the incredible luxury of being able to rehearse from

Tuesday to Saturday for a segment that lasted only six or seven minutes. This meant I could practise the sound effects and polish the scripts until they were perfect.

In 1955 commercial television arrived in London and I was approached to come up with a segment for their children's programme. Here was my chance to resurrect Oliver Polip the Octopus.

I tossed around ideas for an octopus puppet with Bob Harbin. All of the suggestions had fiercely complicated controls or were almost impossible to make. Finally, Bob said, 'Why don't you just use your hand?'

I looked at my hand and, arching my wrist, put my fingertips on the table. Then I walked my hand across the surface, paused and spun it round. The effect was instantly and magically perfect. Wow!

I whipped out a pen and drew a smiling mouth, two eyes and eyebrows on the back of my hand and walked it up and down. Oliver came to life.

I couldn't thank Bob enough.

'I did nothing. It was all you,' he said.

What a man!

The people at Associated Rediffusion loved the idea. I made a bowler hat out of papier mâché, with an elastic band as a 'chin-strap'. This went round my wrist and made it look as though Oliver was wearing his bowler at a jaunty angle.

I also made exquisite little Oliver-sized bits of furniture such as tables and period chairs. I painted them in various shades of grey (of course, colour television was still far in the future). Then I practised for hours in front of the mirror, getting all the movements right. I could make him lean on things, slip over, or sit down on chairs. He could appear excited, or bored, or angry.

As the day approached for the launch of the station the atmosphere at the Wembley studios was a mixture of nervous tension and excitement. There was a great feeling of being involved in something special. Yet we also knew that many cynics were predicting that commercial TV would fail.

The cameramen, wardrobe, make-up, props and technical staff worked horrendously long hours. It got so bad that some of the cameramen's eyesight started to fail, but we all felt like one great team, pulling together.

The rivalry with the BBC was instantaneous and almost like a war. Anybody who worked for commercial TV was almost automatically blackballed by the Beeb. If you made the mistake of switching sides you were a traitor and a turncoat. Yet for some reason, children's TV didn't seem to count. Perhaps they just assumed that it wasn't important enough. As far as I know, I was the *only* person regularly working on the BBC and ITV in those first years.

Working on both sides of the fence meant that I became quite well known as a children's presenter. When I left Lime Grove or Wembley studios after a show, kids would wait outside and ask for autographs. I was always so thrilled to be asked that I took the time to draw a little cartoon self-portrait with a whiskery face. I figured it was a bit different and people might appreciate the effort and remember me.

Chapter Seven

'WILL YOU MARRY ME?'

EVERY YEAR SINCE ARRIVING IN ENGLAND I HAD SUBMITTED A couple of paintings to the Royal Academy Summer Exhibition. In 1956, to my amazement, I had two works accepted for hanging.

The first, *Deep Water Blues*, was a portrait of one of my television producers, Roger Jenkins. It was done in oils on an old piece of hardboard which had all sorts of knife slashes across the surface. Roger was leaning back in a chair smoking, playing guitar and looking suitably debauched. Most of the colours were deep blues, hence the title.

The second picture, a watercolour, showed Mrs Squirrel standing inside her first floor window with flowers blooming in the window box. She had a bored look on her face (probably because I had kept her standing there so long), so I called it *Window Box Boredom*.

When the Royal Academy accepts an artist's work, they send an invitation to what is called Varnishing Day on the eve of the exhibition opening. Members of the public aren't allowed in, but the artists can come and retouch or repair their work if it has been damaged in transit or in hanging.

I had no idea of this at the time. I was just so chuffed to be a part of the exhibition that I went along to soak up the atmosphere and feel special. As I walked up the imposing steps of the Royal Academy, I came face to face with Alwen Hughes. She looked just as stunning as she had done in my first year at art school. She also looked just as lost as I did.

'God, you look beautiful,' I said, sweeping her up in my arms. I turned and ran the whole length of a near empty gallery, still carrying her.

'Put me down! Put . . . me . . . down!' she hissed at me through clenched teeth.

I suddenly realized the enormity of what I was doing. (Perhaps I was starting to mature a little.) I put her down gently and we stood there, red-faced, not knowing what to do or say.

'I wanted to show you something,' I said sheepishly. I took her with me while I found where my paintings were hanging. She said all the right things.

'But what are you doing here?' I finally asked.

She laughed. 'The same as you.' She took me to see two terrific life-sized sculptures of animal heads. The works had such energy and power that clearly Alwen had an amazing talent.

'Do you fancy a coffee?' I asked, not feeling very confident.

'OK.'

I almost did a double take. She had said yes!

We walked up and down Piccadilly for an hour looking for a coffee shop. Isn't it typical! Just when I get this stunning lady to go out with me, I couldn't find a place to take her. Eventually, we shrugged our shoulders and exchanged phone numbers.

In the weeks that followed, I tried to call Alwen but the number always rang and rang without anyone answering. Out on the town with a host of admirers, I thought. Eventually, I gave up ringing.

By then Barbara and I had finally broken up for good. I think she got fed up with waiting for me to take life seriously. I had also moved out of Mrs Squirrel's boarding house. After four years my long-suffering room-mate Malcolm Lipkin had outlasted me.

He no longer had to lock up his piano, or put up with paint fumes.

I found a single room with bathroom all to myself just round the corner in Bramham Gardens. Mrs O'Gorman, a cleaning lady, came in every day and kept the place tidy and I still had meals provided. Eating out was definitely a luxury.

My cousin Halcyon, Auntie Pixie's eldest daughter, was on holiday in London. I remembered her as a kid in pigtails, but now she was all grown up. She invited me for a meal and I went over to where she was staying. That night I heard a Harry Belafonte LP with a wonderful calypso song called 'Hold 'im Joe'. It had a bit that went:

> *Don't tie me donkey down there.*
> *Let 'im bray, let 'im bray, everybody.*
> *Tie me donkey down there.*
> *Let 'im bray, let 'im bray . . .*

It was a great sing-along chorus, just perfect for the Down Under Club. For the next few days the tune spun hypnotically in my head. I wondered if I could write an Australian set of lyrics to go with it. I changed donkey to kangaroo, but it didn't fit the rhythm. It had one syllable too many. Pity.

That weekend Alex asked me to do him a favour. A young doctor and his wife from New York were on honeymoon in London and Alex had promised to take them sightseeing in the countryside. Unfortunately, he had a dinner party that evening in the depths of Surrey. He asked if I could come sightseeing with them and drive the couple home afterwards in my car.

'Not a problem,' I said.

After a wonderful day together, we three headed back to London and the newlyweds invited me out to dinner. 'Is there someone you can call? We can make up a foursome.'

'Well, there *is* a girl . . . but I barely know her.'

I took a detour back to my place and found Alwen's number. I didn't hold out much hope. Either she was the most popular girl in London, or she'd given me the wrong number.

'Hello?'

'You're home!'

'Who's this?'

'It's Rolf. Rolf Harris. Ah . . . I just sort of wondered if you'd like to come out to dinner?'

'Tonight?'

'Yes. I know it's short notice . . .'

There was a long pause. I crossed my fingers.

'OK.'

'It's not formal or anything fancy,' I said. 'Don't get all dressed up. I'm just in a polo-neck sweater and a sports jacket.'

She gave me her address in Warwick Avenue, Maida Vale and I arranged to pick her up at seven thirty. I found the place and knocked on the door. It swung open to reveal a vision dressed in a stunning little black dress, with high heels and hair beautifully arranged on top of her pretty head. She wore big dangly earrings that she'd designed herself.

I thought to myself, 'What on earth would she have worn if I'd said to *get* dressed up?'

We went to the Lyons' Corner House Grill & Cheese at Marble Arch. It felt wonderful to walk in the door with a beautiful woman on my arm. I could see heads turning to look at us.

The evening couldn't have gone better. The American doctor and his wife were great company and Alwen seemed to shine. At art school I'd imagined her to be a bit stuck up and snobbish because she ignored me. In reality, she was painfully shy and I was a big, hairy, uncouth Australian. I had frightened the life out of her by jumping out from behind her easel with my 'Give us a big smile' act.

As we left the restaurant and walked along Oxford Street, I said to her, 'Aren't you nice!'

She stopped, turned and looked me directly in the eye. 'Yes . . . I am.'

I was so stunned that I took a step backwards from the footpath. Brakes squealed and Alwen screamed. A red London bus bore down on me. The driver swerved at the last moment and blasted his horn.

Despite almost finishing under the wheels, I was still thinking about Alwen's last words. Her look had said it all. She was giving me fair warning that she wasn't cheap, or easy, or to be messed around with.

The American doctor gave me a nudge. 'You're a dark horse,' he whispered. 'You said you barely knew this girl.' I smiled and glanced at Alwen. It felt so right . . . so perfect.

I dropped her home and drove back to Earl's Court feeling like a man who had just found a winning lottery ticket in his pocket. The next morning, on the spur of the moment, I bought a dozen red roses and turned up at her door. She burst into tears and I was lost. What had I done?

She kept shaking her head and wiping tears from her cheeks.

'I'm sorry . . . if you don't like them . . .' I said.

'It's not that,' she sobbed.

'What's wrong?'

'Nobody has ever given me flowers before.'

By then I was truly lost.

We made a date for the following Saturday night. All week I floated about in a daze. All those clichés about love were true. I had never felt like that before. This was special. She was special. When I looked at Alwen I saw someone who was pure and sweet and different from the show business crowd. She wasn't trying to impress, or show off, or shock.

I counted down the days until Saturday. When I picked her up in my car she was wearing the same little black dress. I found out later that the only reason she had worn it was because she had no other outfit apart from her scruffy old clay and plaster-covered artist's jeans.

We drove to a party in south London and I parked outside the house. Music thumped from inside and people were spilling out into the small front garden.

We sat in the car and talked. Both of us seemed to be putting off the moment when we'd have to go inside.

Finally I said, 'I really hate parties. I don't drink and I don't smoke. I never know what to do with myself.'

Alwen nodded in agreement. 'I know what you mean. You're always hoping you'll meet someone and you never do.'

We sat in silence, lost in thought. I could hear her soft breathing and smell her perfume. Then from nowhere I heard myself say, 'Will you marry me?'

Even more startling was her answer, 'Yes.'

We turned and looked at each other, open-mouthed . . . stunned. Neither of us could believe what had just happened. Yet there were no sudden second thoughts or delayed giggles. The words had been spoken and they were genuine.

After a while I turned on the engine and we drove aimlessly around, alone in our thoughts. London looks beautiful at night, with the great buildings lit up by spotlights. The Thames was a river of reflections and young couples snuggled against each other on park benches. Neither of us wanted the moment to end. Yet both of us were staggered by the enormity of what we'd just agreed to.

A week later Alwen introduced me to her father. We had arranged to have dinner at the same restaurant as our first date. Arriving early, I felt quite apprehensive. What would he say? The engagement had come out of the blue. Would he give his blessing?

While waiting, I began toying with the lyrics of the calypso song I'd heard Harry Belafonte sing. Although I couldn't simply replace the word 'donkey' with 'kangaroo', I got rid of the word 'don't', and kept repeating the line, 'Tie me kangaroo down there.' If I threw in a small pause after 'down', and let the accents fall naturally, it created a whole new rhythm. A new melody just flowed naturally along with it. It was as though somebody had simply handed me the finished tune on a plate.

I still didn't like the last word, 'there'. It seemed too gutless for such a strong beat in the music. How could I make it more Australian? I tried using the word 'mate' but still wasn't happy. Then I came up with 'sport'. It was perfect.

> *Tie me kangaroo down, sport,*
> *Tie me kangaroo down.*
> *Tie me kangaroo down, sport,*
> *Tie me kangaroo down.*

I had no idea what the lyrics meant, but they just seemed right. I could imagine the crowd at the Down Under belting it out.

I began working on the verses. First I wrote down a long list of all the Australian animals I could think of – the funnier sounding the better. I also wrote a list of all the slang Aussie names like Bluey and Curly.

The first verse created the template for the rest.

> *Keep me cockatoo cool, Curl,*
> *Keep me cockatoo cool.*
> *Don't go acting the fool, Curl,*
> *Just keep me cockatoo cool.*

By the time Alwen's father arrived I had three or four verses mapped out, in the traditional manner, on the back of a menu. The one that tickled me most was a lovely piece of nonsense about the duck-billed platypus. I spun it around and wrote:

> *Mind me platypus duck, Bill,*
> *Mind me platypus duck.*
> *Don't let 'im go runnin' amuk, Bill,*
> *Just mind me platypus duck.*

I thought it was hysterically funny.

Major Hughes was an ex-military man who seemed to march rather than walk. I didn't know whether to shake hands or salute.

I chose the former and my knuckles cracked as he gripped my hand.

In a typically blunt piece of straight-faced Aussie humour, I told him, 'You'd better watch your tone of voice when you speak to me, because I'm going to be taking your daughter off your hands.'

The major blustered and blew out his cheeks. There was silence.

Oh my God, he'd taken me seriously! I thought he'd come back with an equally tongue-in-cheek retort. I went hot and cold. How could I retrieve the situation?

'What do you think of these?' I said, showing him the verses. I started singing the new song. Major Hughes sat unmoved during the entire rendition.

When I finished, he realized that some response was expected. 'Humph, humph,' he said, clearing his throat. 'Sounds like a load of old rubbish to me, old boy.'

I didn't know what to say. I folded the menu and slipped it into my pocket. Alwen gave my hand a squeeze under the table. I looked at her and realized that it didn't matter what her father thought of me. Nothing was going to change the way I felt about her.

A few weeks later, I journeyed down to Devon to meet the rest of her family. Her mother, Mrs Elsie Hughes, was a quiet no-nonsense sort of woman, who made me feel very welcome.

She and the major ran a small hotel that was fully booked for the weekend. I ended up sharing a tent on the lawn with Alwen's younger brother, Hugh. He still tells people how he slept with me in my early days.

Although nothing was said, I think Alwen's parents thought I was good news. I was too frightened to ask them. I think they were relieved that Alwen had found someone. She was twenty-six years old and most girls of that age were married.

The most important member of the family I had to win over was a dog. Puggy, her black standard poodle, was absolutely devoted to Alwen and guarded her like a jealous husband. From the beginning, Puggy sized me up and decided I was up to no good. She watched me constantly, trying to make sure I wasn't left alone with Alwen.

At one point, we managed to sneak a cuddle in a quiet room. Puggy trotted in and stopped dead. I swear she changed the expression on her face. She turned her back to us, sat down and put her nose in the air. No amount of talking from Alwen could make her turn round.

'We'll have to get some balloons,' said Alwen.

'Balloons?'

'There's a newsagent round the corner.'

I jumped in the car and came back with a packet of party balloons. Puggy was still in a sulk. As soon as she heard a balloon being blown up, her head spun round and her ears pricked. I let go of the balloon and it shot randomly around the room. Puggy set off in chase, barking like a playful puppy.

We played this game for hours and from that moment I rarely moved without a packet of party balloons in my pocket.

I had no idea why Alwen had agreed to marry me. Every so often I had to pinch myself to make sure it was real. Typically, I tried too hard to impress her. I sang songs, whistled, yodelled and generally made a lot of noise. I thought that's what she loved about me.

And then one day she took me walking on Dartmoor, a place she'd always loved. I couldn't leave such vast emptiness unfilled, so I kept making funny sound effects or singing. Finally, she said, 'For goodness' sake, just be quiet for a moment.'

'Why?'

'Listen.'

I stopped and listened. 'What am I listening to?'

'To the silence. If you don't shut up you won't hear any of it.'

It was like a slap in the face. The noise, the songs, the sound effects, the funny voices . . . they were almost the essence of me. That's what I did everywhere I went – I jumped in and grabbed people's attention.

I lay on the grass beside Alwen feeling the heat of her thigh against mine. The sun was shining and the sky seemed impossibly blue. I snuggled closer and tried to sneak a kiss.

'Oh, for goodness' sake, just lie still. Take in the silence around you.'

Finally, I swallowed my pride. I lay back and listened to the birds, the insects, and the breeze rustling through the grass. I was dying to burst into song, but at least I made an effort. My education began that day. Alwen tried to show me how to stop and listen. It was a revelation.

Before we left Devon, I nervously broached the subject of taking Alwen away on a holiday. Her mum smiled nicely and said, 'She's old enough not to need my permission. She can do anything she wants.'

We decided to go to Spain and began making all the preparations. Firstly, we needed to buy holiday clothes for Alwen. She couldn't go travelling in her work clothes and a single little black dress.

I had some money, although I had no idea how much. IAR, my agency, collected my earnings from TV and cabaret work. I didn't question how much I was being paid for jobs, or how much I'd earned in the past. I didn't ask to see accounts – it didn't even occur to me. I still laboured under the misapprehension that money was a vulgar subject.

If I needed cash, I mentioned it to Phyl and she arranged to have £50 drawn out of the IAR account where all my money was kept. (Earning interest for them, I later assumed.) She gave me the cash and I signed a receipt. Whenever this happened, I felt like a charity recipient receiving a handout even though it was *my* money.

I took Alwen shopping in Oxford Street. It was a magical feeling being able to say, 'If you like it, let's get it.'

We bought her shorts, different tops, a bathing suit, a mask, snorkel and flippers. I wanted her to enjoy the full experience of lazing around in the warm waters of the Med.

Early one morning, we set off in the heavily laden Morris Traveller. Both of us were nervous. Everything had happened so quickly and we still barely knew each other. Yet now we were heading off alone together.

The first revelation stunned me into silence. As we drove towards the ferry I started singing 'Fox Went Out on the Chase' which had a good sing-along chorus.

'Come on, Alwen, sing along,' I said, '. . . town-o town-o . . .'

'I don't sing.'

I laughed. 'Very funny. Come on.'

'I don't sing.'

'Everybody sings.'

'I don't. I can't sing.'

'Oh, rubbish!'

I couldn't conceive of anybody not singing. I thought she just needed some coaxing. I tried again but there was no reaction.

I looked at her in amazement. 'You're serious, aren't you?'

'Yes.'

'You've never been able to sing?'

'Never.'

'Couldn't you just do it quietly?'

'No. It's no good. My throat just closes up. I'm terrified of singing.'

I was flabbergasted. Singing was central to my life. I had grown up in a family where everybody sang. All my mates had their favourite party pieces. We'd sing round the piano, all joining in with the choruses.

Now I had discovered that the love of my life was never going to be able to share this with me. Lamely, I finished the chorus on my own and we sat in awkward silence. I think Alwen felt I was being critical of her. She couldn't change who she was. At the same time, I just needed a chance to get used to the idea.

We drove down through France, retracing the route that I'd taken with Barbara and Marie a year earlier. We camped in the car each night, stretched out on the seats, or lying nearby, staring up at the stars.

When we arrived in San Feliú de Guixols I looked up Luis Figueras, my friend of the previous year. He ran the little beach bar and we found he had a spare room in the house he was renting. Alwen and I moved in.

The holiday almost ended in disaster on the first morning. We set off for a secluded bay where I wanted to teach Alwen to snorkel.

When you're good at something, it's easy to forget that not everybody is so confident. Alwen couldn't swim and had a fear of not being able to see what lay beneath her in the water. I started gently teaching her and soon she was able to float on the surface, watching the tiny fish through her mask.

'Let's go for a swim right around the bay,' I said.

'But I can't swim . . .'

'Don't worry. I'll pull you along.'

I explained to her that deep water was no different from shallow water as long as she lay on the surface and let the water support her.

'The main thing is not to panic. Just breathe regularly through the snorkel.'

All this is absolutely true in theory and in practice, but that doesn't mean a great deal when someone is terrified of the water. I didn't recognize this and blithely carried on.

Hand in hand we swam right out in the deep. Suddenly, Alwen sat bolt upright. The intake end of her snorkel plunged into the water and she inhaled a great lungful of water. She panicked and her fist clenched mine. Down she went, dragging me under with her.

I managed to hoist her out of the water above me and rip the snorkel from her mouth. Although she could now breathe properly, she still clambered all over me, forcing me under. She'd seen a swirling movement in the dark green weed far below. She thought it was a shark or some unnamed terror of the deep.

I kicked like mad with my flippers, dragging Alwen with me, and managed to reach some nearby rocks. By that time she had nearly drowned both of us.

I was furious. 'What the hell were you doing out there! You nearly killed us!'

It was, of course, the worst possible thing I could do. Alwen was terrified and I only made things worse. She started to cry. We were marooned on a rock in the deepest part of the bay and she was inconsolable. It seemed like hours before I calmed her and gave her enough confidence to trust me for the return journey.

To this day I kick myself mentally for that disastrous morning. I should have remained calm. Instead, I lost my temper and totally destroyed Alwen's confidence. She would never swim in deep water again.

I also learned that day never to shout at Alwen. She was impossible to have a row with because she didn't argue or yell. As soon as voices were raised, she began crying, or closed down. In many ways, she reminded me of Dad. He had always walked away from arguments and confrontation.

Alwen's perception of that holiday is probably entirely different from mine. But I'm equally sure that both of us wondered at times what we were getting ourselves into.

During the fortnight I painted the outside of Luis's beach bar in zebra stripes and he rechristened it the Zebra Bar. He was so pleased that he let us stay for free from then on. I also talked myself into a job playing the accordion and singing at a local night-club. I did all the latest American pop songs like Bill Haley's 'Rock Around the Clock'.

With the extra money I earned we stayed longer in Spain than we planned, but, sadly, it couldn't last for ever. I had to be back in England for the next series of *Whirligig* on the BBC and *Oliver Polip* on ITV. On the drive home I came up with a new idea for Oliver's spot. It was a new character – a Spanish dogfish called Perro Caliente (which meant 'hot dog' in my cowboy Spanish translation). I figured that I could make a hand puppet out of papier mâché and have him speaking in a thick Spanish accent.

On the return trip, we stopped at Avignon for the night. The river was so low it had dried into a series of pools separated by great stretches of dusty river sand. It had been so hot that we both went for a swim.

That night was a misery. There were a million mosquitoes waiting to leap on us so we had to sleep in the car with the windows closed. Hot, sweaty and miserable, we jumped into the river again next morning to cool down. Later, we even cleaned our teeth in the tepid water.

Alwen had never been to Paris and we had planned the trip to give us a day there. As we neared the city she started getting appalling stomach cramps. Soon she was doubled over in pain, moaning and gasping. She couldn't sit upright in the front seat so I rearranged our things to let her lie down across the back.

All she saw of Paris were the tops of buildings as we drove into the city. She couldn't care less. She simply wanted me to find a chemist and get something for her stomach.

I found a place to park, gave her a kiss and set off. I didn't know what a chemist was called in France. What the hell was I going to ask for when I found one?

Walking for miles through the twisting narrow streets, I began to worry that I wouldn't be able find my way back to the car. But most of all I was scared witless that Alwen would die before I got back. I had never seen anybody look so sick.

Finally I came to a shop with three gigantic ancient bottles in the window filled with different coloured liquids. Using my best schoolboy French, I managed to pantomime my way through a vague description of Alwen's illness. I threw in words like 'jeune fille' and 'malade d'estomac', while clutching my stomach and doing contortions.

The old Frenchman behind the counter nodded sagely and gave me two bottles of pungent-smelling liquid and a third hastily filled with water from a tap. Clutching the bottles under my arm, I somehow retraced my steps and found the car. Alwen managed to raise a smile. She had been just as frightened as I was that I'd get lost and not find her.

I got a slug of the mixture down her and it seemed to help. The French chemist had said 'o–pital' over and over again but we didn't have the time or the money. If we could just make it back to England, Alwen said, then she wouldn't mind going to a hospital. At least there she could speak the language.

We talked it over and decided to drive as far as we could that night, sleep somewhere by the side of the road and catch the first ferry in the morning. I drove until I couldn't keep my eyes open any longer. With nothing to eat, we lay down under some low bushes and slept terribly. Doped up on medicine, Alwen was a picture of absolute misery.

After a few hours' sleep, I drove like a lunatic to Calais and just made the ferry. To add to our woes, we had a stormy crossing. The boat pitched in and out of huge swells. For a while we had to wait off Dover because it was too rough to berth.

It took Alwen a week to get well again. I cursed my stupidity. How could we have swum and brushed our teeth in those stagnant pools?

Despite the thumbs down from Alwen's dad, I still thought my new song, christened 'Kangalypso', would go down a storm at the Down Under Club. As with all my new material, I didn't announce it as being one of my own. Halfway through the show, I said, 'Here's a song a fella wrote . . .' and I launched into it.

I got through a chorus and verse before I realized they were groaning. 'Corny!' yelled someone.

'Rubbish!'

'Boo!'

'Give it a rest, mate.'

I stopped singing, shrugged my shoulders and got on with something else. Such was my lack of confidence in anything that I'd written myself, I figured that the audience had voted and the song stank.

There was a strong feeling that anything to do with Australia was second-rate. It had to be American. The only Australian songs that were acceptable were the classic ones, like the ballads about convicts, bushrangers and swagmen.

I would never have sung the song again if it hadn't been for an Aussie dentist called John Lattimer. He was a mate who had fixed my teeth a few times in his little surgery in Fulham. His main trade was in repairing the molars of Aussie blokes who insisted on taking beer bottle tops off with their teeth.

The following week at the club, John yelled out, 'Sing us that mad song about the kangaroo.'

'Nobody liked it.'

'I did. Sing the bloody thing.'

I shrugged and launched into it again. A few people booed but they soon fell silent. By the end of the second chorus, everybody was singing. What a turnaround! From then on it became a favourite. People would suggest new verses and I added the best of them. At one point we had fourteen verses and the song ran for nearly eight minutes.

Some of them fell by the wayside, like these.

> *Brush me bunyip's back teeth, Keith,*
> *Brush me bunyip's back teeth.*
> *If you don't I'll send for the polithe* (lisp), *Keith,*
> *So brush me bunyip's back teeth.*

And this.

> *Let me grey dingo go, Dig,*
> *Let me grey dingo go.*
> *He can't stand all that snow, Dig . . .*

(Then in a different voice):

Poor old coot's gone delirious.
That's not snow, that's his dandruff!

At about this time, Bruce arrived in England on a business trip. He had risen quickly through the ranks at Lintas and become a senior advertising executive. I invited him to the Down Under Club, mainly, I guess, so that I could show him how well his younger brother was doing.

We arrived at about seven fifteen and the place was pretty empty. By eight thirty it had turned into a different beast, with people standing shoulder to shoulder, passing beers to each other across a sea of heads.

Afterwards I asked Bruce, 'What did you think of "Kangalypso"?' We were in my car heading back to his hotel in South Kensington.

'It doesn't *go* anywhere.'

'What do you mean?'

'Well, it hasn't got a story. You need something to tie it all together – a reason for doing all those verses.'

Criticism from an older brother is never easy to swallow. This was no exception – it stuck right in my throat. We drove in silence to the hotel.

'Let's work on it upstairs,' said Bruce. Back in his room, he began scribbling. 'Why don't you do something like this?'

A weatherworn stockman lay dying,
A saddle supporting his head.
Around him the blowflies were flying,
And these were the words that he said . . .

It was a parody of an Australian song we both knew.

Bruce argued that an opening like that would give me a reason for doing all the verses that followed. 'Then all you need is a comedy ending. Otherwise it just peters out.'

Much as I hated to admit it, he was right. There and then, we created the last verse together.

> *Tan me hide when I'm dead, Fred,*
> *Tan me hide when I'm dead.*
> *So we tanned his hide when he died, Clyde,*
> *And that's it hanging on the shed.*

It was perfect.

I tinkered a bit with the introduction, but it was pretty much as Bruce suggested. It had an old Australian stockman, propping himself up on one elbow, turning to his mates who are gathered round, and saying:

> *Watch me wallabies feed, mate,*
> *Watch me wallabies feed.*
> *They're a dangerous breed, mate,*
> *So watch me wallabies feed.*

The next week at the Down Under Club I tried out the song in its new form. They loved it.

In the early years of commercial television, one of the programme ideas devised was an 'advertising magazine'. Basically it was an excuse to put on one 'live' advertisement after another for twenty minutes, loosely linking them with some sort of storyline.

I was hired to front a programme called *Quick on the Draw*. The idea was for me to link the various commercials with comedy drawings. It was broadcast live from Manchester every week, which meant a long train trip there and back.

Advertising magazines were outlawed after six months, but on one of my last trips to the Manchester studio I spotted a piece of hardboard covering a section of the floor in one of the corridors. It was about three feet by two feet six, covered in a wonderful random pattern of spots of white paint that had been dropped, spattered and smudged on it some time earlier.

I'd been meaning to paint a portrait of Bob Harbin for a long time and the piece of hardboard was perfect. I could put a translucent layer of deep blue paint over the whole surface and the pattern of the white spots and smudges underneath would hopefully give the painting a magical, mystical look – just the effect I needed when painting a magician.

Nobody wanted it, so I lugged the board back on the train with me and arranged for Bob to come over for a sitting. On the day in question I realized that I hadn't coated the board in blue. Quickly, I squeezed Prussian Blue out of a tube and smothered it in turpentine, spreading it thinly with a big brush.

I had half an hour before Bob arrived and the paint just stayed wet and tacky. Coming up with a brainwave, I propped the board face down between the table and the back of a chair and put my portable room heater underneath it. Pretty soon the whole place was stinking of turpentine and oil paint. I opened the window and the door to get a through draught.

Ten minutes later, I tested the paint with my finger to see if it was drying. I let out a yelp and jumped backwards. A great blister rose on my finger. I couldn't believe how much heat was coming out of the little heater. I had visions of the board bursting into flames.

Grabbing the edges, I found I couldn't hold it with my fingers so I propped it between the open palms of my hands and frantically shook it back and forth trying to cool it down. The most wonderful *whoop whoop whoop* sound filled the room. I stopped. Wow! I tried it again. *Whoop whoop whoop*. What a sound!

I held the board vertically between my palms and wobbled it like mad. It seemed to settle down into its own regular rhythm. Then I started emphasizing every second beat, *Whoop, WOP, whoop, WOP*.

It sounded even better when I held it horizontally.

Without even thinking, I found myself whistling the tune to 'Kangalypso'. It fitted perfectly.

All thoughts of the painting had gone.

The fellow who lived in the flat below yelled up the stairs, 'Hey, Rolf, I think there's a pipe burst in the attic. I can hear water pumping everywhere.'

I stuck my head out the door. 'Don't worry. It's just this.' I wobbled the board – *whoop, WOP, whoop, WOP*. He looked at me as though I was crazy.

When Bob turned up, I couldn't resist giving him a demonstration too.

'What about the portrait?' he asked, sounding slightly put out.

'Oh, I'll still do it,' I said, putting the board on the easel.

I did a cracking good job, even if I do say so myself, but I sort of knew with every brush stroke that the portrait would never decorate a wall. I had a very different future in mind for my 'wobble board'.

The children's department at Associated Rediffusion devised a new show to appeal to older youngsters. The set-up took the form of a house with five different rooms – one for each day of the week.

The owner of the 'house' and main presenter was to be Jimmy Handley, the famous actor son of Tommy Handley, whose BBC radio programme *It's That Man Again*, or ITMA, had been required listening in our house in Bassendean during the war.

Jimmy visited a different 'room' in this imaginary house each day and introduced the various entertainers and comedians who lived there. On one of the days, lanky Jack Edwardes and tiny cockney comedian Charlie Drake played a pair of odd job men who managed to screw up the simplest tasks, from changing a washer to hanging a picture. They were called Mick and Montmorency.

My segment was called 'Bearded in his Den' and I played a mad artist who lived in the basement, painting pictures and singing songs. My set had huge white walls and a little upright piano to one side. Using a house painting brush, loaded with black paint, I did a big picture on the wall. Then I played the piano and sang a song which was somehow related to the painting.

When I first suggested the big painting format it didn't enter my head that I couldn't do it. I simply worked out the drawing beforehand on a small bit of paper and then changed the scale enormously for the real thing.

I used Bill Veal's trick of half closing my eyes to get a blurred image. The tiny details disappeared and I could see the big picture. This helped me capture the perspective of the drawing even though I was standing only a foot or so from the wall.

I also worked out beforehand how I could change the first painting into something completely unexpected and different for a second song. It might start as a picture of a mermaid sitting on a rock, but with a few black lines across here and a splodge of white paint there, I turned the rock into a hippopotamus and the mermaid into a palm tree or whatever.

The idea of using a big brush and painting on a huge scale came to me totally by accident. Alex had invited me to spend another Christmas in Germany and, having crossed the Channel, we found ourselves on a train waiting to depart. It was freezing outside and the compartments were heavily heated. The windows inside were completely misted over. Wonderful!

Using my finger on the glass I did a full-sized caricature of a man with huge buck-teeth, a bald head, big ears and freckles. Throughout all of this, Alex had been loudly and persistently clearing his throat. I turned round and said, 'Hey, have a look at this.'

Sitting opposite us was a chap who was the dead set spitting image of my drawing. Alex had been trying to warn me. With one sweep of my overcoat sleeve I wiped off the likeness and tried to act as though nothing had happened.

One of the things that had struck me about drawing on the misted window, was how I could do a perfect black line instantly because of the darkness outside. When I drew things on television I had to use black chalk (felt-tipped pens hadn't been invented), and no matter how hard I scrubbed away with the chalk, it always came out as a dark greyish colour. I could never get a decent solid black. The only alternative would have been to use black paint, but that would have meant constantly dipping a small paintbrush into a pot which would have taken for ever.

Now I began thinking, what if I did it big? What if I used a house painting brush which could hold loads of paint?

Back in London, I began experimenting. Bill Veal had taught me that if I wanted to do a long thin straight line, instead of dragging the brush across I could do it as a dotted line with the flattened edge of the brush, making sure I kept it straight. From a distance it looked perfect. These were the same techniques that I used on the big paintings.

Those early works on 'Bearded in his Den' were really just big cartoons – larger versions of the black chalk drawings that I was still doing for Willoughby and Oliver Polip. Gradually, however, they became more complicated and I began using different tones of grey.

The complex paintings were lovely to work out beforehand. I planned them on scraps of paper and on the backs of old scripts. One of my favourites was really simple and involved painting a light fitting and a light switch on the wall, with painted wires leading between them.

I made sure the fitting was painted directly over a real one which I'd previously covered with a sheet of tissue paper. This meant that I could take a real light bulb, punch it through the flimsy paper and slot it into the real fitting underneath. I pretended to flick the painted switch and then traced my finger slowly along the painted wire to indicate the route the current was taking. As I reached the bulb a technician backstage flicked the real switch.

Let there be light!

Chapter Eight

AND PUGGY CAME TOO . . .

ALWEN AND I WERE MARRIED ON ST DAVID'S DAY, 1 MARCH, 1958.
Since we both had Welsh blood running through our veins,
we thought it appropriate to share our day with the patron saint of
Wales.

Alex Haussmann was my best man. To avoid any family
jealousies, Alwen chose Puggy to be her bridesmaid. She was
given a brand new bright red leather lead and collar for the
occasion.

Although I felt a bit braver about the idea of marriage, I still had
butterflies. At twenty-seven I was definitely ready to settle down,
but I kept thinking about the extra responsibility of worrying
about two people instead of just myself. Then I pictured my life
without Alwen and knew the answer.

I drove myself most of the way to St Mark's Church, near
Warwick Avenue station, and parked a mile or so away. I was determined that nobody was going to write 'JUST MARRIED' all over
the car in lipstick or shaving cream.

I caught a bus the rest of the way and found Alex already at the
church. He was in charge of recording the proceedings on his tape

recorder so I could send it back to Mum and Dad. He set up the recorder beside the altar and did the sound checks. It worked perfectly as the organ swelled up to a dramatic pause just before the 'Wedding March' commenced. Suddenly the verger sneezed. He was standing only an inch and a half from the microphone and when we played it back later it sounded like a three-megaton bomb going off.

As the 'Wedding March' played, I lurched to my feet. Turning, I saw Alwen coming down the aisle. She wore a pencil-slim dress in a floral pattern of different colours of soft brown. There were flowers woven into her hair which was piled high on her head. She looked radiant.

Dear old Pugs was in front of her, head held high, carrying her lead folded twice in her mouth. She kept in perfect step with Alwen the whole length of the aisle.

It was a lovely ceremony. Afterwards, we had some press shots taken outside. Despite her shyness, Alwen handled the photographers and journalists like a seasoned professional. We held the reception at her studio a hundred yards away from the church. Tables were set up amid her finished and half-finished sculptures.

Alex read the telegrams. One of them said, 'All is forgiven. Come back to me. Love, Fifi.'

I turned scarlet and tried to explain to Alwen's parents that I didn't know anyone called Fifi. I was so embarrassed and protested so vehemently that I'm sure some people didn't believe me.

Alex was recording the speeches when the phone rang. It was Mum and Dad. At the time it didn't occur to me that it must have been night time in Western Australia. They must have walked up the road to a public phone box and waited with hands full of coins for an operator to put through a long distance call.

It was the first phone call I'd had from them since I left home six years earlier. To their generation the telephone was a new-fangled invention to be treated with distrust. Mum kept shouting, perhaps thinking her voice had to carry the 9,000 miles. I could hear Dad in the background telling her to hush.

I introduced Alwen and we had a wonderful four-way chat. I felt homesick, but at the same time incredibly close to them. The world wasn't such a big place after all.

When it was all over I said to Alex, 'That was great! Did you get it all?'

His face fell. When the phone rang he had just naturally switched off the tape recorder.

Newlyweds are supposed to leave before the guests, but we enjoyed our reception so much we stayed to the very end.

Robert Combe, an old family friend of Alwen's, drove us back to my car. At least, he tried to. I couldn't quite remember where I'd parked. Well I could, but a no entry sign and a series of one way streets drove us round and round in circles getting even more lost. Adopting a different approach, we went back to my flat and I retraced my nervous drive of earlier in the day. An hour and half after leaving the church we finally pulled up alongside my Morris Traveller.

Robert took his leave and left Alwen and me alone for the first time as husband and wife. Not entirely alone – we had Pugs sitting in the back.

It was still quite early and we had to decide what to do next. Normally, on a spare afternoon we went to the pictures. Twenty minutes later, I parked in the West End and we left Puggy in the car with the windows slightly open. We bought tickets to see *Around the World in Eighty Days* but had half an hour to wait before the movie started. Going next door for a hamburger, we were sitting at a table when a cabbie came wandering over.

'That's you, ain't it?' he said, holding up a copy of the London *Evening Standard*. The headline read 'And Puggy Came Too'. The photograph showed all three of us lined up on the church steps.

'You just got married – what are you doing here?'

We laughed.

After the movie, we drove home to my top floor flat on the edge of Regent's Park, near London Zoo. Lying in bed, we could listen to the sounds of lions roaring and wolves howling from across the canal.

Straight away Pugs jumped onto our bed. I was having none of it.

'Off!'

She jumped down and curled up on the carpet. Five minutes later, she hopped on the bed again. I ordered her off. But Pugs was very wise and persistent. Four more times she tried, leaving it longer and longer between attempts. When we woke in the morning, she was fast asleep on top of the covers at the foot of the bed. She had just outwaited me.

Neither Alwen nor I had a career that was regarded as 'safe'. It wasn't in our make-up. We were both creative people and nine-to-five jobs were never going to suit either of us. Despite this, Alwen was a real worrier about things like money and bills. The financial security that I brought to the marriage took some of this away. She didn't have to be concerned about where the next cheque was coming from.

She and I were very different, yet we got on famously. She was quiet and pensive, while I was all noise and spontaneity. She loved classical music, riding, milking cows, collecting eggs and gathering firewood. I came from a different world.

Alwen laughed out loud at accidents and mishaps, whereas I hated practical jokes and pratfalls. She laughed hysterically the night I casually leaned on my wobble board and had it suddenly disappear beneath me, through a narrow gap in the stage. I tumbled to the floor, totally stranded without an instrument. Another time I split my trousers and had to wear my jacket tied around my waist through the whole show. Alwen was beside herself with laughter.

We spent a lot of time together, although I was away some nights doing cabaret spots. Neither of us knew how to cook. Our first attempt at roast chicken ended in disaster. Having bought the bird, we popped it into a baking dish and into the oven. A beautifully browned chicken emerged which I carved with great ceremony. The first taste told a different story. The innards had been cooked inside and the gall bladder had broken, making the flesh completely inedible.

Next I attempted roast beef which finished up as a solid block of charcoal when I forgot the time. Even the dog wouldn't eat it. And when I tried to cook rice, I poured the entire contents of the bag into the boiling water. It swelled and swelled until eventually it stood a foot proud of the saucepan like a huge white cylinder.

We persevered, however, and ultimately each of us learned a handful of dishes. I could do a really good roast beef, medium rare, and Alwen did a wonderful sweet vegetable curry.

Four months after we married I had a call from two young hotshots from West Australian Newspapers, Jim Cruthers and Brian Treasure. Their company had won the licence to launch the first television station in Western Australia and they were on a scouting mission to London to gain experience. One of their tasks, I discovered, was to talk me into coming back to Perth to run the children's programmes on the new station, TVW7.

During the previous six years WA Newspapers had known exactly what I'd been up to in England. Mum made sure of that by sending them press cuttings and calling journalists to say, 'Rolf has just done this . . . or that.' She was my number one fan and my Aussie press agent rolled into one.

Jim and Brian offered me a contract for a year to produce and star in a half-hour children's show five days a week. Although excited by the possibility, I didn't want to be typecast as a children's presenter. I wanted to branch out and try a few things, so they agreed to let me do some late night variety shows as well.

They mentioned a salary of £1,200 for the year, which sounded like a fortune, but I never thought to break it down and work out how much it meant per week.

Phyl Rounce said it was 'ludicrous money'. 'You haven't said yes, have you?'

I nodded and she threw up her hands.

I thought her nose was out of joint because I had negotiated the deal myself. Of course, I was wrong. I had done my usual thing of accepting the first figure mentioned to get the awkward subject over with.

IAR did the very decent thing and didn't ask for a percentage. I think Phyl assumed I was off home for good and they'd never hear from me again.

When I broke the news to Alwen, it didn't enter my head that she wouldn't want to go. I just assumed that she'd be happy to come with me. I'd spent so long telling her about Australia, and here was her chance to see it.

'I get to produce and star in my own daily show,' I said excitedly. 'Five days a week. And I get to do a variety show. It's going to be great.'

Alwen nodded. 'And it's only for a year?'

'Yeah. Did I tell you about the variety shows? They'll pay me extra for each of them . . .'

She let me prattle on. I was consumed by dreams of wowing them in my home town. The boy from Bassendean was going to return like a prodigal son and be beamed into all their living rooms.

The contract didn't start for another year, so in the meantime I continued working for the BBC and ITV. In between times I had the odd foray into British night-time television. In particular I had a couple of parts in the TV version of *Hancock's Half Hour*.

Tony Hancock was a real hero of mine and his show was enormously popular. The Aussie actor Bill Kerr had been a regular in previous episodes, playing a half-wit from Wagga Wagga, but he was away filming. Bill was a wonderful harum-scarum ratbag of a bloke who thought nothing of driving flat out down the wrong side of the road to jump a queue at traffic lights.

I had to play an Australian naval officer and I arrived early at the rehearsal, dying to make a good impression on all these legendary characters. Sid James introduced himself and the other regulars wandered in, chatting and grabbing cups of coffee. Sid had a cigarette hanging out of his mouth and was studying the racing form guide.

The great man hadn't arrived. We waited . . . and waited . . . and waited.

Forty minutes after the rehearsal was due to start, a taxi drew up outside. The door of the rehearsal room crashed open and Tony Hancock strode in, larger than life, with his overcoat draped over his shoulders like a cape.

'Can somebody lend me ten bob to fix up this taxi?' he cried.

'Sure,' I said, rushing forward and dragging out a ten shilling note. He took it without a word.

Sid James glanced at me over the top of his paper and said out of the corner of his mouth, 'That's the last you'll see of that.'

He was right.

The rehearsal and show went off reasonably well. Tony Hancock had one of those deadpan faces that could convey the most amazing range of emotions by just the lifting of an eyebrow, or the pursing of the lips. And from looking quite bored and uninterested, he would suddenly get a fit of the giggles and set everybody off. I was so in awe of the cast that I felt like a Boy Scout doing bob-a-job tasks. Try as I might, I couldn't be cool and laidback.

Later that year I was invited to be part of a Christmas radio show that was being recorded to be broadcast in Australia. It featured all the well-known Aussie entertainers who were working in the UK. I don't know how I managed to get included. I was best known for being on children's TV.

Among the famous names were Wilfred Thomas, Dick Bentley, a group called the Horrie Dargie Quintet (Horrie was the brother of the famous Aussie painter William Dargie) and the beautiful actress Kitty Blewitt.

I first set eyes on Kitty when she arrived for rehearsals. This very glamorous lady walked in looking slightly dishevelled, having spent all night on a train. She'd been forced to change at Crewe as she came down from the north after a performance.

Kitty shrugged off her coat, glanced at herself in the mirror and curled up her rosebud lips. 'I had a compartment all to myself as far as Crewe,' she explained. 'Then I was just going to stretch out in my new compartment when some ghastly-looking bloke came in with a hairdo on him like a burnt-out armpit.'

I will never forget those words coming out of her exquisitely shaped mouth. The description was just so vivid and so typically Australian. At that moment I realized I had been away too long. It was time to go home.

I sold my dear little Morris to an Aussie mate, who claimed the engine was shot to bits and couldn't 'pull the skin off a rice pudding'. I took his word for it and accepted his offer of £300. What did I know about engines?

Large wooden trunks were packed with our things and Puggy was delivered down to Devon to stay with Alwen's parents. This was hard for Alwen. The skinny black poodle, with the fussy ways, was like a soulmate.

We boarded the ship in the heart of London, in the shadow of St Paul's Cathedral. Some of the guys from the Down Under Club came down to say goodbye, giving us a rousing rendition of 'Waltzing Matilda'.

Departure was delayed for some reason and we gave up waiting and retired to our bunks. I woke next morning thinking the sea was incredibly calm. Instead, I looked out the porthole and saw the dome of St Paul's gleaming in the morning light.

Engine trouble kept us mid-stream until four o'clock that afternoon. By then most of the passengers were going stir crazy because the crew hadn't been allowed to open the bars or serve any alcohol.

It was the *Straithaird*'s last voyage and it was plagued by breakdowns. We spent a night wallowing in the Channel on our way to the Med, and, later, a whole day marooned in the Suez Canal, with no movement, no breeze and no air-conditioning.

We stopped at Aden, one of the world's few duty-free ports, and found it crammed with German tape recorders and cameras. According to the Arab salesmen, these were offered at only a fraction of their normal prices. I knew nothing about cameras, but I knew it was time I owned a decent one.

The salesman flashed his gold teeth and boxes were produced. He spoke complete double Dutch about two and a quarter inch square formats, aperture controls and shutter speeds. I left the shop lighter by £41, clutching a Rolleiflex and 35mm attachment. Despite my inexperience, they proved to be one of the best buys I ever made and started my lifelong love of photography.

Back on board the *Straithaird* I finally plucked up the courage to try out my new contact lenses. I'd always worn glasses on television but they were forever catching the studio lights and sending great flares back into the camera. This meant the lighting boys had to keep adjusting the position of the lamps.

Since nobody had seen me on TV in Australia, it seemed a good idea to launch my new image – minus the glasses. What nobody had told me was that contact lenses directed all available light inwards. The blinding glare of the tropics was channelled directly into my eyes as though coming through a magnifying glass.

To make matters worse, the first time I wore them a tiny piece of grit got caught behind the right lens. It felt like a piece of sharpened concrete sawing on my eyeball. Alwen helped me back to the cabin as I stumbled like a blind man. Safely in front of the mirror, I pulled up my eyelid and took out the lens.

'Phew!'

That little sigh of relief had a major repercussion. The contact lens, which had been delicately balanced on my fingertip, had disappeared.

Surely it couldn't be far away. We searched every square inch of the floor and found nothing. For two hours we ransacked the cabin. Working out from the centre on our hands and knees, an inch at a time, we were like forensic scientists studying a crime scene.

Just when I reached the point of complete despair, we found the offending transparent quarter-inch hemisphere on the blanket of the top bunk, hard against the wall. It must have bounced off the mirror, flown over my head and landed behind me. Not surprisingly, my desire to create a new image was rapidly wearing off.

The *Straithaird* steamed across the Indian Ocean and we arrived in Ceylon for a day-long stopover. All sorts of tourist boats and local fishermen buzzed around us in the bay. Alwen and I were on deck, leaning over the railing. I noticed a group of women in sunhats, bobbing up and down in a tender.

'Gee, that looks like my mum,' I said.

I looked again. 'And that woman next to her looks just like Nellie Phipps, a friend of ours from Bassendean.'

'Where?'

I pointed out the boat.

'They're waving at us,' she said.

It *was* Mum and Mrs Phipps! Mum was half standing, waving like mad and shouting 'Cooee!'

What a glorious reunion! Mum explained that she and Nellie had discovered they could get a passage from Ceylon to Perth on the *Straithaird*. On the spur of the moment they decided to surprise us.

She steamrollered her way through Alwen's shyness and immediately took charge, fussing over me and making decisions for all of us.

After a day ashore we set sail again. Immediately, Alwen was in trouble. She had eaten or drunk something on shore that didn't agree with her. Her stomach pains were so severe that she was put in strict isolation in the sick bay. The ship's doctor feared she might have contracted cholera.

For the rest of the voyage Alwen stayed in bed, isolated from the rest of the passengers and crew. Even I wasn't allowed to visit her. By standing outside the sick bay door on tiptoe, I could just manage to see her upside-down reflection in the high gloss paint of the ceiling. The two of us spoke in whispers.

Alwen's abiding memory of that trip was the nightly showing of

The Bridge on the River Kwai on the outdoor cinema, just outside her window. She lay in bed feeling dreadful listening to the sounds of the bridge being built and blown up over and over again.

As we sailed down the coast of Western Australia, I got my first taste of home. Somebody had tuned their radio to a local station. It was Saturday afternoon and a very nasally-voiced race caller, with a machine gun delivery, was broadcasting from the track. It sounded totally Australian and at the same time totally alien to my ears. I'd obviously been away a long time.

A day out of Fremantle, Alwen was allowed to get up for the first time. I walked her up and down the deck for hours, trying to get her legs working. I think she dreaded our arrival. She was hoping to make a good impression, but still felt weak and feverish.

Now within sight of the shore, I gazed at the burnt, scorched landscape and began to wonder how Alwen was going to cope with her new surroundings. For her it must be like looking at a different planet. A heat haze made the headlands shimmer and beyond lay thousands of miles of scrub and sandy terrain.

By the time we reached Fremantle, I had started to look at my homeland through her eyes. We had just come from one of the busiest cities in the world, but now we looked across row after row of buildings, none of them above single-storey. The rust-streaked tin roofs and drab exteriors looked like something from a B-grade Western movie.

I caught my breath as the hot air scorched my lungs. A swarm of flies buzzed around my face. I hadn't mentioned the flies to Alwen. I hadn't even thought about them! They are such a fact of life in Australia you don't notice them. They land on your back in their thousands, or circle your head like an honour guard. They crawl into your mouth, eyes, nose and ears. Inhale too quickly and you're likely to swallow a few. And each time you wave them away, they lift off and then settle again.

The comic image of Aussie headwear – the hat with dangling corks – isn't a fiction created for tourists. It's almost essential whenever someone has to work outside using both hands. Without such a hat, you finish up continually doing the great Aussie wave to keep the flies away.

I think Alwen was too sick to be horrified. Even wearing make-up, she still looked deathly white.

Dad was there to meet us along with the whole Hagen family who had emigrated from England a few years earlier. Mum's cousin, Beryl Hagen – we all called her Boo – took charge of Alwen.

'Right, first thing we do is undo that belt. It's too tight. Tut, tut. Just look at you . . . well, don't you worry . . . we'll take care of you, dear.'

All the bars on board were closed so Boo talked her way into the captain's cabin where she commandeered a large slug of brandy for Alwen.

'Get that down you. Now forget the passport thing. You're coming with me.'

Somehow Boo managed to bypass all the landing formalities. She whisked Alwen off to their home in Claremont and dosed her up with Chlorodyne for her stomach.

Meanwhile, I had to go through the formalities of clearing our luggage. All went well until the customs officer asked me to open the suitcases. I suddenly realized the keys were six miles away in Alwen's handbag. Dad had to go and collect them and bring them back.

Two hours later I cleared customs and stepped onto home soil. I had been away for seven and a half years.

Alwen recovered quickly thanks to Boo's care and was soon able to take in her new surroundings. Mum and Dad's house in Bassendean came as a shock. It seemed smaller than I remembered and a little run-down.

Naturally, they both assumed we were going to stay with them. This meant sleeping in the same separate beds that Bruce and I had grown up using, in the sleep-out with fly screen netting around the walls and shutters that had to be closed when it rained.

There was no privacy. Doors were never locked, or curtains closed. I woke in the morning to hear Dad scraping his burnt toast in the sink only a few feet away. Keen to start work, I went straight to TVW7's temporary offices. The studios were only half built and people were starting to panic about being ready on time. I began planning the shows and suddenly realized that I had no experience of interviewing people for jobs. Added to that, I had virtually no money to spend on hiring anyone.

Brian Treasure said to me, 'Get them to do it for free, mate. They'll jump at the chance to be on TV.'

Before I left England Bob Harbin had told me what to expect. He'd just come back from Bermuda where he'd been running TV shows on the tiny island.

'They'll have no money,' he told me. 'They'll tell you there's a budget, but by the time you get there it won't exist.'

His words now sounded prophetic.

'So what do I do?' I'd asked him.

'Contact the local clubs like swimming and diving and dog breeding. And the local societies that are full of amateur historians and naturalists. They'll do things for nothing.'

I had no conception of how much work was involved in producing half an hour of television, five days a week. I arrived with all sorts of grand ideas. First, I thought I could repeat the success of Willoughby. All I needed was to find somebody to operate the eyes and mouth and do the voice.

Four factors soon changed my mind. 1) I couldn't find anybody. 2) All the people in showbiz wanted to appear in *front* of the camera. 3) I didn't have a budget and 4) there wasn't any rehearsal time.

The only ideas that were going to work were those that were totally self-contained, in which I controlled every element. I told the story, did the drawings, sang the songs and moved the scenery. Oliver Polip was perfect, but he could only fill ten minutes of the show. Taking Bob's advice, I began looking for interesting people who could entertain children.

The search brought me back in touch with a bloke called Harry Butler whom I hadn't seen since teachers' college.

Harry came from wheat-belt country, east of Perth, and I first met him when he worked at the power station with Dad. He was sixteen years old back then – the same age as me – and his work-mates treated him like a real country bumpkin. The only way that Harry could get any respect was by impressing people with his bushcraft.

He had no background as a naturalist. He'd taught himself. Of a weekend he'd go out into the scrub and on Monday morning he'd come to work and say, 'Hey, fellas, have a look at this.' He'd open a sugar bag and hold up a live King Brown, the deadliest snake in the State.

By the time I reached teachers' college Harry was giving lectures on wildlife and nature studies. Now he agreed to come on the show and talk about different animals. He proved to be an absolute natural in front of the camera. Eventually I had a stable of regular presenters from various clubs and hobby groups, but Harry was always the most popular.

As I battled to get the show off the ground, Alwen was at home with Mum and Dad. She found it quite awkward living in some-one else's house in a strange country. Hardest of all, however, was her difficulty understanding what people said.

It wasn't just the broad Aussie accent. Most Australians don't move their mouths when they speak, so you can't easily lip-read. People would ask her something and Alwen would look vainly at their mouths, hoping for some clue. Even if they repeated the question she still didn't understand. As a result she found herself saying yes or no without knowing if she had said the right thing or not. Most of the time she hadn't.

Conversations with visitors withered and died. Uncomfortable silences filled the gaps. Unfortunately, through no fault of her own, Alwen got a reputation for being a bit stand-offish and stuck up. She was too polite to explain that she hadn't understood what had been asked. And her very quiet, nicely spoken accent collided with the same old Aussie prejudices that I had taken with me to England.

I was oblivious of this. I was too busy working. The new station was launched on schedule surrounded by hoopla and teething problems. The impact was just as dramatic as it had been everywhere in the world when TV arrived. It changed the way people lived. People stayed at home rather than going out to the cinema or the theatre.

The children's show proved to be a big success. Kids all over Perth sat in front of their sets, counting the legs of the octopus and singing the songs. I made up stories with a local flavour, weaving in current affairs and introducing Australian animals.

Within days I had children waving to me in the street and asking me for autographs. Early one Sunday morning, I dragged myself out of bed to go to the bathroom. I wore a pair of daggy underpants with elastic perishing round the waist. I was constantly tugging them up.

With the toilet still flushing behind me, I emerged scratching my stomach and yawning. Standing in the middle of the sleep-out, staring at me, was a middle-aged woman with two little children.

Alwen lay in bed, wide-eyed, holding the sheet beneath her chin. I was speechless. Then I suddenly realized I was scratching my private parts.

'The kids just wanted to see you,' the lady said.

'Oh.'

'This is Kenny . . . he's five. And Mary . . . she's three. Say hello to Mr Harris.' She nudged them.

'Hello, Mr Harris,' they said in unison.

Still in shock, I scrabbled around for a bit of paper and a pen. I signed autographs, keeping one hand on my underpants to stop them falling down.

After they'd gone, Alwen said, 'Who were they?'

'I have no idea.'

When the shock wore off, I became angry. The old casual Rolf of ten years earlier would probably have laughed and enjoyed the attention, but now it seemed like a real invasion of my privacy.

I didn't mind people asking me for autographs – I was enormously flattered. But in the UK, they had always waited outside the studio, or chosen a moment when I wasn't busy. The difference in Perth was that people didn't think twice about barging into conversations, interrupting restaurant meals and almost driving me off the road.

Why was it so different?

Then it dawned on me. No matter what I did, I would always be the boy from Bassendean to these people. It didn't matter what I'd done before, or what success I'd achieved overseas, the locals would say, 'Well, it's just Rolf. He used to live down the road,' or 'I used to wipe his nose when he was four,' or 'I remember young Rolf. He used to live opposite the Maddafords.' Anybody who had ever brushed up against me felt as though they could pop round any time with their friends or complete strangers.

I don't know what I was expecting. Maybe I thought my success would mean they treated me differently.

Much later I heard St Matthew's line: 'A prophet is not without honour, save in his own country.' I knew exactly what he meant. I pictured him trying to preach on his home patch and having the locals say, 'Oh, little Matt, I remember changing his nappy and wiping his bum. He was always trying to make speeches . . .'

At first I was disappointed that friends and locals treated me the same as always. Then I realized that they were doing me a tremendous favour because they brought me down to earth and stopped me getting too big for my boots. In egalitarian Australia, the tall poppies get chopped down if they hog the sunlight.

Our Sunday morning visitors prompted a change of address. It simply wasn't practical for Alwen and me to stay with Mum and Dad. Soon afterwards we moved into a rented flat on the south side of the river, looking across the water to the Esplanade and the buildings of Perth.

Hadden Hall had once been a big old mansion and it still had

jarrah hardwood floors and high ceilings. A developer had turned it
into flats that were large and airy, but infested with fleas. I bombed
them with kerosene and flea spray, but it still took weeks for the last
of them to perish. Alwen's legs were covered in bites. What is it
about English skin that seems to attract fleas and mozzies?

We had no furniture apart from a bed. I rigged up a table using
a piece of wood roped to the ceiling. Then we went shopping for
everything from saucepans to cutlery and linen for the bed.

In one department store, I asked an assistant for sewing cotton.

'You'll get that in Habbo,' she said.

'What?'

'Habbo.'

She had to repeat the word twice more before the penny
dropped.

'Haberdashery!'

'Yeah, what did ya think I said?'

No wonder Alwen was having difficulty. Even I had trouble
understanding some of the short cuts in the language.

I ploughed on with work, leaving home at seven each morning and
rarely returning before eight of an evening. Despite the workload
I still wanted to broaden out and try some comedy ideas. As
promised, TVW7 gave me a regular weekly slot at ten o'clock on
Tuesday night. The half-hour show, called *Relax with Rolf*, was
full of songs and my attempts at comedy sketches.

I had no budget and had to do everything from painting my own
scenery to writing the scripts. It was all very rough and ready. If
things didn't work (which happened quite often), there was just a
painful silence. It never occurred to us to get some pre-recorded
laughter tracks to swell the response from the tiny audience of
twenty that could fit into the studio.

The camaraderie at the station was wonderful. We all pitched in
to help. I often worked all weekend painting scenery in four tones
of grey for plays that local schoolkids would put on (for no fee of
course). This was television run on a shoestring.

It didn't take long for me to realize that the money I was earning didn't go very far. I had rent to pay each week, along with the hire purchase payments for a new station wagon that I'd bought.

To earn extra money I took a regular Saturday night gig at the Charles Hotel, playing the accordion and singing. Alwen used to come along at first but she still found it hard to understand people and make friends. Eventually, she chose to stay at home.

When we first decided to return to Australia, she had great plans to continue doing her sculpture. Sadly, Perth proved to be such a backwater that she couldn't find the right clay. This meant she didn't even have the joy of any creative outlet to fill her time.

I had no idea how lonely she became. She said nothing to me. She could see how much I loved the challenges I faced and didn't want to disappoint me or become a burden. In this strange new country, full of people she couldn't understand, she locked herself away or went walking alone.

Once or twice she took the bus the five miles to the coast. The long white sandy beaches that most people thought were wonderful Alwen found boring. She saw them as just sea and sand. There was no shade, or shells or interesting stones to collect. The wind blew constantly, tossing up sand, and the sun was too fierce. Of course, she didn't say any of this. She knew it would rub people up the wrong way.

All of this put a fierce strain on our marriage, although I didn't realize it then. I didn't discover Alwen's unhappiness until years later, back in England, when I was cleaning up one day and found her old diary in a pile of rubbish to be thrown out. Flicking through the pages, I came across a passage she had written in Perth.

'I don't know what I am going to do,' she wrote. 'I feel like killing myself I'm so bored. My days are filled with such emptiness. Please take me away from here.'

The words struck me like hammer blows. I sat on a packing box and tried to remember all those nights I came home late and weekends I filled with extra work. Everything had been about *me*. I had been so absorbed in my own career and desire to impress people that I had totally forgotten about Alwen. I'm crying inside now as I write this.

Why hadn't she said anything? Because she was in love with me, I guess, and could see that *I* was happy.

Added to this was the sense that I had become public property. Everyone in Perth knew me either from before, or from their daily dose of television. Alwen felt that she had no stake in my life any more.

I read that diary entry over and over again. I felt terrible and I kicked myself for my selfishness. Yet I said nothing to Alwen. I was too embarrassed. How could I say I was sorry so long after the event?

I have never been very good at discussing anything emotional. I'm always afraid that it might open the floodgates and become too much. What if there were terrible recriminations? What if I couldn't make amends?

I wish that Alwen had told me at the time. And I wish I could have said to her, 'Next time, tell me if you're unhappy.'

Instead I chose not to rock the boat.

Chapter Nine

KEEP ME COCKATOO
COOL, CURL

WHEELING THE STRANGE MACHINE IN FRONT OF THE cameras I began cranking levers and turning pedals. It looked like a real Heath Robinson contraption, with arms, pulleys and bicycle wheels.

'Now if I can just get this going we'll be able to record the sound of this board on this bit here,' I said to the audience. I gave Bob Harbin's portrait a wobble or two. 'Not many people realize you can make a recording this way.'

I got the bicycle wheel moving and a weight attached to a string and looped over a pulley kept it turning. Then I started wobbling the board in tempo.

When I finished, I 'rewound' the weight and started the gadget again. 'I'll just play it back to you,' I said.

At that precise moment, out of sight in the control room, a soundman flicked a switch and a pre-recorded version of the wobble board came booming through the speakers.

'Wow! It worked!'

I rushed to grab my accordion and started singing 'Kangalypso',

Early publicity shot: who is that handsome smooth-shaven fella?

EARLY DAYS IN LONDON

(Above left) Outside Mrs Squirrel's boarding house in Earl's Court.

(Above right) My long-suffering room-mate, Malcolm Lipkin.

(Below) A home away from home: the Down Under Club in Fulham.

FARM LIFE IN SHROPSHIRE

(Clockwise) A postcard from Shropshire. Perro Caliente, the Spanish dogfish puppet. Oliver Polip meets vegetable, 1953. I win a welcome fiver for a cartoon in a *Picture Post* competition. <small>Dick Dyerson</small> My portrait of Alex Haussmann.

BEAUTY AND THE BEAST

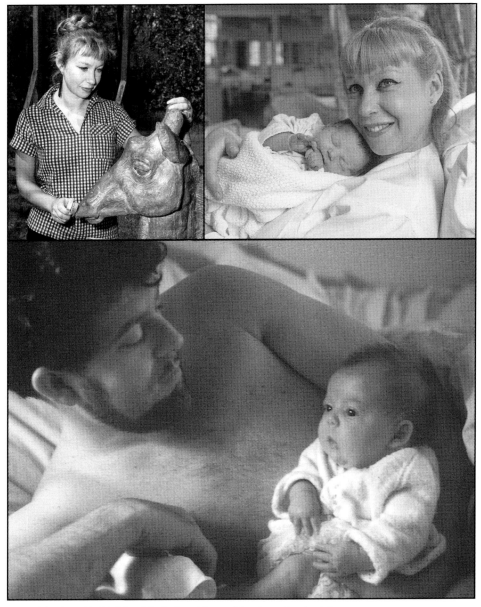

OPPOSITE (Left) My fair lady, Alwen Hughes. I asked her to marry me on our second date. *(Above right)* Getting engaged in London. © Express Newspapers
(Below right) On our wedding day with Puggy the poodle as bridesmaid.

THIS PAGE (Top left) Alwen with her giraffe sculpture. *(Top right)* Baby Bindi's first photo call in March 1964 (only one photographer turned up – the rest were taking pictures of the baby Prince Edward). © Hulton Archive
(Below) How can anything be so small and so perfect?

'SIX WHITE BOOMERS, SNOW WHITE BOOMERS
RACING SANTA CLAUS THROUGH THE BLAZING SUN
SIX WHITE BOOMERS, SNOW WHITE BOOMERS
ON HIS AUSTRALIAN RUN'

OPPOSITE (Top) Painting scenery for a play on TVW channel 7 in Perth; the scene grew from my smaller painting of Regent's Park in London.
(Centre) The first genuine Aussie Christmas carol, 'Six White Boomers'.
(Below left) Larking about with Alwen and Harry Secombe in Sydney in 1963.
(Below right) Alwen on the run from the flies.

(Clockwise from top left) Vancouver: demonstrating my original wobble board (with Bob Harbin's portrait) to Jack Webster and his son. Plugging my Australian recording of 'Sun Arise' on Jack's radio show. My original two-colour linocut rough for the sheet music of the UK recording of 'Sun Arise'. Cooking with Victor Borge on TV in Canada. A signed publicity photo from the Cave nightclub in Vancouver. Ken Stauffer is on the right.

I drew this cartoon after hosting the Beatles' Christmas Show in London in 1963.
Check my self-portrait in the corner. Later it grew to become the Rolfaroo.

with the wobble board providing the rhythm. I'd re-named the song 'Tie Me Kangaroo Down, Sport' because it was easier for people to remember and sounded more Australian.

It was the first time I'd risked singing one of my own songs on *Relax with Rolf*. The best I hoped for was to get a few laughs, which is why the reaction was so amazing. Over three hundred letters arrived at the station in the following days. Many of them were asking for a copy of the lyrics so I typed up the words and had them duplicated to send out.

A week later the Horrie Dargie Quintet arrived in Perth to do a promotion for a new car. I hadn't seen the guys since the Aussie Christmas radio special we recorded in London. They came out to the TV station with the local EMI man, Peter Howard.

I was still ecstatic about the reaction to 'Kangaroo'.

'It went down a storm,' I said excitedly. Then I proceeded to sing the whole song to them there, in the middle of the office, using Bob's portrait for the tempo.

Horrie loved it. 'Can I get a copy?'

'Sure.' I gave him a cyclostyled sheet of the lyrics. I was going to write out the music, but Horrie said he had the tune firmly in his head.

The Dargie Quintet had a weekly television show in Melbourne and a few weeks later I had a telegram from the band.

'Great audience response to "Kangaroo" on our show. Can we have your permission to record it?'

Wow! This was fame indeed!

I sent a telegram straight back: 'Yeah, go for your lives.'

Then I rang up Peter Howard at EMI to tell him the good news. 'Isn't it great? The Dargies want to record my song.'

'What have you told them?' he asked.

'I said go ahead.'

'Don't *you* want to record it?'

'Well, yes, I suppose . . . I'd like to . . . yes.'

Peter then explained the facts of life to me. Whoever records a song first is credited with having the definitive version. Whatever other versions come out later are considered to be copies, or covers, of the original. 'They're like poor relations,' he said.

'But I've already sent 'em a telegram saying yes.'

'So send them another one and tell them no.'

'Won't they be upset?'

'Tough. It's your bloody song.'

I sent another telegram that same day. Cold silence followed. I don't know if Horrie ever forgave me.

Now it was up to me to record the song. As soon as I had a tape, Peter promised to send it to EMI in Sydney.

I'd shipped out with me my old Ferrograph tape recorder which weighed a ton and required the dexterity of a watchmaker to get the spools threaded. Carrying it into the bathroom at Hadden Hall, I propped it on the sink and hung a microphone over the clothesline above the bath.

This was the quietest room in the flat and I didn't want any background noise. I recorded the song using my accordion. Of course I couldn't play Bob's portrait at the same time so it had to be sacrificed.

I took the tape straight to Peter Howard.

'It sounds like you recorded it in your bloody bathroom,' he said.

'Yeah. I did.'

'Jesus. Look . . . these people in Sydney get sixty tapes a day to listen to. They're going to play eight seconds of this and throw it in the bin. If you're going to send them a tape then at least do the *best* job you can do. Hire a bloody studio! Get some musicians! Spend a few bob. I'll lend you the money.'

He talked to me like a Dutch uncle and I felt very chastened. I went away and tried again.

This time I hired a close harmony trio called the Rhythm Spinners who had performed on *Relax with Rolf*. I also hired an English guy called Brian Bursey who played the double bass.

We gathered in a studio at TVW7, standing round a single microphone slung from the sound boom above our heads.

Rehearsing it beforehand, all the guys sang with American accents. I stopped them.

'I don't want "Tar mah kangaroo dayown, sporrrt". It's an Australian song. It's got nothing to do with America.'

'But we do everything in American accents.'

Bizarre as that sounds it was true. Most Aussie entertainers at the time were singing with broad American accents. Maybe this is what was meant by 'cultural cringe' – they didn't think their own accents were good enough.

I put my foot down. 'Just sing it the way you talk.'

'You'll never sell a copy. It's a fact of life,' they argued.

'Well it's my bloody song. Just do it my way.'

I could hear them grumbling to each other, but we tried again.

The end result sounded fantastic, with the wobble board going *whoop, WOP, whoop, WOP* in the background.

Afterwards, I said to the guys, 'OK, about the money.' (Discussed after the event, you'll notice.) 'Do you want ten per cent of the royalties, or a straight fee up front?'

They all chorused, 'We'll take a fee, thanks very much.'

I paid them £7 each. I bet they kicked themselves for years afterwards.

Peter Howard liked the new recording and sent the demo tape to Sydney. A month later, without any communication from EMI, without a contract being signed, or even suggested, I discovered that 'Tie Me Kangaroo Down, Sport' had been released as a single. The B-side was 'Nick Teen and Al K Hall', a song of mine which I'd recorded at the same session.

I was thrilled. I had my *own* record. If nothing else, my friends and family would buy a copy each.

Yet something remarkable happened in the weeks that followed. Bob Rogers, the top DJ in Sydney, picked up the song and began playing it regularly. Other radio stations followed.

Bruce kept a close eye on what was happening and phoned me up. 'This song could be something big,' he said. 'How soon can you get here?'

Using his instincts as an advertising man, Bruce knew the record needed a push. He organized a publicity tour, which included radio interviews and an appearance on *Bandstand* – Australia's top TV pop programme.

I took a week off from TVW7 and flew to Sydney. Bruce met me at the airport and we drove directly to a radio interview with Bob Rogers. From there I was whisked across the city for another interview and then another.

The next day I had an afternoon rehearsal for *Bandstand*. The producer explained that I had to lip-sync the song.

'What do you mean lip-sync?'

'We want you to mime it.'

'Why?'

'It's the show policy.'

'But I can get everybody singing.'

'Nobody will sing here, mate.'

'They will. I'll stop and make them.'

He looked aghast. 'Not on live television, you won't.'

I had no choice. We rehearsed the song a few times, but I had great difficulty miming the spoken introduction about the dying swagman. The same thing happened on the show proper and I looked as though I was singing a totally different song. The teenagers who normally danced to the pop songs didn't know what to do with 'Kangaroo', so they just stood around.

As it turned out it didn't matter. Four weeks later I had the number one song in Australia. My first song . . . a No. 1. How easy was that!

Here was an Australian song, sung in an Australian accent, and people were buying it. It proved to me, once and for all, that I could be myself. I didn't have to put on a phoney accent, or wear a dinner suit, or sing like an American. I could *be* unashamedly Australian and succeed. It changed my life.

At the height of my new-found fame, I was booked to appear on the same bill as Crash Craddock, Johnny O'Keefe and the Everly Brothers at Rushcutter's Bay Stadium in Sydney.

All these famous rock 'n' rollers wore amazing stage outfits with spangles and sequins. Dressed in a pair of R. M. Williams-style trousers and an open-necked shirt, I looked more like a roadie than a rock star.

Up until then, the biggest audience I'd ever performed in front of was 200 people. Now I could hear the roars of 2,000. I ducked to the lavatory for a nervous wee. I propped Bob's portrait against the wall and stood at the urinal. A bloke walked in, so tall his head almost touched the ceiling. He had forearms decorated with tattoos.

'So this is the famous wobble board,' he said. 'How does it work?' He picked it up by the top, tried to wobble it and snapped both corners off.

My mouth dropped open. He handed me the board and took off. I couldn't speak . . . couldn't think of anything to *say*. I looked down at Bob's gentle face and felt sick. Holding each edge in my palms I gave it a bounce. It still worked. Thank goodness!

The stage at Rushcutter's Bay Stadium was an old boxing ring, with the audience all round you. During each performance a mechanical device would slowly turn the stage through 180 degrees and then slowly back again. It meant that all the time you had your back to half the audience.

The Rushcutter's Bay crowd had a reputation for being ruthless. As I waited backstage I was told the story of one poor girl, with a lovely voice, who was singing a medley from various comic operas. Halfway through a bloke bellowed, 'Turn round, love. Let's see your face.'

She continued singing and graciously turned to face the voice.

'Bloody hell, turn aback again, would ya.'

The poor girl stopped in mid-note, burst into tears and left the stage with laughter ringing in her ears.

What were they going to do to me? I wasn't a rock 'n' roller. I didn't have a fancy costume. I was this innocuous Aussie, with a beard and glasses, wobbling a painting.

I bounced onto the stage and blinked into the bright lights. I was thankful to have something to hold to stop my hands shaking. I started singing, but it didn't take long to realize that everybody in the audience behind me was talking and laughing.

I figured that I had two choices. I either went down with a fight, or I let them win.

In mid-song I suddenly stopped. The band was caught by surprise. I turned and signalled them to stop playing. I don't think they had ever seen anybody go straight to total silence mid-verse. It certainly got the crowd's attention.

I turned to the section of the audience behind me and said, 'Can you hear me alright over there?'

'Yeah,' some bloke yelled back.

'Good! 'Cause I can hear you loud and bloody clear from here. Shut up, you *bastards*, I'm trying to sing a song.'

The whole place erupted into laughter and applause. From that moment I had them. They all joined in the chorus and wanted me to do an encore.

Back in Bassendean, Mum was so excited she didn't know where to turn. Normally, she'd have been calling the local newspaper and telling all her friends, but they already knew. 'Kangaroo' was being played on the radio and there were interviews and profiles about me in the papers and magazines.

Alwen seemed happy because I was happy. Sadly, I had so many new demands on my time that we spent even less time together. Alwen didn't once complain. I'd come home and ask about her day and she'd describe how she went for a walk and picked up some things from the shops. Inside, she must have been thinking, 'Surely he's going to see.' I never did.

Having the number one song was amazing, but I don't think I appreciated the magnitude of the achievement. It had happened too easily. Perhaps if I had struggled to break through, I would have understood it better. Instead, I just assumed it was my right. I also thought, OK, I did it once – I can do it again.

I was in for a rude awakening.

My next single was a double A-side. 'Big Black Hat' was a light, whimsical song, that got longer and longer with each verse. The flip side was 'I've Lost My Mummy', the song that I'd written in Earl's Court but been too afraid to show any music publishers.

Another Aussie singer, Johnny Ashford, had just had a big hit with 'Little Boy Lost', based on the true story of a four-year-old boy lost in the New England Ranges and found alive. Stupidly, I thought I might piggyback on some of this success, so I re-named my song 'Lost Little Boy'.

It was a terrible mistake. To begin with, when you have a song with the same line, 'I've lost my mummy', repeated throughout, you don't change the title to something else.

Likewise, you should not (repeat *not*) try to create any kind of tenuous link between a comic song about a kid lost in a department store and an emotional real-life rescue in the wilderness. Needless to say, my new record disappeared without trace.

Not to be deterred, I wrote 'Tame Eagle', a weird parody of a big rock 'n' roll hit called 'Teen Angel'. The original was a ballad about a girl riding on the back of a motorcycle who drops her high school ring at a railway crossing. She runs back to fetch it and is killed by a train, thus becoming the 'teen angel'.

In Australia nobody seemed to bother about parodying other people's songs. It was done all the time, without anybody seeking permission from publishers or writers. A few weeks after 'Kangaroo' hit the No.1 spot, a Sydney club comedian called Joe Martin brought out a parody of the song using the same chorus. He claimed it was a 'traditional' Australian song and therefore was out of copyright.

I was furious. I phoned EMI in Sydney, who chased up Joe Martin's record company. Instead of being apologetic and immediately withdrawing the single, they shrugged and said, 'What's the fuss about?'

Eventually, I had to go before a Justice of the Peace in Perth and swear that the words and music were written by me. That should have been the end of it, but a few weeks later, EMI contacted me again.

'Look,' they said, 'Joe's spent a lot of money on the recording. They've only pressed a couple of thousand copies and they're all out in the shops. They want to know if you'll give them permission to sell the existing copies so Joe can get some of his money back. They're guaranteeing not to press any more.'

I spoke to a few people and they all took the view that the parody wasn't doing any harm, so I shrugged my shoulders and agreed.

My comic version of 'Teen Angel' disappeared without trace. It taught me that when people love a particular song, they don't appreciate somebody mocking it.

EMI was keen to release an album to take advantage of 'Kangaroo'. I went into a recording studio and put together an odd mix of tracks, which was called *Relax with Rolf* and had a self-portrait on the cover.

As part of the promotion, EMI organized a concert for me at Sydney Town Hall. It was billed as 'Rolf Harris playing all his hits', which was rather an overstatement since I only had the one.

The town hall was only about a third full when I arrived. I walked on stage in my ordinary pair of beige trousers and open-neck shirt. A bloke called out, 'Where's your flash stage suit?'

I didn't know what to say.

From that moment I lost the audience. All my clever songs were ignored or fell flat. Nobody was listening. They had bought tickets expecting to see a rock 'n' roll star and I hadn't delivered. It taught me another important lesson about knowing my audience. I couldn't compete with guys who relied on gutsy electric guitars and pounding rhythms. Hopefully, once they knew me better, audiences would know what to expect.

Back in Perth I enjoyed a great burst of songwriting. One of the technicians at the TV station, an American called John D. Brown, had suggested that I write an Australian Christmas carol. He couldn't believe that radio stations were playing all these songs about snow, sleighbells and reindeer when outside it was 104°F in the shade.

He was right, of course. Australians just took this for granted. We put up Christmas trees and spray-painted snow on shop windows. Our Christmas cards were covered in snowmen and Santas in red woollen suits.

'Why don't you write a song about what Christmas is really like in Australia?' said John.

Fired by the idea, we set about inventing an Aussie Christmas legend. The result was 'Six White Boomers' – a song about Santa's sleigh reaching Australia and being pulled by six white kangaroos instead of reindeer. Over time, it became a Christmas favourite in Australia, sung at carols by candlelight and end-of-year school concerts.

Another song that surfaced during that period was an Aboriginal lullaby called 'Carra Barra Wirra Canna'. Morva Cogan lived just up the road from Mum and Dad and had watched me grow up. When I had a hit with 'Kangaroo' she revealed to me that she was a songwriter. She pulled out a scrap of paper with five lines of prose and she wanted to know if I thought it was any good.

My mind immediately flashed back to Earl's Court, when I showed Ray Hartley my first effort at songwriting. I really wanted to give Morva some encouragement.

'Do you have a tune?'

She hummed a couple of disjointed bars of melody, which sounded quite nice. But when I tried to make the melody fit her lyrics, it didn't work. I tried to explain that the song needed some sort of structure. I got her to hum the start of the tune again and began writing down the music as best I could.

Eventually, I changed the entire 4/4 rhythm, slowing it down to the tempo of a waltz, with a two-beat rest at the end of every second bar, giving the singer time to breathe. I sent the finished song to EMI publishing, crediting Morva as the writer.

Another song from that time was 'Sun Arise' which was inspired by the Aboriginal music that Harry Butler had introduced me to. He had travelled all over the outback and become accepted by the 'elders' of the tribes that he visited.

As I listened to his tapes, I was stunned by the juxtaposition of the voice, the didgeridoo and the beating sticks. No single element fought the other. Each had a separate register – the nasal-sounding voice in the middle, the didge an octave lower and the piercing metallic-sounding sticks way up high. The rhythm was absolutely mesmerizing.

Up until then I had no idea what a didgeridoo sounded like. I'd used the word in 'Kangaroo' because it sounded funny and was associated with Australia. Now, listening to Harry's tapes, I fell in love with the instrument.

When 'Kangaroo' became a hit, Harry Scrivener, a friend of my dad's, sent me a didgeridoo from northern WA. It had instructions scrawled on a scrap of paper, 'Blow, suck, blow, suck, blow.'

I drove Alwen crazy trying to make it work. I practised every night in Hadden Hall, but could never get any further than making a loud blast.

Not long afterwards I was sitting in my office at TVW7, when a secretary poked her head round the door. 'Quick, there's someone playing a didgeridoo on the lunchtime show.'

I dashed round to the studio and stood in the control room, watching through the window. Trevor Jones, Professor of Music from the University of Western Australia, stood in front of a microphone holding a four-foot-long wooden tube to his lips. The low rolling, rumbling sound seemed to resonate right through the middle of me. As soon as the show was off air, I introduced myself to Trevor and asked how I could learn.

Within days I was sitting in his office, watching how he made the basic sound on the didgeridoo. Almost effortlessly he created that deep 'pedal' note that went on and on, like the drone of the bagpipes.

The practical side of cycle-breathing seemed to come easily to me, although often it's the hardest part, according to Trevor. It means using the muscles of your cheeks to squeeze air out of your mouth, while simultaneously filling your lungs through your nose. When done successfully, you can hold a note indefinitely, alternating between lung pressure and cheek pressure, without ever stopping to grab a new breath. But although I mastered the breathing technique, I still couldn't make it work on the didgeridoo.

Harry Butler and I wrote 'Sun Arise' together, trying to capture the magic of Aboriginal music by reproducing the repetition of lyrics and music that makes it so mesmerizing.

The lyrics for the song came from a story Harry told me about Aboriginal beliefs. Some tribes see the sun as a goddess. Each time she wakes in the morning, her skirts of light gradually cover more and more of the land, bringing back warmth and life to the earth.

Alwen helped me polish the lyrics on a holiday we took to the south-west of WA – our first break since we arrived in Australia. We drove through the famous jarrah forests around Pemberton, pulling off the road each night and sleeping in the station wagon. At one point, we climbed all the way to the canopy of a massive jarrah tree, using metal steps driven into the side of the trunk. From the fire look-out at the top, 150 feet above the ground, we could gaze for miles across the grey-green foliage.

I love the chaos of the Australian bush. There is nothing neat or uniform about it. The scrub is cluttered and confused, with muted colours and a shimmering heat haze. I think Alwen found the scenery quite foreign, but beautiful in its own way. The flies, however, drove her crazy. In the sandy soil of the south-west, they bred by the thousand and would settle on our backs in a black swarm wherever we walked.

It was a wonderful two weeks. We were totally alone and wrapped up in each other. I wish Alwen had told me how lonely and unhappy she'd been. I guess she didn't want to spoil the moment.

Back in Perth, I began recording several songs including 'Six White Boomers' and 'Sun Arise'. The latter featured Trevor Jones on didgeridoo. I thought it was going to be groundbreaking because it was so unusual and Australian. Instead it barely made a ripple.

Rather than prompting a greater appreciation of Aboriginal music, I seemed to be upsetting people. An anonymous letter arrived, I assumed from an Aborigine, who simply wrote, 'How could you say that about my people in "Tie Me Kangaroo Down, Sport"?'

I felt myself go hot and cold. I knew the verse the letter referred to.

> *Let me Abos go loose, Lou,*
> *Let me Abos go loose.*
> *They're of no further use, Lou,*
> *So let me Abos go loose.*

> *All together now!*

When I wrote the song in London for a noisy, beer-drinking bunch of Aussies at the Down Under Club, I didn't think about the sensibilities of Aborigines. I was simply trying to pack the song full of every Australian reference I could think of. I had imagined Aboriginal jackaroos working for the stockman and once he died, he wanted them to be paid their wages and let go. I guess I was very naive. Now I could see how easily this could be misconstrued.

From that moment on, I never sang the verse again. And every recording of 'Kangaroo' since then has had the verse removed. Unfortunately, the original version is still played sometimes, but I can't control that.

My contract at TVW7 was coming to an end. The station wanted me to stay for another year, but I said no. It was time to move on. I didn't want to get stuck doing children's TV for ever. It was time for a new challenge.

Early in 1961 we left Sydney on a US cruise ship owned by the Matson Line. For some reason, the vessel was kept at refrigeration temperature all the way to Hawaii. It was so cold inside and so hot outside that we had to take summer clothes to wear on deck and woollies to change into when we came back indoors.

After two weeks in Hawaii we boarded the P&O liner *Oriana* on her maiden voyage. She was magnificent – nothing broke down, nobody fell sick and the air-conditioning maintained a perfect, sensible temperature.

We sailed across the Pacific and reached Victoria, the lovely old capital of British Columbia in Canada. A group of local journalists joined us on board for the short trip from Vancouver Island to the mainland. The *Oriana* was the first big ocean liner to ever visit Vancouver and P&O had spared no expense in promoting the inaugural voyage.

Dean Miller from the company's promotions department had seen my name on the VIP passenger list and mentioned my Australian No. 1 record to journalists. I did a lot of interviews, including one with an abrasive Scot called Jack Webster, who was the top talkback radio star in Vancouver. Jack had a very aggressive style, but I managed to hold my own and get him laughing at every mad Scottish joke I could remember. We finished up having a ball.

Afterwards he offered to arrange somewhere for us to stay for a few weeks while we looked round. He also asked if I'd thought of doing any shows in Vancouver.

'It hadn't even occurred to me.'

'Well, I have a friend who runs a nightclub. I could put you in touch with him.'

As we were speaking, the *Oriana* moved very slowly under Lion's Gate Bridge in brilliant sunshine. We looked in awe at the snow-covered peaks of the Rockies that seemed to be only a few miles away.

As we docked, a school choir began singing from the pier. My ears pricked up. That sounds familiar. Glancing from the upper deck, I saw about forty kids singing 'Tie Me Kangaroo Down, Sport'. What a thrill!

Someone from P&O had tracked down my record at CKLG, a

local radio station, and borrowed their only copy for the choir to learn. I rushed down to the cabin and came back with Bob's portrait. Giving a big thumbs up to the kids, I began singing and 'wobbling' along with them. God knows what the other passengers made of it.

It took hours to get through customs. The customs officer didn't believe me when I told him the didge was a musical instrument.

'Would you mind playing it for me, sir?'

'I can't.'

'So why are you carrying it?'

I shrugged. 'I live in hope.'

I could see Alwen rolling her eyes. She probably wanted to see it confiscated.

'What's in this box?' he asked, eyeing another strange object.

'A Spanish dogfish,' I replied, giggling. That nearly got me deported.

He watched me stony-faced as I explained that Perro Caliente was a TV character and gave him a demonstration. I'm convinced he almost smiled.

True to his word, Jack Webster had organized us some good, cheap accommodation. The next day the sun disappeared and the rain arrived. It fell non-stop for the next sixteen days and nights. After two days in the flat, waiting for the skies to clear, we dashed through the downpour until we found a shop selling umbrellas and raincoats.

Through Jack, I arranged to meet Ken Stauffer, the owner of the Cave nightclub, and Ben Kopelow, who did publicity for the up-coming acts. I was under no illusions – we weren't talking about headlining Vegas. They'd snap me up, I thought.

I started telling them about my cabaret act but soon realized that it was impossible to explain. So much of it depended upon getting the audience participation.

'You won't believe me unless you see me do it with an audience,' I said. 'Why don't you give me a trial run for a week?'

Ken explained very nicely that they didn't work like that.

'We're booked two months in advance,' explained Ben. 'People don't just turn up.'

'I did.'

Finally Ken suggested that I go across to a smaller place that he owned called the Arctic Club. 'Go and see Bert Williams. He's the manager. Tell him to put you on next Monday night.'

'Just the one night?'

Ken laughed. 'You're lucky to get that.'

I trooped down the road and round the corner to the Arctic Club, which the locals pronounced 'The Ardic'.

Bert Williams was even less enthusiastic about giving me a live audition. He phoned Ken for confirmation. Apparently, Ken told him, 'He's either as mad as a hatter, or he's good. There's only one way to find out.'

The following day I met the band at our only rehearsal. Bert did the introductions. 'This is the Chris Gage Trio. That's Chris on piano, Jimmy Whiteman on drums and Cuddles Johnson on double bass.'

'G'day, guys.'

They only just bothered looking up. Chris was chewing on a matchstick and Jimmy and Cuddles were reading the paper.

I put my accordion down in the corner. 'Right. I'm gonna do this song called "Tie Me Kangaroo Down, Sport". I use this board as an instrument. I do the verses and I get the audience singing the chorus.'

They all stopped chewing gum in unison and looked at me in disbelief. '*Who* is going to sing the chorus?'

'The audience. I'm going to get them singing.'

Chris snorted with laughter. I caught the sideways amused look that passed between Jimmy and Cuddles. From then on they mucked about and it was hardly worth rehearsing.

On Monday night I turned up early. The Arctic had a capacity of about 125, with seats all round a central dance floor. As the nine o'clock show drew nearer, the place was only about a third full.

Three young women were sitting at a table nearest the stage. They were all attractively dressed and made-up.

I crouched down next to them and spoke in a whisper. 'Listen, it's my first night and it's important that I make a good impression. I'm going to sing this song. The chorus goes, "Tie me kangaroo down, sport . . ."' I went right through it with them and explained that I needed them to sing it with me. 'It'll give me the lift I need. Is that OK? Fantastic.'

Bert introduced me, sounding hopeful rather than enthusiastic. The applause was equally lukewarm. 'I've just had this hit song in Australia,' I said. 'It goes something like this.' I started on the wobble board and the band joined in. 'There's an old Australian stockman . . .'

When I reached the chorus, I gave a big, 'All together now . . .'

I was on my own. Not a soul joined in. I stopped the band in mid-chorus. The place went dead quiet. I looked down at the women at the ringside table and said, 'What happened to you three? This is it – the chorus. You promised faithfully you were going to sing it with me.'

I could see them turning the colour of their lipstick.

I started singing again. When I reached the chorus, I again found myself singing alone. I stopped the band and left the stage carrying the microphone.

'Aren't you going to sing?' I asked quietly, standing next to their table. 'This is my big chance. If you don't sing with me, I'll be lost.' The microphone picked up every whispered word.

There was a lot of good-natured laughter as I went back on stage and started again. This time the girls were brilliant. They started singing and soon everybody else had joined in. It was a great night. All my jokes seemed new and the songs were fresh. Chris and the boys had a ball.

Afterwards, Bert Williams asked, 'You know those women you were talking to?'

'Yeah?'

'They were prostitutes.'

My mouth dropped open. Innocent old Harris had no idea. It hadn't even crossed my mind why such glamorous girls might be sitting on their own.

The following morning Bert had a call from Ben Kopelow and Ken Stauffer asking how my audition had gone.

'He was absolutely terrible,' said Bert. 'Totally amateurish.'

'So we can't use him?' said Ken.

'Hell no, I want to book him for a week. If you ask me, he does it all wrong, but the audience just loved him.'

Ken gave the go-ahead and I was offered 125 Canadian dollars for the week. I didn't stop to translate this into pounds and thought it sounded like a fortune. In fact it was only a quarter of what I imagined.

By the Thursday night's performance, word of mouth had packed the Arctic Club. Bert booked me for another six weeks at $200 a week. 'If business gets better, I'll raise that,' he said.

Business did get better. By the last week they were queuing on the stairs waiting for the second show. By then Bert was paying me $700 a week – unheard of money to my mind.

It was a watershed moment for me because I found it so liberating. Nobody knew anything about me in Canada. I was free to be anything or anybody I wished. In England I had always been very conscious of the fact that I was a raw colonial and that upper crust accents intimidated me.

But in Canada it didn't matter whether I was Sir Giles McPhirtlesquirt or Fred Nurk. I had arrived on my own terms and there was no issue of accent, or schooling, or class. Nor was it like Perth where people would say, 'Oh, yeah, it's just Rolf. He grew up down the road. I used to sit next to him on the school bus.'

Canadians had no preconceived ideas about me. I no longer felt like tugging my forelock, or making excuses for other people's rudeness. If someone talked during my act, I stopped the band and said, in a nice way of course, 'Could you shut up? I'm busting a gut to entertain you here.'

It was wonderful. I was free of it all. For the first time in my life I felt like a man rather than a boy among men.

When the rain finally stopped falling, Alwen and I explored Vancouver. Although eager to get home, she liked the change of scenery and being back in a place where you could see the seasons passing clearly. That was something which she missed in Australia . . . looking out the window and knowing instantly whether it was spring, summer, autumn or winter.

We did a joint interview on CBC television talking about our shared interests. One of the things we mentioned was collecting rocks. This had nothing to do with geology. Neither of us had a clue what most of the rocks were. We just liked picking up interesting pebbles and fossils on our travels, just as a child collects shells on a beach.

After the show a man called the studio and asked if we'd be interested in learning how to cut and polish stones. Greig Marotte, an Australian living and working in Vancouver, was a member of a lapidary club. He invited us along one day and introduced us to what became one of our favourite hobbies. Here was something we could learn to do together and share.

On another television show, I sang 'Carra Barra Wirra Canna', the Aboriginal lullaby that I'd written with Morva Cogan. A few nights later, on stage at the club, I heard a woman call out, 'Sing us that lullaby you did on television.'

'It's hardly a cabaret song.'

'Why not?'

'Well, it's not exactly comedy, is it? It's a lullaby.'

'What difference does that make?'

'I'm just saying it's not nightclub material.'

Once again out of the darkness she asked, 'Why not?'

By then I'd run out of excuses. I sang the song and got a great reaction. Up until then I had always laboured under the misapprehension that cabaret was about whimsical songs and comic set pieces. Now I realized there were no hard and fast rules. I could do ballads, or sing lullabies. I could move people, or make them think.

Doing two shows a night for seven weeks was absolutely exhausting. I had never worked at that sort of pace before. Bert wanted me to stay on for another month, but it was time to go.

There was a club in San Francisco called The Hungry I that I wanted to check out. It was where the Kingston Trio had started. The owner had heard about my Arctic Club success on the grapevine and sent me a letter saying, 'If you're ever in town look me up.' I suddenly had visions of being 'discovered' and wowing them in America too.

After an emotional farewell from Vancouver, we boarded a train and headed south, eventually crossing a border into California.

In San Francisco I went straight to The Hungry I and suggested a live audition with an audience. Mr Banducci, the owner, wouldn't hear of it. 'Audition for me,' he said.

'You won't believe me when I tell you what I'm going to do and what's going to happen. You need to see me with an audience. I'm really good. I killed 'em in Vancouver. They were queuing every night.'

'Show *me*.'

'No, you don't understand. It won't work at an audition like this. I haven't got terrific band arrangements. I'm not that great a singer. I'm just good with people . . .'

'Permit me to know my clientele, young man,' he said, in a deep, rumbling American accent.

I had a sinking feeling in my stomach. Mr Banducci sat on a chair, with a cigar clenched between his teeth, waiting for me to start. Oh well. Here goes. I ploughed through a couple of songs, but I could see his eyes glazing over. He brushed cigar ash off his trousers as he stood up. His only word on the subject was 'Sorry'.

I left the club and trudged back to our hotel. We hung around San Francisco for another two weeks seeing the sights. I rang Mr Banducci every day, but it was no use. He was never going to give me a chance in front of an audience.

Feeling disheartened, I suggested we scrap the rest of the rail trip down to LA and hop on a plane to New York. Alwen jumped at the chance. She was all fired up to get back to England.

From the airport we took a taxi into Manhattan. As it raced along a six-lane motorway, I whispered to Alwen, 'It's weird seeing cars driving on the right hand side of the road.'

Our driver turned round, still doing sixty miles an hour, and said, 'Oh, yeah, what side of the road do they drive on in your country?'

'On the other side.'

'Oh, yeah,' he scoffed. 'What about the *on-coming* traffic?'

He had me there!

We stayed with Frank Devine, an Aussie journalist I'd met during my TV stint in Perth. He was now doing very well in New York and had an apartment in Queens.

Giving America one last throw of the dice, I touted my Australian record of 'Kangaroo' around the various record companies. Henry Onorati at 20th Century-Fox Records eventually agreed to release it.

Riding my luck, I also tried for an audition at the famous Blue Angel nightclub. I phoned beforehand and arranged to see the manager. It taught me something interesting about how entertainers are labelled in America. Unless you have a slick-talking, high-powered agent selling you up-front, people figure that you're from Hicksville, or a no-hoper.

It was no good quoting my success in Vancouver. 'Where's that?' I was asked.

'I really need to audition in front of an audience,' I said, feeling like a broken record.

'Try *me*.'

'No. I mean a *real* audience.'

The guy laughed. I had more chance of flying to the moon than of being let loose on the patrons of the Blue Angel.

So I went through another excruciating trial, singing songs to a lone figure sitting in judgement from the darkness. It was so awful that by mutual consent not a word was spoken afterwards, and we left by separate doors.

Alwen had started counting down the days until we flew home. I had arranged the flights and shipped our excess baggage. On the day before we were due to leave, a telegram arrived from Bert Williams. It said simply, 'Come home. We need you.'

It was the word 'home' that did it.

'I want to go back to Vancouver,' I said.

Alwen looked horrified. 'But we're going home. The tickets are booked. Our cases are packed . . .'

I tried to help her understand. The terrible audition at the Blue Angel had left me feeling like an unwanted failure. Now I had a chance to feel good about myself again. In Vancouver I'd been appreciated.

'You don't have to come,' I told her. 'You can go home and see Puggy and your family. It's only for a month. Then I'll be home.'

She caught the plane the next day. Saying goodbye was truly awful. We hugged for a long time and I didn't want to let her go. I flew off in the opposite direction, feeling totally lost without her.

Business at the Arctic was amazing. People were lined up outside for both shows and Ken Stauffer insisted on giving me $1,000 a week. I didn't protest. He was a very persuasive man and convinced me to stay another month and then another. Thirteen weeks later I was still there.

It's a wonder Alwen didn't send me an ultimatum, 'Come back or else!' Instead she flew from England to join me. Again she probably felt completely abandoned in our relationship, but didn't say anything. Typically, I just assumed that what made me happy would make her happy.

Although the Arctic had a great crowd, occasionally I had to deal with drunks and hecklers. I had all sorts of advice from well-wishers on what I should do. The general consensus seemed to be that I should learn some 'squelches' (put-downs). Lines like, 'Sit him over by the wall, that's plastered too'; or, 'The last time I saw a mouth like that it had a hook in it.'

One night, I felt the need to try out one of these squelches. I had just started introducing 'Six White Boomers' and was explaining that in Australia, Christmas came in the middle of a long hot summer. I got as far as saying, 'In Australia, Christmas comes . . .' when a voice from the darkness completed the line, '. . . but once a year.'

The audience laughed and I did too. Suddenly, this fella began delivering a string of rapid-fire one-liners. I couldn't think of a thing to say. Soon everybody was listening to him, while I stood totally ignored in the spotlight. Then I remembered a 'squelch' I'd been given only that evening.

'Give me a break, sir,' I said, interrupting his jokes. 'Did I pester you earlier in the gents' toilet when you were making a date with that fella? Did I pester you then?'

The line got a great burst of laughter and applause. But as it died, the same voice came back at me from the darkness. 'Well, is the date still on, or is it off now?'

The audience exploded and I joined in the applause. 'You win,' I said.

From that day onwards, I never used another squelch. Embarrassing people is not what I'm about. I want to be friends with my audience. Admittedly, there are times when this hasn't been easy. Like every other entertainer, I've had to fight for my life on stage against very clever and sometimes cruel hecklers.

In total I spent thirty-one weeks at the Arctic Club and it is still one of the highlights of my career. It ended very sadly and suddenly. Early in the morning on Christmas Eve in 1961 I was woken by a phone call from my mate Greig Marotte.

'Have you heard the news? The Arctic Club has burnt down.'

I laughed, thinking he was joking.

'Seriously. It's on the radio.'

'Oh, shit.'

I threw anything on, jumped in a cab and went down to the club. Fire engines blocked the street and hoses snaked across the asphalt. Firemen with blackened faces were packing things away. They looked exhausted.

The club was a smouldering ruin. The only thing still standing was a staircase leading up to nowhere. The first floor had collapsed, along with the piano and the bar. Apparently, the boiler in the basement of the adjoining premises had blown up and set the building alight. The fire had spread quickly until everything caved in on itself.

Picking my way through the puddles and smoking timber, I reached the cupboard beneath the lone staircase. This is where I kept my piano accordion, propped in its cardboard case. I opened the door and there it was. It was sitting in three inches of water. Miraculously it had survived the fire. Next to it, in a canvas carry-case stinking of acrid smoke, was Bob Harbin's portrait.

I rescued both and took the accordion to a repairer, who dismantled it and dried the parts. Slowly it was rebuilt until it sounded brand new.

The Arctic had been destroyed. Ironically, Ken Stauffer's larger nightclub, the Cave, was closed for renovations at the time of the fire. He immediately reopened and booked me into the new venue.

The Cave had a capacity of 950. Up until then I had only ever worked in small intimate places, where I found it quite comforting to see the silhouettes of everyone in the audience. Now I was entertaining a much larger crowd, filling two storeys.

The fact that I couldn't see everyone in the audience worried me at first. I tried to remember what Hermione Gingold had told me. Even if I made eye contact with just one person, by some indefinable magic everybody else in the room would believe I was talking to them personally.

Every night I would circulate among the audience beforehand, shaking hands with the regulars and introducing myself to newcomers. This meant that later, when the spotlight was in my eyes and I couldn't see their faces, I still felt as though I knew them. And if I made a mistake, or wasn't particularly good, I knew they'd forgive me because they'd met me. I was just an ordinary bloke, having a go.

After a month at the Cave I decided it was time to leave. England beckoned. I had been away for nearly three years and had learned a great deal about television, songwriting and life in general. It was time to put all of this to good use.

Chapter Ten

'SO, RINGO, WHAT DO YOU THINK ABOUT SPAGHETTI?'

HAVING CONQUERED AUSTRALIA AND A CORNER OF CANADA, I arrived at EMI in London clutching my recordings and feeling certain the company would automatically release the songs in the UK. It would be like having a second bite at the cherry, on the other side of the world.

'No, it doesn't work that way, old boy,' I was told. What a familiar refrain . . . and accent.

'What do you mean?'

'I tell you what, go and see George Martin. See what he says.'

George was then a young record producer with EMI. Later I discovered that anybody who was considered oddball, musically weird or hard to categorize was sent to George. He was considered to have the Midas touch when it came to knowing what worked and what didn't.

I sat in his office as he listened to the recordings. Although only four years older than me, he spoke like a wise uncle.

'I'm sorry, but we can't put any of these out. They're not well enough recorded.'

My hackles went up. 'What do you mean?'

'Just that. We'll have to do them all again.'

As the shock sank in, he added insult to injury. 'And this song "Sun Arise" . . .'

'What about it?'

'Well, it's boring.'

'It's authentic,' I said, defensively.

'Yes, it might be authentic, but it's boring. It just goes on and on.'

'That's what makes it authentic . . . the repetition. It becomes a mesmerizing thing.'

'Exactly.'

'But . . .'

George put his hand on my arm and said, very gently, 'Look, Rolf, let me put it this way. If you recorded an Eriskay love lilt in the original Gaelic, you might sell eighty-seven copies to enthusiasts. But if you were to take that same melody, put some English words to it and release it as "A Scottish Soldier" you could sell half a million. All you're doing is giving people something they can understand.'

Although it was hard to accept, I could see that he might have a point.

George began weaving his magic. 'Listen, I think the song has great potential. Why don't you go away and try to think of a middle bit? Keep the same feel, but write a middle-eight with a new tune in the same vein. That breaks it up and relieves the boredom. Then when you come back to the original melody, everybody knows it and wants to hear it again.'

Sitting at my ramshackle piano, I set about writing a new section. Having worked for a few hours, I ran the changes past Alwen. She loved the additions and so did George. He immediately arranged for me to record 'Sun Arise' at Abbey Road Studios in North London.

The problem, of course, was that nobody in the UK could play the didgeridoo. I still had mine but it was in the wrong key and I was no closer to playing it properly.

Johnny Spence, the inspired arranger George had brought in, solved the problem by using eight bass fiddles sawing away on the bottom E for the whole of the song. Afterwards I heard one of the bass players complain that it was the most boring recording session he'd ever done.

It might not have been entirely authentic without a didgeridoo, but the bass fiddles sounded great. Johnny Spence also added a stunning thumping drum beat to complement the beating sticks.

Apart from his creative input, George threw his weight behind the promoting of the song. He told EMI, 'Now this is totally different. Nobody will understand it, but it's marvellous. You've got to have faith and keep plugging it.'

Singles usually spent about three weeks on the plug list. If a song hadn't picked up airplay or interest by then, the record company would drop it. 'Sun Arise' spent three *months* on the plug list. Every week the reps went out and tried to convince radio producers to play the song. EMI paid Radio Luxembourg to have it constantly on their pop programmes, which was standard practice in those days. Radio Luxembourg was the only commercial radio station that could reach into British homes.

In September 1962, 'Sun Arise' began being picked up.

Roger Henning, a gauche and rather brash Aussie with flaming red hair, got in touch with me. He had all sorts of ideas about how to promote 'Sun Arise'. Roger had a background in newspapers and knew exactly what buttons to push to get publicity. He took it upon himself to become my informal public relations officer – dashing here and there, filling my diary with press and photo calls. He even convinced the West Australian Agent General to allow me to paint a nine-foot-high poster of myself advertising 'Sun Arise' in the front window of his offices in the Strand.

In the meantime, I was back on the books with IAR and had Phyl Rounce as my manager. Roger drove Phyl mad because she couldn't understand his motives. He was charging around the place drumming up publicity, when that was supposed to be her job. She was even more suspicious when word filtered back that Roger was claiming to be my manager when he arranged interviews.

In the early sixties the music scene was incredibly exciting. Rock 'n' roll was filtering across the Atlantic from America, along with the new dance crazes and hairstyles. Most of the music was being imported from America and even the home-grown acts were singing American songs. All that was about to change with the emergence of stars like Johnny Leyton, Marty Wilde and Gerry and the Pacemakers.

Amidst all this, people didn't know how to categorize me. Some remembered me vaguely from my days on children's TV. Others didn't know whether 'Sun Arise' was a novelty song, a folk song or something completely different. Yet it became one of those tunes that people couldn't get out of their heads.

On a Sunday afternoon in October, Alwen and I were wandering through the back streets of Camden Town, looking at houses and flats for sale. We were in a cobblestone mews, admiring window boxes, when Alan 'Fluff' Freeman's voice drifted down through an open window. He was introducing *Pick of the Pops* on BBC radio.

'And at seventeen we have a new entry – Rolf Harris with "Sun Arise".'

We stood on the pavement, staring up at the first floor window in disbelief, listening to *my* record. What a wonderful moment!

'Sun Arise' climbed to No. 12 and then No. 9. I appeared on *Top of the Pops* and *Thank Your Lucky Stars*. During an interview with Kingsley Amis on *Kingsley Amis Goes Pop* I did a huge Australian bush painting and then sang the song. I told Kingsley right at the beginning that I couldn't talk sense and paint properly at the same time. For some reason, he totally ignored this and kept asking me questions. When I didn't answer, he panicked and began firing even more questions at me.

For some reason, I thought he was being sarcastic and asking me loaded questions about my qualifications to be a pop star. I refused to be intimidated and mildly mocked him. Afterwards, I overheard him say that it was the worst programme he'd ever done. It embarrasses me when I think back on it. My little bit of success had gone to my head and made me a very obnoxious young man.

'Sun Arise' had reached No. 2 in the UK chart and everybody seemed convinced that I was destined for the top spot. I was at risk of becoming insufferable.

The following Sunday, 'Fluff' Freeman announced the new No.1. A young fella by the name of Elvis Presley had jumped from nowhere straight to the top spot with 'Return to Sender'. I came down to earth with a bump.

Our two-room flat near Regent's Park had been sub-let while we were away in Australia. We moved back in and discovered the last tenants had been allergic to cleaning. The walls were covered in cooking grease and a saucepan of rotting green mildewed soup had been sitting in the oven for weeks.

Having saved a bit of money, I had ambitions of perhaps buying the whole house. It had been on the market for £11,000 before we left. We came home to find it up for sale again – for £22,000 – an obscene amount of money. If I could have guaranteed myself a successful career, I might have bought it on the 'never never', but there are no certainties in show business.

Alwen's parents had moved from Devon to Swiss Cottage, only fifteen minutes' drive away. It was nice to have them so close. Alwen also became friends with Don and Anne Charles, who lived in the flat below us. Don was a singer, who was also managed by Phyl Rounce. His wife Anne was an ex-dancer from Bradford and they had a baby girl, Julie.

I didn't quite know what to make of Don. On the surface, we were best of mates, swapping jokes and laughing, but he was quite a smooth operator. He was always trying to sell me lengths of cloth for flash stage suits. The cloth was incredibly cheap, but there was never a mention of where he got it from. Don was also full of ideas for money-making schemes. Whenever I had misgivings, he somehow managed to talk me round.

Even before 'Sun Arise' became a hit I'd started putting together an album with George Martin. We re-recorded most of my Australian stuff and added some new material. A very smart young Scottish entrepreneur called Andy Lothian saw the possibility that 'Sun Arise' would be a hit and booked me to do a tour of Scotland. By the time the tour started, I had the No. 2 song and a brand new album.

This was my first experience of touring. Andy drove me between the different venues – some of them hundreds of miles apart across huge and empty distances. I think some of the audiences expected a rock 'n' roller rather than someone wobbling a bit of hardboard and playing the accordion.

In East Kilbride, just outside Glasgow, I faced a dance floor full of Scottish teenagers, who were suddenly forced to stop dancing because of the floorshow – namely me.

I started with a song from the new album – a whimsical rendition of 'An English Country Garden'. As I sang the first line, I suddenly remembered that the Scots hated the English – or so I'd been told. I figured they wouldn't take kindly to my singing about anything English, so on the spur of the moment, I changed the end of the first line and sang, 'In a Scottish country ga-arden.'

In the next instant my mind flashed ahead to the end of the song. The parody made a mockery of English gardens as being soggy and scraggy with the immortal lines, 'Littered garbage dropped among/Little bits of doggy dung.'

I was now about to sing these things about *Scottish* country gardens! They'd lynch me!

Rapidly losing confidence, my voice began to falter and I broke into a cold sweat. The stage lifted me only a few inches above the teenagers who were less than impressed. A lad of about fifteen, standing right in front of me with his arm around his dance partner, said, 'Why don'cha fuckin' pack it in, Jimmy, and let's get back to the fuckin' dancing!'

The little girl with him, all of about twelve, said, 'Aye, why fuckin' don't ya?'

My mouth fell open. I looked around the room and the feeling seemed to be unanimous.

'Yes, why don't I,' I said. I turned and left the stage. It must have been the shortest floorshow ever.

Later in the tour, I arrived at a dance hall which was totally empty.

'Don' worry,' said the caretaker. 'The pubs are nay closed yet.'

By ten thirty the place was packed to the rafters and jumping with drunks. In the middle of a song, something flashed past my head. I realized it was one of those old pennies, just over an inch in diameter.

I caught the tail end of the arm movement from the corner of my eye. I looked at the bloke who'd thrown it and said laughingly into the microphone, 'You missed.'

The next one didn't.

A lethal copper disc came skimming towards me. I just had time to raise my hands in front of my glasses. I had a vertical bruise on my wrist for a week. It was better than losing an eye.

Thankfully, not all the venues were this rough. I sang at a theatre in Glasgow which was quite posh, with velvet seats and proper stage lighting. I was in the dressing room getting ready when a total stranger walked in, wearing a kilt and full Highland regalia.

'Have a drink,' he said, producing a bottle and pouring about an inch and a half of whisky into a glass.

Very politely I said, 'No thanks. I don't drink.'

'I don't think ye heered me,' he said. 'I says, have a fuckin' drink.'

Working on the theory that a soft answer turneth away wrath, I said, 'No, seriously, thanks very much, I honestly don't drink.'

He gripped my shirt-front and hoisted me out of my chair. He was about six foot eight and very good at hoisting. With my face now an inch from his, he spoke very slowly and quietly, as though dealing with a complete idiot.

'I don't . . . think . . . ye heered me, Jimmy. I says . . . have . . . a . . . fuckin' . . . drink! OK?'

'Sure, why not.'

I forced down my first ever gulp of whisky. It tasted like medicine.

'Have anither,' he said.

'No, really, I've had en—'

'I . . . says . . . have anither!'

'Fantastic.'

I downed a second gulp. My head was spinning. Thankfully, my new acquaintance seemed satisfied and left without another word.

Most of my act was based on the album material, with a few parodies and folk songs thrown in. Normally, I finished with a rousing version of 'Waltzing Matilda', getting the audience to join me for the chorus.

In Dundee, I was singing the verse that goes, 'Down came the squatter, mounted on his thoroughbred. Down came the troopers, one, two, three.' I wanted the audience to do the counting with me, so I stopped the song and said, 'I want to really hear you shout that out.'

We started again, but they sang the line rather tentatively. I stopped the band.

'Come on, really *belt* it out. ONE! TWO! THREE!'

We had another go, but it still wasn't right.

I stopped the band yet again. 'Listen. Stop pussy-footing around. I want you to really let rip. Raise the roof.'

The band struck up and we sang the verse once more. Our drummer was a quiet Scotsman who rarely made eye contact with anyone. But at the precise moment the audience yelled ONE, TWO, THREE, he took it as a count in, and launched into the classic Scottish drum roll that precedes all Highland marches.

The rest of the band and I were stunned. We couldn't believe this shy, retiring, self-effacing guy could suddenly snap and of his own volition do something so spontaneous and unexpected.

At the end of his drum roll, don't ask me why or how, I launched straight into 'Scotland the Brave'.

The band laughed out loud in amazement and then joined me. I can't explain how beautifully this all worked. The audience roared with laughter and in one thrilling instant, we had turned the arrangement on its head and sent a buzz through the whole place.

From that moment on, I used the routine whenever I played 'Waltzing Matilda'. I'd rehearse it over and over with any new band until it seemed as spontaneous and accidental as the first time it ever happened. I would never have dreamt up this piece of material in a million years, but it was just perfect.

The following year, 1963, I did my first big packaged pop tour. The promoter was Larry Parnes, who had discovered and promoted stars like Adam Faith and Billy Fury.

The tour was a real eye-opener for me. On the same bill we had a seventeen-year-old called Shane Fenton, whose real name was Bernard Jury, but who later became Alvin Stardust. Also featuring were the Tornados, Peter Jay and the Jaywalkers, Eden Kane and Jess Conrad.

We did concerts all over the country in dance halls and theatres. In one gig, at a dance in Epsom, I walked on stage amid the bright lights, while the audience was in semi-darkness. I suddenly realized that half of those watching were children, who looked to be eleven or twelve years old. And they were the best-dressed kids I'd ever seen, in expensive suits, jackets and ties. To my horror, some of them were smoking – not just cigarettes, but cigars!

They seemed totally uninterested in my spot and I got no reaction at all. I came off stage feeling uptight and angry. 'Never again,' I said to the stage manager. 'Did you see those kids out there? Half of them were drunk and some of them were smoking.'

'What d'ya mean kids?' he said. 'They're jockeys!'

The dance hall was the 'local' for a lot of the racing folk from the nearby stables and Epsom racecourse.

At the age of thirty-three, I was the grandfather of the touring party, along with Al Paige, the comedian. I felt like a weird fish alongside all these young rock 'n' rollers. I had never quite fathomed the appeal of rock 'n' roll. It was like a foreign country to me. I loved pop music, but the rockers did all that strutting and posturing. I tried it once when I was singing in Spain during my first holiday with Alwen. It worked really well where nobody knew me, but I simply couldn't imagine being taken seriously doing it.

I'm sure that's why the sixties didn't swing for me. Everyone else was appealing to the screaming young girl fans in the crowd, who gathered backstage in their hundreds after every show. The stage doormen at the various theatres fought a running battle to keep them outside but somehow the girls always managed to get in. Two girls in particular followed the tour around and earned rather unflattering nicknames which I don't think I'll repeat here. In one venue they were smuggled backstage one at a time in a big suitcase.

For me it was all rather unnerving. There were semi-clad young women in dressing rooms, shower stalls, wardrobes and on tables. I tried not to watch – or be *seen* watching – but it wasn't easy. I spent most of my time reading the same page of a book fourteen times before realizing I was holding it upside down.

A part of me wanted the courage to get involved, but I was petrified. I was almost twice the age of the young blokes and I was married. And I kept asking myself, 'How did I miss out on all this when I was their age?' Yet the sheer mindlessness of it all threatened to shatter my illusions about women. I wanted them to be up there on a pedestal, not scrabbling around in dressing rooms with very little on.

Almost straight after the tour I went into my first summer season at Great Yarmouth. I was on the same bill as Joe Brown, a cockney comedian and singer with a shock of spiky hair.

I nearly didn't make it on stage. On the first morning, as I unloaded my gear, I started lugging the Ferrograph tape recorder upstairs. Alwen and I had rented a first floor flat for the season. As

I reached the top, I bent over to put the Ferrograph down. Big mistake! The pain was mind-blowing and I couldn't straighten up.

Hunched over, I crept down the stairs, crawled into the car and somehow managed to drive in first gear to a doctor's surgery.

'You've slipped a disc,' he said.

'Can you slip it back again?'

'No.' He handed me a metal waistcoat which looked like something from a medieval torture chamber. 'From now on you'll have to wear this.'

'For how long?'

'Permanently,' he said, quite matter-of-factly.

It sounded like a life sentence. I phoned Phyl Rounce and told her the terrible news. 'Don't do a thing,' she said. 'I'll be there tomorrow morning.'

The next day she arrived with a masseur called Carl, who was apparently the saviour of showbiz people who pulled muscles and slipped discs. The man was a total sadist and my back was covered in bruises for a week. But to his credit, he got me walking.

I dispensed with the metal waistcoat and was back at rehearsals the next day, grateful to be mobile again. Alwen spent the season in Great Yarmouth rather than having to spend sixteen weeks back at home without seeing me. The fact that she couldn't drive had always made it hard for her to get around. For years I'd been trying to convince her to get her licence, but she refused to drive a manual car, and was frightened by anything too large.

'I'll learn to drive when they build an automatic Mini,' she said, reasonably confident it would never happen.

One Sunday morning I picked up a paper and saw an advertisement for the first automatic Mini. I arranged secretly to buy one and have it delivered. On the day it arrived, the doorbell rang and I said to Alwen, 'Could you get that, love?'

She went downstairs and found a chap standing on the doorstep holding a clipboard.

'Mrs Alwen Harris?'

'Yes.'

'Could you please sign for this?' He pointed to a little red Mini with a white roof.

Alwen refused to believe it at first. How could I have called her bluff?

Stupidly, I made the mistake of trying to teach her to drive. It almost ended our marriage. We set off through the streets of Great Yarmouth, with Alwen clutching the wheel and nervously negotiating each turn. I found myself getting more and more stressed.

'Don't do that! Watch out for that car! You're too close! You're going too slow!'

I should have remembered my lesson from Spain. Never shout at Alwen or she simply freezes, or bursts into tears.

Eventually, she took driving lessons and discovered, of course, that everything I had told her was completely the opposite of what the instructor said. What did I know?

She passed her test at her first attempt and at the end of the season we drove back in convoy from Norfolk to London – her little Mini behind my Vauxhall estate car. I kept glancing in the rear mirror, feeling very proud of her.

We had never talked about starting a family. Both of us had simply assumed that children would come along at some point. But after five years nothing had happened. Neither of us said anything. In my case, it fell into the category of being a 'serious' subject and hence should be avoided.

I think privately we each thought by then that it wasn't going to happen. That's why it came as such a surprise when Alwen became pregnant. I think she knew instantly, at the moment we conceived, although her recollection is different. She remembers being sick and going to the doctor, who broke the news.

She was quite frightened at the thought of being a mother. She wasn't naturally maternal and had never been around babies. There were no younger nieces or nephews in her family. A lot of her fears were for her independence and the sense of quiet that she wrapped around herself. A baby would change all that.

Our first priority was to find a bigger place to live. With Phyl Rounce working on the case, we eventually settled on a terrace house in Sydenham, South East London. It was the end house of a newly built row, with a garden the width of the house. What particularly sold us on the place was the huge old coach house at the bottom of the garden. We thought it would make a perfect studio for Alwen's sculpture and my painting.

As Alwen expanded, my showbiz career was going from strength to strength. I had a weekly show on BBC television called *Hi There!* in which I did big paintings, sang some songs and gave groups the chance to plug their latest pop records.

On top of this, BBC radio offered me a half-hour light music show 'live' on Tuesday mornings at 10 a.m. It was a marvellous opportunity. They had organized a four-piece band – piano, bass, drums and guitar – headlined by a young man from Oldham called Laurie Holloway. (Laurie went on to be musical director for the likes of Englebert Humperdinck, Terry Wogan, Michael Parkinson and Dame Edna Everage.)

Each week I came up with new material, roughly sketching out the chord sequences and the drum patterns. Laurie's genius was in being able to take these rubbishy bits of paper and transform them into wonderfully inventive musical scores. The search for material was constant and over the years I found hundreds of songs, many of which I would never have thought of singing otherwise. It also gave me the chance to work with all sorts of stars from the pop world both past and present.

Meanwhile Epic Records in America had decided to release 'Sun Arise'. It shot to No. 48 on the US Top 100 chart and was expected to rise higher, and Epic urgently asked for material for an album. All the UK recordings were sent to New York and the album released.

'Kangaroo' was chosen as the second single and it began getting airplay, particularly in Denver, Colorado, for some strange reason. Epic got quite excited and wanted me to help promote the song. I jumped at the chance, particularly when I heard that the Blue Angel in New York wanted to book me. Memories of my embarrassing audition were still fresh in my mind. But now they wanted *me*! I wondered if they realized I was the same bloke.

Alwen was six months pregnant when she and I flew to America in mid-November. I did a whirlwind tour of radio stations and appeared on Johnny Carson's *Tonight Show*. To the amazement of the producer, I managed to get the audience singing the chorus of 'Kangaroo'.

The Blue Angel had a reputation for 'discovering' unknown stars. Barbra Streisand had been a teenager when she was plucked from the club and won a role on Broadway. A lot of the Epic Records staff came along to see my first show. One of the producers, Bobby Morgan, said to me afterwards, 'You really like sound effects. I bet you can't do this one from Tennessee.'

He started 'eefing and eyefing', which is a rhythmic huffing or panting, which I've heard described as sounding like Granny having a stroke or a small furry animal reaching orgasm. According to Bobby, it had started in the backwoods of Tennessee, where the poor hillbillies, unable to afford musical instruments, developed a way of making the sound of bass fiddle and brushes just with their mouths.

I loved it. I also dumbfounded Bobby by doing it effortlessly straight back to him. The sound fascinated me and I adopted it as my signature sound effect.

Alwen had been craving curries ever since she fell pregnant but Indian restaurants were very rare in New York. We trawled through the Yellow Pages to find one and then took a taxi from the hotel. Ours were the only white faces there. The food was absolutely appalling and had to be eaten while dozens of people were staring at us. I couldn't work out if we'd stumbled upon an organized crime syndicate or if they were waiting for us to collapse from botulism.

Back at the hotel, we found a telephone message from Alwen's parents. Her beloved poodle Puggy had died. Alwen didn't cry. Instead she went very quiet and I didn't know what to do.

The next morning as we wandered along First Avenue, looking for a coffee shop, a black lady came towards us in a shambling run. She was sobbing. I thought she'd been attacked or robbed.

'Are you alright?'

'The President's been shot!' she said, her eyes wide with shock. She staggered off, running aimlessly along the pavement.

Then I heard people whispering in disbelief. They looked blankly into each other's faces, hoping for some explanation or word that it was all a mistake. Total strangers were crying in each other's arms.

Alwen and I went back to our hotel room and spent most of the day watching news bulletins on television. The streets were all but deserted. When they finally confirmed that John F. Kennedy was dead, it was the blackest day that Alwen or I could ever remember.

I dreaded going in to work that night. I was particularly worried about whether to sing one of my regular songs, 'The Wild Colonial Boy'. It was about a lad from Ireland who becomes an outlaw in Australia and is shot and killed.

I shouldn't have worried. Not a soul appeared at the club. The place was normally packed with 250 people, but now it echoed in its emptiness. Waiters stood around with grief-stricken faces and the bar staff sat in silence on the stools.

The following week the Blue Angel closed its doors.

Four young lads from Liverpool had come from nowhere to take the pop world by storm. The Beatles had first entered the charts in 1962 with 'Love Me Do', just when 'Sun Arise' was making its mark. By April 1963 they were on a roll.

Every month they released a new track – each of them produced by George Martin. The whole country waited with unrestrained excitement to see what the band would do next. And they never failed to surprise and impress with songs that were always totally new and different and staggeringly good.

I first saw them at the Royal Albert Hall when I shared the billing at a concert called 'Swinging Sound 63'. It was broadcast live by the BBC and also featured Del Shannon and George Melly.

Soon afterwards I interviewed John, Paul, George and Ringo for BBC radio. I was worried sick beforehand. Despite being almost twice their age I was totally in awe of them. They were so sharp and quick-witted. Some interviewers and journalists had been made to look complete fools if they asked them banal questions.

I mentioned this to George Martin, who told me not to be nervous. 'They're four ordinary lads.'

'But what do I ask them?'

'Anything you want.'

Every secretary in the building had gathered in the corridors to catch a glimpse of the Fab Four when they arrived at the studio.

I did the introductions and then hit them with my first question: 'So, Ringo, what do you think about spaghetti?'

'Spaghetti! What's that got to do with anything?' They all burst into laughter.

By giving them something unexpected, I had broken the ice. I managed to get through the interview, but I was no Michael Parkinson.

That same year I was asked to compère The Beatles Christmas Show at the Finsbury Park Empire in London. The entire Liverpool connection was performing, including Cilla Black, Billy J. Kramer and the Fourmost.

I did a cabaret-style spot directly before the Beatles and each night as I came to introduce the Fab Four, I made a heartfelt plea.

'Now look. Last night everybody screamed so loudly that nobody heard a word they sang. These guys are fantastic, but please, *listen* to them. Ladies and gentlemen, the Beatles.'

A wall of sound hit me. Teenage girls, shoulder to shoulder, beneath the stage and leaning from the balconies were screaming so loudly that nobody could hear a thing above the racket. Some of them were fainting, while others clutched tear-stained photographs of their idols. The Beatles could have been miming, or singing a totally different song, and nobody would have known.

The Christmas Show ran for a couple of weeks. One night when I was doing my spot, John Lennon got hold of a microphone backstage and started making clever comments. I was explaining to the audience about 'Sun Arise' when his voice boomed, 'I dunno about that, Rolf.'

The audience laughed and I looked round. I started again and the voice said, 'Well, of course, you could say that. But, then again, I dunno, Rolf. Maybe you're just making it up.'

I tried to laugh it off, but inside I was seething. When the Beatles finished their set, I stormed into their dressing room.

'If you want to fuck up your own act, do it, but don't fuck up mine!' I yelled.

'Ooooh, Rolfie's lost his rag,' said John.

'Yeah, Rolfie's upset,' echoed George.

They started laughing and so did I. They had such charm that I couldn't be angry with them. At least I'd made my point and they didn't do it again.

Soon I was back on radio with them – compèring a Beatles New Year's Eve Show on BBC radio. At one point I got them singing 'Kangaroo' with me and I rewrote the lyrics especially for the occasion. The chorus had that wonderful high-pitched 'oooooh' that was so characteristic of the Beatles.

> Don't ill-treat me pet dingo, Ringo,
> Don't ill-treat me pet dingo,
> (In Liverpool accent) He can't understand your lingo,
>   Ringo,
> So don't ill-treat me pet dingo.
> All together now, Tie me kangaroo down, sport,
> Tie me kangaroo down, ooooooh.
> Tie me kangaroo down, sport,
> Tie me kangaroo down.

George's guitar's on the blink, I think,
George's guitar's on the blink.
Well it shouldn't go, 'Mm dinga, mm dinga, plink.'
Hey, that's really on the blink.
All together now (repeat chorus)

Prop me up by the wall, Paul,
Prop me up by the wall.
I'll scream and I'll cheer 'til I fall, Paul,
If you'll prop me up by the wall.
All together now (repeat chorus)

Hey keep the hits coming on, John,
Keep the hits coming on.
At least 'til after I'm gone John,
Just keep those hits coming on.
All together now (repeat chorus)

(Slow, *colla voce*) *Tan me hide when death comes, chums,*
Tan me hide when death comes.
(In tempo, in Liverpool accent) *So we tanned his hide*
    when he died, Clyde,
And Ringo's got it on his drums.
All together now (final chorus)

(Thirty years later I tried to get permission to use the recording. Letters were sent to all the former Beatles and Yoko Ono. They have a long-standing policy that if one of them disagrees then they all disagree. My request was turned down. Ironically, not long afterwards I discovered that a chap in America was distributing a bootleg version of the original recording on the Internet.)

It had been an amazing year. My success in Australia had been repeated in America and the UK. I had offers to do all sorts of things such as product launches, guest appearances and TV commercials.

A BBC producer approached me about a pilot for a new show that would showcase up and coming rock bands. He wanted me to compère the show, although I don't know why he chose me. I didn't know the first thing about the subject and didn't understand the appeal of rock music.

The first band to be featured on the pilot rehearsed and appeared at St Michael's Church Hall, not far from where I lived. They called themselves the Rolling Stones.

We filmed in the church hall and I went down to meet the guys. The young Mick Jagger strutted his stuff, gyrating and pouting during ear-shattering electric guitar solos. I was lost. With all that screaming and posturing, I couldn't hear a word he sang. If you can't hear the words, how do you know what the song is about?

Feeling totally out of my depth, my introductions were stilted and unnatural. Not surprisingly, the programmers at the BBC said, 'No. Dreadful. Couldn't possibly work.' The idea was axed.

Three months later, ITV launched a show called *Ready Steady Go* hosted by Cathy McGowan. It had almost exactly the same format and proved to be *the* hit show of the sixties.

I've often wanted to contact that BBC producer and apologize for my cack-handed handling of what was basically a great idea. He simply chose the wrong presenter.

Alwen was feeling rather tired and looking very pregnant. The baby had started pushing up on her lungs and sometimes she struggled to take even shallow breaths. This made her panicky all the time.

The idea of fatherhood excited me, although I hadn't really thought it through. I didn't imagine it was going to change things much at all. We'd do exactly the same things, I thought, with an extra little person tagging along.

This lack of foresight became clear when I agreed to a return season at the Blue Angel. The nightclub had reopened after its disastrous November and in the meantime 'Kangaroo' had reached No. 5 on the US charts.

As the day of my flight drew closer, the baby still hadn't arrived. We sat in Sydenham almost watching the days peel off the calendar.

Of course, I should have cancelled the Blue Angel gig. It wasn't important in the grand scheme of things. But in those days I looked at a contract as something engraved in stone. Nobody at my agency had advised me any differently, so I just assumed that I had to go.

I was due to fly to New York on 10 March. By the 8th Alwen was two weeks overdue and panic had started to creep in. We talked to our doctor and decided to induce the birth. We arrived at Lewisham Hospital in the early evening and were directed towards the maternity ward.

A matron who looked like Hattie Jacques took one look at me and said, 'Where do you think you're going?'

'My wife is having a—'

'Yes, a baby.'

'I want to be present at the birth.'

'I'm sorry but that's not possible.'

I tried to explain to her that our doctor had said it was OK. I really wanted to be there. She point-blank refused, filling the doorway like a nightclub bouncer. Apparently husbands were considered to be a total liability.

I barely had time to give Alwen a kiss before she was wheeled away. The matron pointed me to the waiting room downstairs. 'We'll let you know.'

It was already dark outside and the weather had been bitterly cold. For the first few hours I paced the floor. When I asked the receptionist if there was any news, he got really uptight. 'They get very annoyed if we ring them,' he said. 'They'll let us know the minute anything happens.'

Feeling chastised, I sat in the waiting room, slumping lower and lower in the chair as the hours ticked by. There was no fire in the grate and the radiator felt as if it should be making ice. I was so cold that I collected newspapers and magazines and put them down the front and back of my shirt. Then I wrapped my overcoat around me. I had visions of being found frozen to death in the morning.

By midnight I began thinking that if nothing was going to happen, maybe I should drive home and get a couple of hours' sleep before coming back. Otherwise I'd be in a terrible state for the flight to New York the next afternoon.

I was too worried about Alwen to leave. Why hadn't anybody told me anything? What was happening up there? Was she OK? What about the baby?

Finally I couldn't wait any longer. I went to the front desk.

'Look, I'm worried about my wife. Could you just check . . .'

'I told you – they don't like us ringing.'

'I don't care. Please. I'm flying to America in a few hours. I have to know . . .' I was so cold my teeth were chattering.

He took pity on me and picked up the phone. All apologetically he started, 'Er, Mr Harris is here. He wants to . . . a girl?'

My stomach flipped over.

'Born at twelve twenty-five . . . mother and daughter fine . . . OK, I'll let him know.'

It was nearly a quarter to two in the morning. Our daughter had been born over an hour earlier and they hadn't remembered to tell me! If I hadn't been so cold I would have been furious!

At least they let me go up and see Alwen. She was all doped up. Something moved in the crib next to her bed. I looked closer and saw a tiny face, eyes closed, with a nose and two little ears. Everything inside me seemed to give a lurch. This was our daughter. How could anything be so small and yet so perfect?

Alwen gave me an exhausted smile and fell asleep. I kissed her on the cheek and slipped away. I figured that I would go home, get a few hours' sleep and then come back to the hospital.

I woke when it was still early and did some last-minute packing. Just as I was about to go back to the hospital, an ambulance pulled up outside.

Alwen had phoned her mum, signed herself out, and the two of them had come home with the baby.

'I wasn't going to stay there any longer than I had to,' she said, 'I hate hospitals!'

She plonked the baby in my arms. 'Welcome home,' I said to the little bundle.

We had a name chosen. We wanted something unusual and uniquely Australian – something that would roll along nicely with the word Harris. We agreed on Bindi – which came from a lovely little town in Western Australia called Bindi Bindi where we'd once found some fascinating stone called Bindi stone, a kind of fossilized asbestos.

Just before I left for the airport, a lone photographer turned up to take some shots of our new arrival for the press.

'There would have been more of us,' he said, 'but they're all covering the birth of Prince Edward.'

A few hours later, I was on the plane. I don't think Alwen could believe that I would leave her. Right up until the last minute she expected me to cancel. She didn't say anything and I didn't say anything. That was the pattern of our lives – we never seemed to discuss anything important.

For a week I wandered around New York feeling totally misplaced and homesick. Then Alwen phoned and announced that they were coming over. 'We're in this together,' she said. 'If you can't be here with us, we'll come to you.'

The next day I went to pick them up from the airport. I walked right past Alwen without recognizing her.

'Rolf?' said a wistful voice. I turned and saw her. She had dyed her hair brown. Bindi was swaddled in blankets, with only her face visible. Already she was wide-eyed with wonder at the world.

I can remember waking the next morning and having them both in bed alongside me. I took a series of photos of Alwen stretched out asleep with Bindi suckling at her breast. I had to stand on the bed to get them in focus. It was a lovely scene.

Later we gave Bindi a bath in the sink. She screamed so loudly that she went purple with anger. I gazed at this little naked girl child, marvelling at the minute size of everything. My eyes travelled down from her neck, to her delicate shoulders and the incredibly smooth skin on her stomach. I reached her genitals and skipped that part. My brain was saying, 'Don't be ridiculous. Why are you so uptight about nudity?' I couldn't help it.

Woody Allen was on the same bill at the Blue Angel, but he didn't make a big impression on me. His humour was very Jewish and self-deprecating.

'He's got no future outside New York,' I told Alwen. Boy, was I wrong!

From New York we flew to Chicago. People were quite surprised to see Bindi, but it seemed perfectly natural to me. She and Alwen were my family and I wanted to be with them. Bindi weighed only six pounds at birth. Alwen had difficulty finding baby clothes small enough to fit her because everything in America seemed to come in large sizes.

We had a cot with carrying handles that could also be put on wheels, but Bindi learned to nap where she could – on planes, in the backs of taxis and the cloakrooms of nightclubs I worked in. The hatcheck girls were happy to look after her.

In Chicago I had been booked to appear at a club called Downstairs at the Happy Medium. On my first night somebody stole my didgeridoo. Although I couldn't play it properly, I still liked blowing a few notes for the audience before I sang 'Sun Arise'. I doubt if America had more than half a dozen people who knew what a didgeridoo was.

Next morning I hit all the radio stations and put out appeals. It was such a strange request all the DJs were happy to help. By that afternoon someone had anonymously left the didge at the stage door.

On my second night, I did thirteen encores and sang every song I knew. The crowd was amazing and left me on a real high. I arrived back in the dressing room soaked with perspiration. I was just about to take a shower when a waiter knocked on the door.

'There's a guy outside wants to see you.'

'OK, I won't be long.'

'He wants to buy you a drink.'

'Yeah, yeah, just give me a minute.'

'He's waiting.'

'OK, but let me have a shower first.'

A few minutes later, as I towelled off, the waiter knocked on the door again.

'Listen, this guy is getting really uptight.'

'Just let me put a shirt on,' I said, becoming a little annoyed.

My visitor was waiting at the bar. 'G'day I'm a master builder from Adelaide. I'm on a world tour.'

'Oh,' I said, shaking his hand.

His first words were, 'Look, I tell you where you're going wrong.'

I raised my eyebrows. I had just done thirteen encores to rapturous applause. At first I thought he was joking, or drunk, but he was neither.

He went on. 'Now let me give you some advice. When I'm travelling around the world I always take a slouch hat and a boomerang with me. And whenever anyone asks me where I'm from I put my slouch hat on, grab my boomerang and sing "Waltzing Matilda". It bloody kills 'em.'

I laughed and then stopped myself. He was being serious.

'Now the Yanks love a good joke against themselves,' he said. 'How about this one. Nore is in the Ark, see, with all the animals.'

'You mean Noah?'

'Yeah, that's what I said, Nore. The elephants've got the runs. They've been shitting everywhere and the other animals are complaining about the smell. So Nore hangs their arses over the side and for days and days they squat there doing their business. Hundreds o' years later Columbus discovered America.' He started cackling. 'Great, isn't it? You can use that one.'

He went on like this, criticizing my act and telling me how badly I had gone wrong. 'Why am I talking to this man?' I asked myself.

Twenty-five years later, after a show in Adelaide, a man came up to me and said, 'You won't remember me. I'm a master builder.'

'Of course I remember you. Bloody Chicago, you bastard.' I told him what he'd said to me.

'Did I really say all that?' he asked sheepishly.

'You really did.'

Another unexpected visitor in Chicago was Bob Hope. He turned up one night and had a meal at the restaurant while I performed the cabaret. I was all excited and kept sneaking glances at him, thinking how nice it would be if he said something or acknowledged the show with a thumbs up, or some applause. Instead, he sat with his back to the stage and totally ignored me.

I tucked this little lesson into the back of my mind. I decided that if ever I became famous, I'd make sure that I didn't act like that. I would always make time for people and if someone was entertaining me I'd listen and give them encouragement. It's not asking much – particularly if you like people.

From Chicago we flew to Vancouver. The local Lions Club had asked me to appear in a charity concert. The rest of the acts were party pieces put on by the members.

As I waited backstage, I heard someone getting enormous laughs out front. I couldn't hear his act, only the laughter. The audience was still chuckling even after I'd made my entrance and started my act.

Later I asked someone, 'Who was the guy on before me?'

'Oh, that mad Dutchman, Frank Roosen, with his three-legged act.'

'The audience seemed to like it.'

'Oh, yeah, it's bloody funny.'

I was intrigued. I called Frank Roosen, who came round to my hotel, carrying a false leg made from a broomstick with a shoe attached. He operated the leg with his hand through a hole in the pocket of his overcoat.

He performed the song in my hotel room and I was in tears of laughter. Frank said he first heard the song at a school concert in Holland when he was only about five years old.

'One of the teachers performed it, with the overcoat and false leg.'

'And you remembered it?'

'As much as I could.'

Frank had translated the song into English and added a few bits.

'Would it be OK if I used it?' I asked, not wanting him to feel obliged. He was thrilled.

I took the song back to England and began toying with the idea of recording it – giving the credit to Frank, of course. I showed it to Laurie Holloway and we both realized that it needed some work. In particular, it lacked a powerful ending.

I rang Frank and asked if he'd mind if I tried to come up with a new final verse.

Again he agreed.

Eventually, I came up with this:

Whatever I did they said was false,
They said 'quick march' I did a quick waltz,
Then they shouted at me 'put your best foot forward' –
  but which foot?
I said, 'It's very fine for you, you only got a choice of two,'
But me, I'm Jake the Peg, diddle-iddle-iddle-um,
With the extra leg . . . diddle-iddle-iddle-um.

George Martin felt we needed a live audience to record the song. That way we could get their reaction and laughter on the track. The 'live' recording session was at Abbey Road Studios and it was the first time I had ever performed 'Jake the Peg'.

All dressed up, I marched down the long flight of stairs from the control room. The audience spotted the third leg and started to giggle. By the time I reached the microphone they were openly laughing.

We should have thought it through a little better. The

microphone was on a stand which meant I couldn't move around. I was stuck in the same spot, unable to do any funny walks to show off the extra leg properly.

I also tried to imitate Frank's Dutch accent, which I thought was a big part of the song's charm. I didn't quite get it right, but the audience didn't seem to mind. They laughed in all the right places.

'Jake the Peg' grew into a classic opening for my act. It had all the elements of a perfect cabaret song and I spent hours practising clever leg moves in front of the mirror. Hermione Gingold would have been proud of me.

Chapter Eleven

THIRTY YOUNGSTERS AND ME

HAVING BINDI TRANSFORMED OUR LIVES, BUT IT AFFECTED Alwen more than it did me. I carried on as before, while Alwen made all the big sacrifices. Instead of continuing her art, she no longer had any spare time. The converted coach house proved to be too cold and isolated to be a studio.

Alwen loved looking after Bindi, but found herself slipping into an artistic vacuum that would last nearly twenty years. It is a big sadness to both of us.

In its place, she busied herself with all the mechanics of running a household and raising a child. I was the traditional breadwinner and she provided the base from which I could go out and forge a career.

Bindi was an absolute delight. Alwen had visions of having to put child-locks on cupboards and being surrounded by noise, but Bindi could happily sit and draw for hours, producing the most amazing pictures.

She began drawing from the moment she first picked up a pencil. We surrounded her with all the tools and would frame her pictures and hang them up the staircase so that she and her friends could look at them.

On a visit to our family doctor she drew an elephant upside down so that he could see it right way up from his side of the table. She was only three years old.

At other times she came out with the most wonderful observations on life. Riding in a taxi one day, she sat very quietly, sucking her thumb and holding her wet tea towel. (It *had* to be wet.)

'What are you thinking about?' Alwen asked.

After a long pause she said, 'I am remembering my past.'

Another time, on a plane trip out to Sydney, Alwen asked her if she knew what the Australian flag was. Again Bindi pondered for a while before saying, 'The Stars and flies.'

Perfect, I thought.

In 1965 I returned to Australia for the first time since the success of 'Tie Me Kangaroo Down, Sport'. Alwen and Bindi came with me, of course.

Roger Henning was back working as a journalist in Sydney. He contacted me before I left England and said, 'Make sure you wear the Jake the Peg gear and come off the plane last.'

I rather self-consciously changed in the toilet on the plane before we landed. What if nobody turned up? I needn't have worried. The pictures appeared on the front page of almost every newspaper.

Roger's next publicity stunt was to have me driving up and down the busiest streets of Sydney, waving to pedestrians from a great flashy car with placards advertising my new show.

In the back of my mind I worried about whether I'd be accepted by Australian audiences, or would they think I had sold out and become a Pom. A lot of Aussie artists and entertainers of my generation gained recognition overseas before being accepted at home. Some claimed that Australia didn't appreciate talent until someone else (i.e. Britain or America) had done so first.

I never believed this, but I knew people would question why I had gone overseas. On my first night at the Silver Spade Room in Sydney I waited for somebody to shout out from the audience, 'So why are you living in England?'

What would I say?

Given the chance, I would have told them this. If I'd stayed in Australia, I would have been a schoolteacher, or just another Aussie amongst many millions. In England I was that Australian bloke who wobbled that board and painted the big pictures. I was a novelty.

As it turned out, I had no reason to fear any negativity. The audiences were marvellous.

From Sydney we went to South Australia and then flew to the Northern Territory for a holiday – our first since Bindi was born. The region had always fascinated me, ever since listening to Harry Butler's stories and hearing his tapes of Aboriginal music. Now I wanted to meet and talk to the people themselves.

The Aboriginal Welfare Department organized a visit to Bagot, an Aboriginal settlement on the outskirts of Darwin. I had no idea these people were being forced to live in settlements on the fringes of communities. I assumed they were there by choice. As I watched barefoot ragged children playing in the dust and men slumped in the shade with nothing to do, I thought how paternalistic the whole arrangement seemed. We white folk were looking after these 'poor benighted people who really didn't know any better'. We were trying to educate them and teach them to live like us.

There was no sense of the noble savage. Circumstances had lessened these people. The authorities were patting them on the head and saying, 'Obey the law, keep your noses clean and you'll get your supplies every month.' We were making them dependent on welfare and a generation later people would call them 'bludgers' and complain that they were milking the system.

We visited another settlement across the harbour where the local tribe was living a more traditional life. They seemed much happier and more self-sufficient. I saw some dancing and heard some didge-playing.

Only days earlier, in Adelaide, I'd come across a didgeridoo in an Aboriginal welfare shop. I bought it for no other reason than that I liked the painting on the outside.

This didge had a much smaller mouthpiece than my original one. To my amazement I found that I could play it with hardly any effort. The cycle breathing worked perfectly and all the theory fell into place. I realized that Aboriginal players, by and large, have much bigger mouths than mine. I'd been trying to play a didgeridoo with a wider bore and it hadn't worked.

Surrounded by Aborigines, I pulled out my new didgeridoo and expected them to be stunned and amazed when they heard this white guy playing. They didn't bat an eyelid. That's when I began to understand that their attitude to life is one of acceptance. If something happens it happens. If it's there, it's there. A refrigerator could suddenly drop out of the sky and it wouldn't surprise an Aborigine one little bit. He'd shrug and think, 'Well, it's there, so it's obviously there.'

Fascinated by the people and the scenery, I promised myself that I'd get back to the Northern Territory. It was a vast, untouched wilderness where very few tourists ever ventured. I felt privileged to be one of them.

In the meantime, I had plans to make another tilt at America, which had become like Don Quixote's windmill for me. My American agent, Fred Harris, arranged to get me on the famed *Ed Sullivan Show*.

During rehearsals, I spied one of my heroes sitting at the front of the empty auditorium. It was Harry Belafonte. I went down and said, 'Excuse me, Mr Belafonte. I've always admired you. My name is Rolf Harris. I had a big hit in Australia with a song inspired by your calypso "Hold 'im Joe".'

He looked expressionlessly at me and then turned his back. It was like being hit with a bucket of ice-cold water. I didn't know what to do. Eventually, I slunk away, feeling totally humiliated. Years later I was told that Harry Belafonte was fiercely anti-white, which, if true, might have explained his rudeness.

To make matters worse, I was bumped off the *Ed Sullivan Show* at the last minute by the Dave Clarke Five. They'd performed the previous week to rapturous applause and the producers decided to put them on again.

I wasn't too surprised to be treated like this. I felt like a poor relation right from the very start. Whenever I brushed up against big-name stars, I would stand there with my eyes shining with awe and admiration. I didn't regard myself as being an equal. In a funny sort of way I had based almost everything I did on the premise that I was a lucky amateur. That's why I used lines like 'Here's a song a fella wrote . . .' or 'Hey, here's an idea, why don't we try to sing it like this?'

I made it look as if we were just trying something for the first time that night, instead of something that had been pre-rehearsed and done a thousand times.

I think Harry Secombe had the same approach of trying to make people believe he was a lucky amateur. It works in Britain because people like to feel as though anybody could come in off the street, get up on stage and, with a bit of luck, be successful. If Harry Secombe and Rolf Harris can do it, then why can't they?

This approach was never going to work in the States. Americans *want* their stars to be totally unattainable, to be up there on a pedestal, high above them, leading glamorous lives that they can only read about in the glossy magazines. They don't want their stars to look as though they're fallible, or the least bit uncertain about what they're doing.

This fact was reinforced for me on another trip to the States to appear on a television special, *Night of a Thousand Number Ones*. The show brought together people from all around the world who had enjoyed a No. 1 hit.

I arrived at the rehearsal and a doorman checked my name off a list. When my turn came to meet the orchestra and record my backing track, the same doorman introduced me as, 'The musical director for Mr Rolf Harris.'

'No, I *am* Rolf Harris,' I said.

Everybody stopped and stared. I shuffled uncomfortably.

'Where is your musical director?' asked the conductor.

'I don't have one. It's just me.'

Apparently no star ever came to rehearsals themselves. Immediately, I was downgraded in their estimation. I could see them thinking, 'He's come himself. He must be really crap. Can't he afford a musical director?'

On another trip to America, I was booked to appear on the *Andy Williams Show*. He and I were going to sing 'Kangaroo', each taking separate verses . . . at least that was the theory.

On the first day of rehearsals I asked, 'When is Andy coming?'

His musical director looked at me sternly. '*Mister* Williams doesn't rehearse.' He emphasized the 'Mister'.

'How are we going to work out what we're each going to do?'

'You tell me and I will relay that information to *Mister* Williams.'

'That's crazy,' I said, scratching my head. 'If he can just give me ten minutes then we can find out what he's comfortable with . . .'

'That's not the way Mister Williams does things. You tell me what you want Mister Williams to do and I will relay that information to him.'

'Well, I don't know *what* I want him to do until I talk to him, but OK, if that's the way it has to be.'

The producer of the show was an Australian, Chris Beard, who had made his name with the comedy show *Laugh-In*. He came to me after the rehearsal and said, 'Andy's not happy with your attitude.'

'What?'

'He doesn't know where you're coming from.'

'What d'you mean, where I'm coming from? I haven't even met him.'

'Well, he doesn't know what you want from him.'

'I don't want *anything* from him. We were just going to sing a *song* together.'

'He doesn't really feel comfortable working with you.'

'*What?* Why not? He's never tried it. We haven't met.'

'It's your attitude. He doesn't know where you're coming from.'

I couldn't believe this. In the space of an hour I had upset the star of the show without setting eyes on him or saying a word to him.

Chris explained that Jimmy 'Schnozzle' Durante was appearing as one of the other guests on the same show. 'Would you be happy if he sang "Kangaroo" with you?'

'Yeah, sure, whatever.'

Jimmy came out and rehearsed with me for as long as was needed, and he was lovely. He had to sing the line 'Keep me cockatoo cool, Curl', which he thought was hysterical because he couldn't pronounce it. He kept saying 'cack-o-too'.

'What the hell does that mean?' he said, trying again and again. He never did get it right, but it didn't matter. We had great fun and the audience loved the song.

I only met Andy Williams during the actual show. We had a chat and he did lots of eyebrow-raising to the audience, sending the message, 'Who is this weirdo?' I was disappointed, but philosophical. It just confirmed to me that I wasn't in the same league as these big stars. And maybe that wasn't such a bad thing.

Back in the UK my children's TV show *Hi There!* was making way for another. The BBC had come up with an idea for a showcase for new magicians. Called *Hey Presto, It's Rolf!*, it had basically the same format with big paintings, occasional songs and appearances by pop bands.

I wanted to come up with a new character for the show. I recalled a wonderful incident from a few years earlier, just before Alwen and I left Australia. I had been invited across to Sydney to appear on *Harry Secombe's Christmas Show* and we stayed with Harry at a house in Whale Beach that belonged to a friend of Bruce's.

At just about dusk, we heard a weird coughing sort of barking sound.

'What's that?'

'A koala,' said our host.

'You're kidding.'

'No. We get them round here all the time.'

'But they don't make a sound like that,' I said.

'Yes, they do.'

The house was set amongst lots of trees and we all headed for the back veranda. Sitting in the fork of a gum tree about six feet away was the first koala I'd ever seen in the wild. I can't tell you how excited I was. I climbed the tree with my camera slung round my neck. As soon as I managed to get close, the koala did a dump on my head. Harry thought it was hilarious. He was singing to me, 'I'm going to wash that koala poo outa my hair.' Amid all the laughter, I managed to get some great photographs.

I dragged them out of storage and chose a few of the best. I went to see the costume designer and said that I didn't want a corny cartoon-type character, but something that looked like a real koala, only bigger. And I imagined it as having the personality and actions of a baby because I wanted to base a lot of the stories on things that Bindi had done when she was only a year or so old. Like the way she would unwrap presents and then play with the wrapping paper for hours, forgetting all about the actual present. Or the way she would try to take a balloon off me as I blew it up and it would go squirting noisily round the room.

We held auditions for the role of the koala and chose a dwarf called George Claydon, who proved to be a brilliant actor.

On the first show, in front of a studio audience, the doorbell rang and I went to answer it. I came back dragging a big basket. Inside was a koala all curled up. The note attached said, 'I can't afford to keep my baby. Will you please look after him until I get back?'

The koala woke, looked round and started crying. The audience let out a collective sigh. From that moment I knew we had a winner.

The storyline developed each week and we ran a competition to find a name for the koala. From the hundreds and hundreds of cards the kids sent in, we settled on the name Coojeebear, or Coojee as he became known.

Tiny children at home, many who hadn't yet learned to speak, understood and identified with everything Coojee did. And parents wrote to us saying how marvellously Coojee mirrored their children's behaviour.

Peter Whitmore, the producer, suggested another segment about a leprechaun. Obviously, we needed an Irishman and I tracked down Paddy Joyce, whom I had met when I was at art school. He'd been one of a bunch of us who'd auditioned for the chorus of *Paint Your Wagon*.

The idea was for the leprechaun to be able to appear and disappear by clicking his fingers, as well as doing other tricks. To make things more difficult, he was going to appear to be only ten inches high.

Nowadays, with computer technology, that sort of thing would be easy, but in 1966 it was groundbreaking. The only way to pull off a special effect like this on 'live' TV was to do a straight superimposition.

The children in the audience would see me totally alone on stage, sitting in front of a table, apparently chatting to nobody. But when they looked up at the TV screens dotted around the theatre they could see me talking to Seamus O'Sean the leprechaun, who did a little jig and disappeared when he clicked his fingers.

Paddy was backstage out of sight of the audience, in a strongly lit area surrounded by black drapes. They had a camera a long way away from him, which gave the impression that he was small. Around him were props that had been built seven times larger than normal size and painted black. This meant that Paddy could appear to be jumping onto a real box of tissues, or walking behind a real teacup, which would be carefully positioned on my table.

The magic came when this whole miniaturized scene was superimposed on screen, to make it look as though the leprechaun was actually standing on the table chatting to me.

In the meantime, I still had occasional cabaret spots of an evening. It gave me a chance to do grown-up songs and comedy for an adult audience. I was appearing at Talk of the Town – a large theatre in London – when a senior BBC producer came to me with a proposition. It was one of those quirks of fate that can change your life.

The BBC had booked American singing star Vicki Carr to do a one-hour TV special with a big band and a live audience. With just over a week to go, doctors discovered that Vicki had nodules on her vocal cords and needed an operation. She couldn't perform.

Normally, the BBC might have cancelled the show, but the Musicians Union had strict rules about such things. If forty-one musicians had been booked to do a show, you couldn't simply 'unbook' them. They had to be paid, even if the show didn't go ahead.

The BBC, committed to this expenditure, began looking for another 'artist' who could front the show at short notice – someone who wouldn't need weeks to rehearse. With a cabaret act already running in the West End, I was the logical choice.

'You can do pretty much the same show,' said the producer. 'We'll just bump up the orchestra and bring in the cameras.'

I tried to be really cool about it, but couldn't believe my luck. My own TV special! It was a huge opportunity for me.

The producer, director and technicians came to see my cabaret for three nights in a row, planning the camera angles and shots. Meanwhile, Laurie Holloway, my musical director, worked on augmenting the arrangements for the bigger orchestra.

The show was filmed on a Sunday night at the BBC Television Theatre on Shepherd's Bush Green. It was the same theatre we used for *Hey Presto, It's Rolf!*.

Backstage in the dressing room, I went through everything in my mind – the introductions, running sheet, jokes, lyrics, etc. My worst nightmare was of me drying up on stage. The scale of the whole exercise terrified me. The last time I'd worked with an orchestra this size had been in this very theatre on *Benny Hill's Variety Showcase* – my first foray into television, which had been a minor disaster.

As I left the dressing room and walked along the corridor

towards the wings, I kept telling myself to forget the cameras and concentrate on the audience. I had to pretend it was no different from any other show.

The next hour passed in a blur. I worked the audience and had them singing along. The show went smoothly and the producer seemed happy. Afterwards I sat in my dressing room while cleaners swept the stage and the lights were dismantled. 'Is that it?' I wondered. I think I expected the excitement to last for longer, or maybe that I'd feel different.

The show had gone out in prime time but it didn't make a huge impact. However, Tom Sloane, the head of Variety at the BBC, liked what he saw. My name was jotted down as someone they might work with again – if they could find the right vehicle.

An idea had been floating around for a while for a musical variety show set in a coffee bar, featuring lots of good-looking teenagers who sang and danced. It had all the right ingredients – pop music, youngsters, hip new dances and all the latest fashions.

I was probably an odd choice to front the show, but the BBC showed a lot of faith in me by allocating one of their top producer/directors, Stewart Morris, to put the show together. They also brought in a crash-hot choreographer, Dougie Squires, and put Alyn Ainsworth in charge of the music. Thousands of young hopefuls were auditioned to find thirty teenagers who could sing and dance. Called the Young Generation, these fifteen girls and fifteen boys were to be my bridge from children's presenter to adult entertainer. They would sing and dance with me, as well as be my audience on stage.

We began work in a big barn of a rehearsal room in Hammersmith. I surprised a lot of people by turning up at all the dancing and singing rehearsals. I also made a point of learning all the dancers' names and getting to know them. I wanted to let them know that I wasn't an aloof absentee star who only appeared for the actual show.

As part of the show I wanted to do a big painting and a song.

Stewart put a stopwatch on me during rehearsals as I painted a nine foot by twelve foot picture.

'No, you'll have to be faster than that,' he said.

We pinned up more paper and I tried again. It was still too long.

Stewart wanted me to cut another four minutes from the segment. He also thought it was boring. 'Nothing else is happening while you're painting. Let's have some music.'

'No, it doesn't need anything else,' I said.

'What do you mean?'

'Well, if it's interesting enough to watch, I don't think it needs any background music. The magic is watching it start from nothing and develop into a finished picture right before your eyes.'

Stewart got more uptight. 'It's not going to work.'

'Well, either we do it this way or we don't do it at all.'

I was adamant. I had never stood on my dignity like that before. Normally, I just went with the flow.

The Rolf Harris Show premiered on a Saturday night in January 1967. The Young Generation, under Dougie's choreography, were an overnight sensation. For the first time dancers were choreographed and cameras positioned specifically for TV rather than for theatre. It meant that kids could slide in on their knees and disappear under cameras, or spin round high-kicking for particular shots.

All the girls were dressed in micro-miniskirts or hot pants – fashions that were coming straight off the King's Road and Carnaby Street. Whenever the girls danced you saw a flash of panties, which is why it quickly became known as the Twinkling Crotch Show.

After the first show of the series we held a post-mortem with Huw Weldon, the head of Light Entertainment at the BBC. Huw was Welsh, with a big booming voice.

'Now, let's get to the painting,' he said. 'I found that a bit boring.'

Stewart chimed in, 'Well, that's exactly what I said. I wanted to have some background music.'

Huw shook his head. 'Background music wouldn't work – it needs something else. You're standing there, with your back to the camera, sloshing paint on. We need to fill the silence. How about doing some sound effects and funny voices. You know the sort of thing. Then stop every now and again, turn back to the cameras and do a one-liner.'

I liked the idea but worried about whether I could pull it off. It meant concentrating on two things at once – painting and talking. The weird sound effects were easy – I'd been making them all my life – but telling jokes was a lot harder.

The comedy writers began sitting in during rehearsals, coming up with jokes and one-liners specifically geared to what was happening with the painting. One of the best ones I remember came while I was painting a huge Aborigine in a white loincloth. He had one leg off the ground as he prepared to throw his spear. As I finished, I turned to the audience and said, 'This particular tribe never used to wear loincloths . . . until the first rehearsal of the painting this afternoon.' It got a great laugh.

From then on the big paintings became a feature of the show. Unwittingly, they also led to a catchphrase that was destined to stick: 'Can you tell what it is yet?'

Each show featured a big production number with elaborate sets and costumes. For one show we recreated Sherwood Forest and I dressed as Robin Hood. Barbara Windsor was Maid Marian. Another had a backdrop of Paris and I sang a song about Toulouse-Lautrec.

Each week we had a special guest performer. Ironically, Vicki Carr was among them, her vocals cords once again in perfect order. Others included Dudley Moore, Dusty Springfield, Buddy Greco, Jose Feliciano and the comedian Jerry Lewis. The show went out live and I had to keep everything in my head – songs, dance routines, harmonies, one-liners and the running order of the show. Surprisingly, I only suffered a complete blank once.

The film musical of *Oliver!* had just been made and Shani Wallis had the role of Nancy. She came on the show to sing a song

Buttons as Jake the Peg:
standing on my own three
feet in panto.

TOURING AUSTRALIA
1960s AND 1970s

(Left) Trying to be a kangaroo.

(Centre left and right) Entertaining kids in Darwin after Cyclone Tracy, 1974.

(Below left) Filming *Rolf's Walkabout* in the Northern Territory, 1963.

(Below right) A customized wobble board.

(Right) King of Moomba in Melbourne, 1975.

(Below) Contemplating upsetting the unions with my royal proclamation.

(Right) Teaching Bindi to swim in the river with Dad.

(Below right) Saluting the half-built Opera House.

THE ROLF HARRIS SHOW

(Top row, left to right) Performing with The Young Generation.

With Sandie Shaw, our 'Song for Europe'. BBC

(Bottom row) 'Can you tell what it is yet?'

ENGLAND
1960s TO 1980s

(Top left) Royal Command Performance, 1967. *(Top right)* Bindi, a budding artist, and her proud dad. *(Bottom left) Quick on the Draw.* © Pearson Television *(Bottom right)* The Stylophone – it was likened to a demented bee trapped in a bottle.

OPPOSITE (Top left and centre left) Rolf on *Saturday OK*, 1977. BBC *(Top right)* Coojeebear, a huge favourite. *(Centre right)* Doing panto. *(Bottom) Rolf's Cartoon Time.*

Honours, ten years apart: an MBE in 1968 and an OBE in 1978.

from the musical and I gave her a big build-up. Then I realized that I had completely forgotten her name.

'Ladies and gentlemen, will you please welcome . . .' My mouth opened, but no sound came out. I started to applaud and Stewart, seeing my blank face, cued the orchestra. Fortunately, Shani entered from the other side of the stage and didn't realize what had happened.

From then on, I made sure that everyone's name was written on cards along the front of the stage, out of camera view. If ever I was lost, I could look down for a prompt.

The series ran for thirteen weeks and climaxed on 11 March with 6.4 million viewers. One of the acts featured that night was David Blanasi, a full-blood Aborigine we'd flown across from Arnhem Land in the Northern Territory.

It was Stewart's idea, and I contacted the Department of Aboriginal Affairs to see if something could be arranged. I was put in touch with district officer Ted Evans and I explained that we wanted to introduce Aboriginal music, and in particular the didgeridoo, to audiences in the UK.

'I don't know if David Blanasi is the best didge player,' said Ted, 'but he's the best guy temperamentally. He'll be least uptight about being on his own and flying to another country.'

Until then it hadn't dawned on me how dramatic a change it would be to take an Aborigine from a settlement in Australia and fly him halfway round the globe, on his own, to one of the biggest cities in the world. The culture shock would be enormous.

I picked David up from the airport and he walked out of a bustling Heathrow Airport like a seasoned flyer. Nothing seemed to faze him. When I first arrived in England I had hung out of a cab window gawping at the sights, but David sat back and half closed his eyes, unflappable and unsurprised.

We'd let Ted know in advance that we wanted David to throw some spears on the show, as well as play the didgeridoo. The props department organized a piece of wood, shaped like a door, to be the target. It was three-quarter-inch vertical pine strips stuck together, with an inset window of toughened glass for the camera to shoot through. David stood thirty feet away and was to aim at the target, just below the lens.

On the night of the show he looked absolutely marvellous, fully painted up in his tribal gear, holding his spear and 'woomera' (spear thrower). He took aim and launched the spear with enormous power. *Whack!* It hit the wood and then fell to the ground. Everybody watching thought, 'How could that happen?'

The next spear stuck in and reverberated. David threw three more, each of them hitting the target and sticking. Seen from the camera behind the target, it looked truly frightening.

After the segment, the Young Generation did a dance routine, while the floor staff retrieved the spears. The first one had lost its nine-inch flat metal blade. Looking closer, they discovered it had gone straight through the plank and finished up six feet behind the camera. It must have missed the cameraman by a fraction of an inch. He was *so* lucky.

The last nine shows of the series featured a young Sandie Shaw, barefoot on stage, singing each of the shortlisted entries for *A Song for Europe*.

I caused a major blue at the end of series party when I was called on to say a few words. I stood up in a bit of a panic, completely unprepared, and made a speech off the top of my head. I mentally ticked off everyone I could remember as I thanked them all for their efforts. When I sat down again, there was a bit of an awkward silence which I couldn't fathom, until Stewart came over to me and whispered, 'You forgot to thank Sandie and wish her good luck for Vienna!'

I felt awful. In two weeks she was going to sing 'Puppet on a String' on the biggest night of her life and I hadn't even mentioned it! Sandie took it as a personal slight and was sure I'd left her name out on purpose. All my apologies fell on deaf ears.

To make matters worse, I was going to Vienna too. The BBC had asked me to host its coverage of the event. The tension was appalling. At the airport before we left, photographers were waiting to get some farewell shots. It was all smiles for the cameras but once the snappers had left Sandie stalked off with her manager, the legendary Evie Taylor.

It proved to be an eventful trip.

Sandie had three backing singers with her, the Ladybirds, who had been on my show from the beginning. They were stunning girls and the most beautiful was a tall, leggy brunette called Glo, short for Gloria.

Hamming it up and flirting with pretty girls came naturally to me. Whenever I saw Glo I made a point of telling her that she was stunning. As usual, I was right over the top, clutching my heart and panting furiously. 'Aaaaah, God you're beautiful. What a vision!' After thirteen weeks of this routine, it was probably starting to wear thin on everybody except me.

In Vienna a big group of us was sitting in the hotel lounge, chatting and drinking. Tom Sloane was next to me, along with Stewart Morris, Dougie Squires, Phyl Rounce and Sandie. Glo walked in and sat down opposite me.

'Oh, here she is. The glorious Glo. What a beauty!' My hand was hammering on my heart as usual.

Without a word, she reached across the open space between our lounge chairs, unzipped my fly, put her hand into my underpants, took a firm grip of my old fella and flipped it out for all to see. Then she looked me straight in the eyes and said, 'Are you gonna do something about this, or are you just gonna keep talking about it?'

You have never heard a room go so silent so quickly. I turned seven consecutive shades of red.

For years afterwards, I thought up good comeback lines, but at that moment, when it counted the most, I couldn't think of a single thing to say. Instead, I wanted to dissolve into a grease spot and soak into the carpet.

Stewart Morris said to me afterwards, 'You should have just grabbed her by the arm and dragged her upstairs.'

'I couldn't do that.'

'Well, you should have done *something*.'

He was probably right. Not surprisingly, I stopped flirting with pretty young women and embarrassing them in public. Glo had given me a taste of my own medicine.

Tom Sloane was coming to the end of his career at BBC television and had his heart set on winning *A Song for Europe*. He was absolutely thrilled when Sandie stormed home and won it for Britain for the first time.

We couldn't find a restaurant where we could celebrate, so Tom paid the staff at our hotel double time to re-open the kitchen, the bar and the dining room for us. After a lovely meal, he made a wonderful speech thanking everyone involved, particularly Sandie, for having 'brought home the bacon'.

When he sat down, everybody called on Sandie to respond to Tom's gracious toast.

'Speech! Speech! Speech!' we cried.

Sandie had had a few drinks. She swayed to her feet. 'I don't know what to say,' she giggled. 'What should I say, Evie?'

Next to her, Evie Taylor growled, 'Tell 'em all to piss off home to bed.'

Sandie did just that. 'Why don't you all piss off home to bed.' She giggled again and sat down.

Absolute silence greeted the speech. Nobody could believe it. Sandie wasn't the arrogant type, but she was young, nervous and drunk. Evie Taylor should have known better, but she was that sort of domineering, high-handed manager who gives managers a bad name.

At the airport the next day, a long line of people waited to get through customs and passport control. Evie arrived with Sandie and took her straight to the front of the queue.

The Austrian official laughingly said, 'She's not ze Queen of England, you know.'

To which Evie snapped a reply, 'Actually, you're wrong. Today she *is* the Queen of fucking England.'

*

That summer I did a family show at Great Yarmouth with Coojeebear and we broke all sorts of box-office records at the theatre. It proved to be a huge season for everybody. Val Doonican wowed them on the pier, as did Morecambe and Wise at the ABC Theatre.

I still felt very unsure as to whether I fitted in with this sort of company. I was in awe of these people.

On a Saturday night towards the end of the season, we put on a midnight matinee for charity. Traditionally, all the shows in Great Yarmouth came together with each of the stars doing a spot.

I went along to the 'talk through' to decide what we were all going to do. That's when I first met Eric Morecambe and Ernie Wise. Ernie was very much the straight man – a lovely gentle chap who was liked by everyone. Eric was the true comic genius of the pair, with a blistering wit that was so sharp it often took lesser mortals minutes to realize that he was making fun of them.

It didn't take me that long. The moment Eric saw me he said, 'Hello, sunshine.' Then he launched into a series of clever jokes about Australians that had everyone laughing. I couldn't think of a thing to say. I can't remember a single one of the jokes now, but they were all very clever put-downs.

I think Eric was expecting me to come back with as good as he gave, but I couldn't compete. I was swamped and went under, looking red-faced and miserable. I don't think he was being malicious. He simply knew what buttons to press to make people laugh.

Occasionally over the years I bumped into Eric at charity photo calls and awards nights. Although always very polite I never went out of my way to strike up a conversation with him. I guess I was too frightened he might do it all again.

I've often wondered if Eric really liked people. I know that probably sounds strange, but quite a lot of showbiz people are painfully shy, or reclusive. Lonnie Donegan is a stunning enter-tainer, but I know he'd run a mile rather than sign an autograph.

I worked with him one summer season and can remember leaving the theatre with him after the shows and walking along the pier towards the turnstiles. Fans would always wait there in the hope of getting autographs. When I stopped to sign, Lonnie would take off, almost knocking people aside to get to his car.

I can't remember ever refusing someone who stopped me in the street or interrupted a meal at a restaurant. This used to drive Alwen crazy. She hated the way complete strangers would suddenly barge into a private conversation, turning their back on her as though she didn't exist, and then monopolizing my time.

Of course I loved the attention and Alwen said I was addicted to praise. She's probably right.

Before a Sunday concert in Blackpool, I was having lunch with the theatre press agent and a couple of comedy writers. A waitress came over and begged me for an autograph for a lady at the next table, who was too shy to ask. I happily signed the bit of paper and did a quick drawing for the lady.

Just as we started our desserts, I suddenly became aware of a dark shape standing slightly behind me. He was a big man with hands the size of dinner plates. I flinched instinctively as his booming Lancashire voice delivered one of the best opening lines I've ever heard. 'I'm not a rich man, lad, but you've made my wife very happy today, son.'

Without even thinking, I replied, 'I never touched her, Your Honour.'

He took me seriously and grabbed my shoulder. 'I know that, lad. Here, I want you to accept this.'

The fingers of his other hand were closed into a fist. For a split second I thought he was going to hit me, but then realized that he was holding something.

'No, honestly, you don't have to . . . er . . .' (I was wondering what on earth he could be giving me . . . a ten-shilling note wrapped round a two-bob bit, perhaps?)

'Take it, lad, take it.'

He uncurled his fingers and an old Boy Scout's lapel badge

covered in verdigris dropped into my outstretched palm. I just had time to read 'Be Prepared' before it rolled off my hand and disappeared with a plop into the custard.

He had my shoulder in a vice-like grip. I didn't know what to say, or do, so I dived into the soggy mess with my fingers and fished for the badge. I found it and used half a bread roll to wipe off the custard.

In the meantime, I was vainly trying to think of something to say. This was obviously one of his most prized possessions. He had taken it off his lapel at that moment to give it to me. His grip on my shoulder was sending my arm numb.

'Say nowt, lad, say nowt,' he said, with his voice shaking.

Then he delivered a final bone-crushing squeeze to my shoulder and departed moist-eyed to where his wife sat smiling at me from the next table.

I looked around at my lunch partners. Their noses were almost touching their desserts and their shoulders shook as they tried to stop themselves laughing. I didn't know what to do. The whole scene was hysterically funny and very touching at the same time. I looked across at the man and his wife and nodded. Then I tucked his badge, still moist, into my breast pocket.

The Rolf Harris Show proved to be so popular that I was voted BBC TV Personality of the Year. It was a huge thrill.

The award ceremony was a gala black tie affair, full of celebrities and TV stars. In my acceptance speech, I described how I'd come over from Australia in 1952. 'That was fifteen years ago and never in a million years did I imagine . . . it would take this long,' I said, getting a great laugh.

Having fallen into the trap of forgetting to thank Sandie Shaw, I went overboard the other way. I thanked everybody, stopping just short of mentioning my dry cleaner and the cab driver who'd brought me. Even so, I still found myself in hot water. When work started on the second series of *The Rolf Harris Show*, I could sense a real chill in the air. Stewart Morris took me to one side.

'What normally happens when someone gets nominated for an award is that they pay for a whole table at the luncheon. Then they invite their producer and the musical director and the choreographer – all the people who helped put the show together – to come and join them as their guests. It shows how much they appreciate the part those people have played in their success.'

I had no idea. It was like a slap in the face. All of the people I owed so much to thought I had snubbed them. Yet nobody had told me the protocol. I just went along, thinking they'd all be happy for me. One of these days, I was going to get things right.

While still trying to atone for this, I had a telephone call at home. Alwen answered and looked at me strangely.

'It's from the palace,' she whispered, holding one hand over the phone.

I thought she meant a local restaurant. I took the phone.

'This is the Honours Secretary at Buckingham Palace,' said a male voice with a very proper English accent. 'I've been instructed to inform you that the Queen has awarded you an MBE in her Birthday Honours List.'

'What for?' I asked.

'Well, ah . . . for services to show business . . . that sort of thing, old chap.'

'Oh.'

'Before we can award the honour we have to make sure that you are willing to accept it.'

'Oh, I see.' There was a pause. 'Yes. Of course I am.'

'Oh, good. Her Majesty *will* be pleased. Would you mind not telling anyone? This is very important. We like to announce all the honours at the same time.'

Alwen was hovering behind me. As I hung up the phone she said, 'You've been given an honour.'

'Shhhhhh. You can't tell anyone.'

'But you have, haven't you?'

'Yes.'

She threw her arms round me. 'I won't tell anyone. I promise.'

*

The Rolf Harris Show was in recess until the next series in the New Year. In the meantime, I went touring Australia and Canada.

In Sydney I did cabaret at Chequers Nightclub. The Australian Broadcasting Commission (ABC) had bought *Hey Presto, It's Rolf!* from the Beeb and were showing the episodes every week-day, Monday to Friday. With this sort of saturation coverage, I was suddenly the best-known children's presenter in Australia.

This meant that a lot of parents brought their children to the early show, which was a bit of a shock for the club. I was in the middle of one performance when I looked down to see a little girl standing on tiptoes with her hands and her chin resting on the stage. She obviously wanted to ask me something.

I stopped the band and thought, whatever she wants, I'll do it. It'll bring the house down. Crouching down with the microphone I said, 'What is it, love?'

She took a deep breath. 'We were hoping to hear . . .' (gulp). She had to swallow because she was so nervous. The audience thought she was wonderfully brave. I kept thinking, 'Whatever she says, I'll play it. Even if the band doesn't know it, I've got my squeezebox. I'll do it just for her.'

The little girl took a big breath and started again. 'We were hop-ing to hear . . . M-M-M-Max Bygraves.'

The audience exploded into laughter. I looked across just in time to see the girl's mother lift the tablecloth and try to crawl underneath it, she was so embarrassed.

Apparently, the little girl wanted me to sing a song that Max Bygraves had recorded which spelt out the letters of 'Australia'. She hadn't managed to get the whole story out.

The Queen's Birthday Honours List was made public on the morning I flew from Sydney to Vancouver. It was all over the Australian newspapers. Standing in the check-in queue, I had a bloke slap me on the back.

'Good on yer, son!' he said loudly. 'Ya know the difference between the MBE and the OBE, do ya?'

I shook my head.

'OBE stands for some "Other Bastard's Effort", but MBE stands for "My Bloody Effort".' He thumped me on the back again and disappeared into the crowd.

I could just imagine Mum picking up her copy of the *West Australian* that morning. Although absolutely thrilled, she would have said, 'Why didn't you tell me? I could have kept a secret.'

Thank goodness I didn't! Mum would have been stopping complete strangers to tell them, or screaming it from the rooftops of Bassendean.

Sadly, the other story dominating the front page that morning was about Tony Hancock. The legendary comic was found dead in his Sydney flat by the director of the TV series he was filming. The verdict was suicide: barbiturates washed down with vodka. There were two suicide notes. In one of them he wrote, 'Things seemed to go wrong too many times.'

It was a desperately sad end for a man with such amazing talent.

Chapter Twelve

'TWO LITTLE BOYS'

D AVID BLANASI HAD BEEN SUCH A HIT ON THE SHOW THAT I suggested another Australian for the new series of *The Rolf Harris Show*. Frank Donellan was a champion boomerang thrower who had performed with me at the very first Expo in Montreal in 1967.

Stewart Morris came up with a great idea for an introduction. He wanted to film Frank 'arriving' at Heathrow Airport, stepping off a jet and then throwing a boomerang that would circle the huge tail of the plane and come back into his hands.

The problem was that nobody had told Frank. 'I didn't bring any heavy boomerangs with me,' he explained. 'I only have light-weight ones. You said I'd be throwing them indoors in a theatre.'

'So what are you saying?' said Stewart.

'Well, I don't know whether a lightweight one'll carry that far,' said Frank.

'I'm sure it will,' said Stewart dismissively.

'But any breath of wind could deflect it.'

'I don't think we need worry.'

Stewart had managed to get permission from Qantas to use a jet parked beside a gate. We did a mock arrival filming the Young Generation waiting on the mobile stairs. As the stairs were driven towards the jet, the back wheels slowly started lifting off the ground. The dancers had made the stairs top heavy and they were about to topple.

The driver began yelling, 'Get off the top! Get off the top!'

People scrambled back down the steps. For a brief moment the stairs seemed to teeter on the brink of uncertainty and then the back wheels landed with a thump on the tarmac again. It was so nearly a disaster.

The jet door opened and Frank stepped out to a great cheer. He moved down the stairs between the dancers and stood on the tarmac. Raising his lightweight boomerang, he gave it a decent old throw. It spun away and began turning in a wide arc that would take it round the tail of the jet. Then, bang! It crashed into the fuselage and bounced off onto the ground.

Collectively we said, 'Oh shit!'

The jumbo jet had to be taken out of service for twenty-four hours to check for any damage. It cost the airline £10,000 in delays and didn't make us very popular. Worse still, the film footage couldn't be used because the boomerang hadn't done what boomerangs are supposed to do . . . come back.

The postscript to the story is even quirkier. During rehearsals at the Television Theatre, Frank was throwing indoor boomerangs one after another. They spun out over the audience area to within inches of the balcony seats and then curved back again where he caught them every time with a clap of his hands.

Stewart had set up a camera on stage that followed the boomerang perfectly, so the viewers at home would see it spinning and flashing in the lights for the entire flight.

Despite this, Stewart announced, 'It doesn't work.'

'What do you mean?' asked Frank, looking mortified.

'Well, they make absolutely no sound that our microphones can pick up. We need a sound so the viewer gets a feeling for the danger of it all.'

He turned to me. 'What do you reckon, Rolf, can you create a sound effect and match it to the action?'

So that's what we did. On the night of the show, I stood in the wings just out of sight and did a very dramatic *whee whee whee* sound into the microphone. I started loud and went softer as the boomerang arced away from the stage and then got louder again as it returned to Frank. It sounded quite scary and worked like a charm.

On Monday morning the head of programming was on the warpath.

'The sound of those boomerangs was absolutely terrifying,' he ranted. 'I can't believe you could have done something so dangerous. It was the most irresponsible thing I've ever seen on television. It must never happen again . . .'

Nobody had the courage to tell him that the sound effect was totally fake and done by yours truly. The whole affair ended with an edict being drafted into the BBC's rules and regulations, which is still there today. It states that boomerangs must never be thrown in a television theatre or studio where there is a live audience, for fear of causing serious injury to members of the public or staff.

In that same series I introduced a new musical instrument to an unsuspecting world. It was called a Stylophone and was the precursor to the synthesizers that would later revolutionize popular music.

The Stylophone was fashioned from an old transistor radio case and had a flat nickel-coated keyboard. It was played one note at a time with a pen-shaped rod or 'stylus'. Nowadays even the simplest of kid's toy has more sophisticated circuitry, but in 1968 it was groundbreaking. (Unfortunately, the sound was pretty awful. Someone once likened it to a demented bee trapped in a bottle.)

The inventor Brian Jarvis and Burt Coleman, one of the manufacturers, had been everywhere trying to market the device. People thought it was amazing, but the musical instrument makers said it was a toy, and the toy makers said it was a musical instrument.

They needed to get a big name involved. I was an obvious choice because I had a reputation for using unusual instruments like a bit of bouncing hardboard, the didgeridoo and the aptly named 'lagerphone' (an Australian bush instrument made from dozens of lager bottle tops loosely nailed to a broomstick).

Burt tried to contact me through the BBC but nobody would put his calls through. Eventually, he turned up at rehearsals, walked past the doorman and interrupted me having a cup of coffee with my guest star Georgia Brown.

'Look, I know I shouldn't be here,' he apologized, 'but I just want you to hear this.'

He shoved a Stylophone into my hands and then showed me how to play it.

I told him he was a cheeky bugger, but admitted the Stylophone was pretty amazing.

I chatted to Stewart Morris and then gave Burt a call. He was just about to appear with it on the *David Frost Show*, but Stewart convinced him to give it to us instead.

On the next week's show I introduced the Stylophone as a new British invention and began playing 'Moon River'. A gentle orchestral accompaniment crept in halfway through and made it sound wonderful. The following week we had six members of the Young Generation playing with me, doing harmonies on 'Yesterday', the classic Paul McCartney song.

The feedback was amazing and the phones didn't stop ringing. The Stylophone went into mass production and four million were sold worldwide in the next few years. As it became more and more popular, bass and treble versions were introduced. For a while it became the 'in' instrument, with David Bowie using one when he recorded 'Space Oddity'.

Yet the phenomenon ended as quickly as it began. Four years later Casio came up with an electronic organ that had actual keys that went up and down like a piano. Overnight the Stylophone became obsolete.

*

One of the biggest names to appear on *The Rolf Harris Show* was Mickey Rooney, a real hero of mine. I'd grown up watching his 'Andy Hardy' movies at the pictures in Bassendean.

Judy Garland had died only a few weeks earlier and Mickey wanted to include a special tribute to her. The two of them had been the golden kids of Hollywood, appearing in dozens of films together, as well as being great friends.

The idea of Mickey talking about Judy and telling the audience what was in his heart could have been marvellous. But he came up with a tribute that involved his playing schmaltzy music on the piano to accompany his recollections. He was obviously very sincere, but the overall effect was quite the opposite. It seemed phoney and trite rather than genuine.

During rehearsals I realized that it wasn't going to work, but I didn't have the courage to tell him how sickly it sounded. Who was I? Maybe it would have worked on American TV, but I knew that British audiences would think it was being manufactured purely to milk their sympathy.

Just as I feared, the spot died on the night. I still didn't say anything to Mickey. It was sad seeing a hero brought down to earth.

The American stars were always quite surprised at how their British counterparts were treated. They were used to having every whim catered for, whereas at the BBC you were lucky to get a plate of sandwiches and a cup of tea.

This perception that the 'star' had unlimited powers created occasional problems. When a bigwig from Epic Records came across on holiday from New York, he looked me up and I arranged for him to see the show. He took a liking to Wei Wei Wong, the beautiful young Chinese member of the Young Generation. Afterwards, backstage, he said to me, 'You were really great, man. Great show. I want you to fix me up with the Chinese chick.'

'What?'

'The dancer. The Chinese girl. I want you to fix me up with her.'

'I can't do that.'

'Listen, man, you're the star of the show. Just use your influence.'

'No, I can't do that.'

He became really annoyed as I tried to explain that I was just another performer on this show. I had no jurisdiction over other people. The concept was totally foreign to him. Apparently in America the star of the show could pretty much hire, fire, bed or boot out anybody he pleased.

When the flamenco guitarist Manitas de Plata appeared on the show he caused a sensation. Flamboyant, charismatic and brilliant by turns, he had the audience in raptures. Even before he came off stage we knew that we had to get him back again. Without anybody's checking first, I was told to announce over the closing applause that Manitas would be on next week's show.

His manager, however, didn't seem so confident. The following day a list of conditions arrived. Manitas would appear again provided that a car and driver were despatched to the West End to pick up eight prostitutes and deliver them to his hotel room.

'Eight?' queried Stewart Morris.

'Yes, it has to be eight.'

Having already announced that Manitas would be appearing, we had painted ourselves into a corner. Hiring prostitutes wasn't the sort of expense that you could claim on petty cash at the BBC, so perhaps they were called 'exotic dancers'. Whatever happened, Manitas appeared on the show the following week as announced.

Having my own show was like a fairy tale, but at any moment I expected somebody to tap me on the shoulder and say, 'You're not supposed to be here.'

The big name stars who appeared each week seemed so much grander and worthier than I was. When it came to music, there were better songwriters. When it came to singing, there were far more magnificent voices.

Even as a painter, I knew that what I did on television each week was unique, but was that enough? One critic wrote, 'Who does he think he is throwing up this crummy attempt at painting each week and trying to convince us he's some sort of modern-day Rembrandt? He isn't.'

I took criticism like this very personally. It added to my sense of being an impostor or gatecrasher. One of the worst moments was when I appeared with the Young Generation at a Royal Command Performance.

The invitation arrived while I was on holiday. Stewart replied on my behalf and also chose the song that we'd perform. It was something I'd written in Spain and we'd done it on the show quite recently. 'Pukka Chicken' was basically a piece of nonsense with lyrics that sounded like a chicken ('Ta pukka pukka, ta pukka pukka') clucking and scratching for food. It was ideal for entertaining kids on a beach in Spain but I doubted if it was appropriate for the Royal Variety Show.

By the time I returned from my holiday the decision had been made and it was too late to change it. A bright yellow chicken suit had been fashioned by the wardrobe department. It made me look like a huge ball of feathers, with just my face visible.

On the night of the performance I shared a dressing room with Dickie Henderson, Val Doonican and Tommy Cooper. I looked around the room and felt totally out of my depth. The others were getting dressed in dinner suits, while I looked like a ridiculous 'chook'!

Tommy had the strangest figure I'd ever seen. His body was totally out of proportion, as though he'd been put together from leftover spare parts. He was incredibly tall, with huge feet, a long, long body and very short legs. This meant his underpants hung below his knees like Bombay bloomers. As he paced around trying to find his bow tie it was like watching one of his comedy routines. I sat quietly in the corner, trying to put the finishing touches to a papier mâché egg that I was supposed to 'lay' towards the end of the song.

'Hey, Tommy, tell Rolf the stripper gag,' said Val and Dickie, sounding like a couple of naughty schoolboys.

'No, no.' Tommy shook his shaggy head.

'Oh, come on.'

After a little more persuading he launched into the joke, with all his trademark asides and wonderful timing.

Val and Dickie urged him on to tell another gag and then another. Our laughter drew half the cast to the dressing room and soon we had people queuing at the door trying to see Tommy's impromptu performance. It was a magical moment.

I'm sure there were great moments in the Royal Variety Show, but my chicken song wasn't among them. I literally laid an egg in front of the Queen. Afterwards, I promised myself that next time – if there was one – I'd choose what song I performed and it wouldn't involve wearing a chicken suit.

Thankfully, Her Majesty was too polite to mention it afterwards in the line-up backstage. Nor did she bring it up at Buckingham Palace when she presented me with my MBE.

Alwen and Bindi were there in the audience. Bindi was only four years old and wore her favourite party dress, with her hair tied up in ribbons. When she saw the Queen chatting to each person she announced to Alwen in a big loud voice, 'I suppose she's thanking them all for coming.'

Until she started school Bindi spent almost four months of every year touring in Australia or Canada. She remembers a great deal although she wishes she could remember more.

It didn't occur to me at the time, but it was a pretty unusual childhood. Alwen says that Bindi was quite a lonely child. Whenever she met other children, it was only for a day or two before we moved on. At the same time she became very self-assured around grown-ups. She could eat out at restaurants and strike up conversations on long flights.

Holidays were her favourite time. I taught Bindi to swim in Darwin in 1969. We were back in Australia as a family to film *Rolf's Walkabout* – the first documentary series to be shot in colour by the ABC. Part travelogue and part natural history, it gave me the chance to show Australians the magnificence of their own Northern Territory.

Before meeting up with the film crew in Darwin, we flew to Gove on the eastern edge of Arnhem Land to get a glimpse of that part of Australia. Arriving by light plane at the dusty airfield, I carried Bindi down the steps. Suddenly a battle cry sounded and spears came flashing over our heads. A rampaging mob of Aboriginals charged at the plane and swarmed around us. I held Bindi tightly. It scared the hell out of Alwen and me. Bindi didn't seem worried at all.

The 'welcome' was arranged by Ted Egan, an Aboriginal Welfare Officer in charge of smoothing relations between the Aboriginals of Gove and the aluminium mining operation.

Ted was a real man's man, who had grown up in the Territory and loved every spike of spinifex and every tree. He also spoke several of the native languages fluently, which meant he could talk to the Aboriginals as equals rather than treating them like exhibits in a natural history display. I envied him. I would have loved to communicate with them more directly.

Gove was a ramshackle, sprawling frontier settlement, fashioned from fibro and corrugated iron. All the vehicles were four-wheel drive and most of them lasted only a couple of years in the rough terrain.

We stayed with Ted, and over breakfast the next morning he mentioned that he had a song which would be perfect for my TV show back in England.

'My mum used to sing it to me when I was a child,' he said. 'It's the sort of song that makes kids sit up and be quiet because it's got a good story.'

He began beating time on the table and then sang:

> *Two little boys had two little toys,*
> *Each had a wooden horse.*

(Oh dear, I thought. This is dreadful.)

Gaily they played each summer's day,
Warriors both of course.

(What am I going to say to him? He's such a nice guy and it's such a namby pamby song.)

One little chap then had a mishap,
Broke off his horse's head.
Wept for his toy then cried with joy
As his young playmate said:
'Did you think I would leave you crying
When there's room on my horse for two . . .'

Ted carried on singing as I struggled to think of something positive I could say. Eventually, he reached the second verse:

Long years passed, war came so fast,
Bravely they marched away.
Cannon roared loud, and in the mad crowd
Wounded and dying lay.
Up goes a shout, a horse dashes out,
Out from the ranks so blue.
Gallops away to where Joe lay,
Then came a voice he knew.
'Did you think I would leave you dying,
When there's room on my horse for two?'

My scalp suddenly tingled and the hair on the back of my neck and my arms stood on end. I couldn't remember ever hearing a song that moved me like this.

There was a long pause when the song finished. Ted got a little self-conscious.

'Well, it was just a thought,' he said.

'It's brilliant.'

He grinned.

'I can't tell you how great I think it is. I've got tears in my eyes.'

I dashed upstairs and grabbed my tape recorder. By now I had a new one, about the size of a briefcase. Ted sang the song again, tapping out the beat on the table. A morning chorus of birds could be heard in the background.

It wasn't until much later that I realized how closely the song mirrored the fate of my father and his brother Carl. Dad had always believed that if they had stayed together during the war, they would have both come out alive together.

From Gove we flew to Darwin and I met up with the documentary team, which included the producer Alan Bateman along with a cameraman and a soundman. We were also joined by Vin Serventy, my old physics teacher from Perth Modern School, who had been making low budget 16mm documentaries about the Australian bush and its wildlife for years.

Vin had suggested that Harry Butler join us. Apart from being brilliant in the field, Harry had a long-wheelbased Land Rover that would become our transport for the next six weeks. He would also cook for us and set up camp each night.

Harry was so charismatic and likeable that he became the unexpected star of *Rolf's Walkabout*. Subsequently, the ABC commissioned him to star in his own wildlife series, *In The Wild, with Harry Butler*.

Although Harry laughs it off, I've always believed that he is the true model for 'Crocodile Dundee'. You only had to look at him. He had bullets in his bandolier hatband, a knife slung on his belt and a battered aluminium boat strapped to the top of his Land Rover. He also seemed to be able to talk to animals and could catch snakes with his bare hands. Topping it off, he had that wonderfully dry laconic sense of humour that is so typical of Australian bushmen.

We had a magical six weeks, bumping over dirt tracks to remote waterholes and gorges. Mind you, it was stinking hot by ten in the morning and you could fry an egg on a flat rock by midday. I worried about Alwen being able to cope, but she and Bindi breezed through it.

The documentary was basically the story of us going on a holiday to the Territory. It was shot on 12 ASA film, which is such a low rating that we normally couldn't shoot anything before ten in the morning and had to stop filming at four in the afternoon. There just wasn't enough light. Sadly, this meant we couldn't do any of the campfire scenes, or spectacular shots of sunsets and sunrises.

Tucking into breakfast one morning, I noticed a round bald patch the size of a two-shilling piece at the back of Alwen's head. It was as though somebody had cleanly shaved a circle of hair from her scalp.

We both laughed it off because there was little else we could do. The nearest doctor was two days' drive away and we had a strict filming schedule. It would just have to wait until we got back to civilization.

After we shot the final scenes at Ayers Rock (now called Uluru) we prepared to fly back to Sydney. Then we discovered a mix-up over money. Harry had given up six weeks of his time but hadn't been paid. The ABC crew had already left saying it had nothing to do with them.

Alwen and I had no spare money, but we decided to cash in our air tickets back to Sydney and give the proceeds to Harry. He, in turn, was going to drive us down into South Australia and from there across to Sydney, a distance of 1,500 miles.

On the first night we stayed at Cooper Pedy, an opal-mining town, where most of the buildings are underground to escape the heat. The generators are switched off at 11 p.m., plunging everything into darkness. Answering the call of nature in the middle of the night meant tackling almost complete sensory deprivation! In total blackness it took me hours to find my way there and back to bed.

Setting off early, we drove all day before stopping in a tiny town somewhere near the Victorian border. The place looked like a ghost town until we noticed a crowd of people gathered outside a shop window. We parked the Land Rover and went to investigate.

The crowd was staring at a TV set, watching history being made. With our faces lit by the flickering bluish light from the screen, we watched Neil Armstrong step onto the moon. It was spellbinding.

'One small step for a man, one giant leap for mankind.'

I looked across at Harry and saw tears rolling down his cheeks. We had spent weeks in the wilderness, where nothing had changed for thousands of years, and now we emerged to find that humankind had reached the moon. I wondered what David Blanasi would have made of it. He would probably have shrugged and accepted it, as always.

Then I thought of my dad. What must he have been thinking? So much had happened in his lifetime. At the age of four, he had seen his first motor car, with a man walking in front of it waving a red flag to warn people that it was going at the alarming speed of four miles an hour. Now, two world wars later, a man was walking on the moon. Staggering!

Back in Sydney we spent a few weeks looking at rushes of the documentary and re-shooting one of the scenes.

We decided to organize a dinner for everyone involved in the project just to say thank you. Alwen had been to lunch at a nice curry restaurant, so we made a booking at the same place for dinner. Nobody told us that the restaurant underwent something of a transformation of an evening. It was a popular meeting place for transvestites and had its own transvestite cabaret.

We turned up and were slightly stunned to say the least. The place was packed with six-foot blokes dressed in frocks and wigs.

Bindi, who was only five, found this fascinating and kept asking us why particular ladies had dark blue chins or really hairy arms. The crowning moment came in the middle of the cabaret when Bindi's high piping voice cut through the music with, 'Mummy, what does silicone mean?'

It was soon time to say goodbye to Harry, who was heading back to Perth. He had become like part of our family during the previous few months and we were desperately sad to see him go.

Rolf's Walkabout proved to be a big hit for the ABC and had the best ratings in the corporation's history until their coverage of the Commonwealth Games in Brisbane more than ten years later.

Before leaving Sydney, Alwen went to see a specialist about her hair loss and was diagnosed with alopecia – a nervous disorder. The doctors could do nothing about it and her hair continued falling out at an alarming rate. Not surprisingly, she became very self-conscious. Back in England she bought a blond wig and began wearing colourful hippy headbands. One afternoon as she parked her Mini outside Bindi's primary school in Sydenham, she was bumped from behind by another car. Her head jerked back and the wig dislodged. The other mothers on the footpath stared at her baldness. Alwen died inside. She gave up wearing wigs after about a year. By then her hair had begun growing back. Although it was never as thick as before, it returned as a fine snow-white fuzz which slowly lengthened.

The fourth series of *The Rolf Harris Show* was in the planning stage. I sold Stewart Morris on the song that Ted Egan had sung to me, 'Two Little Boys'. I went through reel after reel of my tapes but couldn't find the recording. As usual, I hadn't catalogued anything.

In desperation, I phoned Ted in Australia. He was back working in Canberra at the head office of the Aboriginal Affairs Department and he quite happily sang the song for me again. I recorded it by holding the microphone jammed into the earpiece of my phone. I still have the tape of that scratchy faraway voice recorded across twelve thousand miles of phone line. It is one of my most prized possessions.

Alan Braden, a musical arranger for the BBC, did a wonderful job creating a very Victorian sounding accompaniment, with the strings providing a crisp marching rhythm. A snare drum came in sparingly in the middle, like a lone drummer boy, and at the end came a haunting trumpet call.

The effect on the audience in the Television Theatre was

electric. When I reached the line, 'Did you think I would leave you dying?' I knew they were feeling exactly as I did when I first heard the song. As the final note of the trumpet faded there was a long silence. Then people erupted into applause. Many had tears in their eyes, myself included.

Hundreds of letters arrived in the following week, most requesting the lyrics, or asking me to sing the song again.

I went straight into the studio to record it using Alan Braden's arrangement. Our first attempt sounded a bit too fast, so we slowed it down fractionally and tried again. This time it sounded too slow. Alyn Ainsworth suggested we start at the slightly faster speed and then slow down fractionally during the drum roll just before the line, 'Did you think I would leave you dying?' It worked like a dream.

At the very end of the recording session, we had one track left unused. I asked the trumpet player, Freddie Clayton, if he could play the final bugle-style bit again. 'We'll give you everything in your earphones except your original trumpet call,' I said. I didn't want him to phrase the two takes in exactly the same way.

Afterwards, we laid the second trumpet call over the first. This created a haunting, irregular echo, like a lone ghostly trumpeter playing on a deserted parade ground. It was just what the ending needed.

'Two Little Boys' went to No.1 on the UK charts and stayed there for seven weeks. It became the last No.1 of the 1960s and the first of the 1970s.

Having done a little research, I discovered the song was about the American Civil War and had been written in 1901 by two of Al Jolson's favourite songwriters, Edward Madden and Theodore Morse. Realizing it was out of copyright, I planned to claim it for Ted Egan and make him a good few bob. But I'd left it too late. EMI had renewed the copyright as soon as they heard me sing 'Two Little Boys' on TV. Instead of Ted Egan getting the writer's royalties, they went to the publishing company.

To make up for this, I gave Ted 10 per cent of everything the song made. My accountant thought I was crazy and Phyl Rounce was speechless, but I reasoned that without Ted, I would never have heard the song.

Throughout the previous seven years, I had continued doing my weekly radio slot on the BBC with Laurie Holloway and the band. In the early days the show had gone out live, but was now pre-recorded and broadcast a few days later.

Phyl Rounce turned up one afternoon at Aeolian Hall in Bond Street. She had never bothered coming to a session before. She waved at me from the control room and I waved back through the studio window.

Dusty Springfield was the guest artist that week. She was a stunning girl, who seemed quite insecure about her beauty. She used make-up like a mask, plastering it on her face.

We had just finished a take for my final song, which I thought sounded fine.

'We'll try it again,' said the producer.

'What was wrong?'

'I think you can do it better.'

'In what way?'

'I just think you can do it better.'

He couldn't give me any reason but I shrugged my shoulders and nodded to the band. They spent a long time getting their instruments together and re-tuning the guitar and bass. The sound levels were checked and re-checked.

'What's wrong with everyone today?' I said.

Finally, we started the song but halfway through had to stop. Someone in the control room had forgotten to start the tape. I was getting really frustrated. We could have all been home by now.

We finally recorded the song and I heard it played back in the control room.

'I honestly think the first one was better,' I said. The producer nodded in agreement. Why then had we been faffing around for half an hour?

Phyl and I left together and emerged into the arcade which led out to Bond Street. A book caught my eye in a shop window. Phyl was one pace ahead of me and didn't realize that I'd stopped to look at a lovely big glossy picture book of Egypt. She emerged through the doors into Bond Street and a TV camera started rolling. Eamon Andrews stepped out.

There was no Rolf!

Phyl dashed back inside and grabbed me by the arm. 'What are you doing?'

'Just looking at this lovely book.'

'OK, but come on.'

'What's the hurry?'

'No hurry.'

She kept hold of my arm this time. We emerged from the doors and Eamon started again. 'Rolf Harris, star of stage, television and radio . . . this is your life!' I looked like a kangaroo caught in the headlights of a road train.

All the delays in the studio had been orchestrated by Phyl and the producer. They knew the camera and crew wouldn't arrive until 5 p.m. and couldn't let me leave early.

It was an amazing evening. Ted Egan and David Blanasi had been flown across to London. But the biggest surprise came when the door opened to reveal Bruce and then Mum and Dad. It was a huge thrill.

By the fourth series of *The Rolf Harris Show* I had used up all the songs I knew that had an Australian or New Zealand flavour. I had also done every cabaret-style spot or comedy number I had ever written or performed on stage. The weekly turnaround meant the search for new material became all-consuming. Eventually, I found myself having to sing songs that didn't suit me. We were choosing stuff from the hit parade by the likes of Nat King Cole, Gene Pitney, or the Walker Brothers.

It was strange how quickly my confidence deserted me. I began to flounder and feel hesitant on stage. I remember having to sing

'You've Lost That Loving Feeling'. I wasn't a crooner with a velvet voice who could sing love songs and I certainly didn't have the 'black' soul sound needed for this one. Halfway through, I grew frightened and jittery. I began stumbling over the words and looking around in a blind panic. It was as though I had suddenly discovered stage fright at the age of forty.

Each week my influence on the show grew less, as did the amount of time I spent up front. The producers and musical arrangers started trying to hide me by using big orchestral arrangements and concentrating more on the Young Generation I began to dread each show and imagine what they were saying up in the control room. 'Get the camera off him. Put it somewhere else.'

Phyl Rounce arranged a meeting with the BBC TV management. Right from the outset she complained about my treatment, saying I was being swamped by the dancers. 'I'm hard pressed finding Rolf in the show,' she said. She lobbied for a change of producer, thinking that was the cause of the problem. Initially, I went along with her, but in my heart I knew it wasn't Stewart Morris's fault.

Bill Cotton, the then head of Variety, rated Stewart very highly. He argued, quite rightly, that we wouldn't find a producer of his calibre, or someone who would move mountains for the show the way Stewart did.

I agreed with him. I knew where the fault lay, but I couldn't admit it to anyone – not even to Alwen.

Phyl was surprised that I changed my mind so quickly. 'Why did you cave in?' she said. 'You should have stuck to your guns.'

She could see I was upset and pressed me to tell her. Over lunch I finally admitted what was wrong.

'They can't put me out front because I'm not confident about what I do any more,' I said.

'Why ever not?'

Phyl couldn't understand how things had suddenly changed. I tried to explain about struggling to find material.

'I'm being asked to sing songs from the hit parade. They're not *me*. You know the stuff I do. I make people laugh, or sing them songs about Australia . . .'

'Can't you write some more Australian stuff?'

I gave her a sad smile. If only it was that easy. I couldn't just pluck songs out of the air on a Thursday night for the following week's show. I had always needed inspiration to write; or songs would come to me almost by accident.

Phyl could do nothing to help me.

By halfway through the series I knew the fairy tale was over. For years I had been waiting for somebody to come out of the wings and tap me on the shoulder, saying, 'We've found you out. You're not really up to this.' This had never stopped me seizing my chances with both hands. In many ways it made me more adventurous. I tried a lot of things that I *hoped* would work and pulled most of them off.

Now I could feel everything slipping away from me. Cabaret had been easier because I was in complete control. I could *see* the audience and work the room. More important, I was doing tried and true material that I knew worked for me. Now I was trying to sing American pop songs that I couldn't relate to.

The crunch came with 'Blowin' in the Wind'. I just point-blank could not learn it. On the night of the show I stood there, in front of a packed theatre and millions of viewers at home, and I dried up. I didn't have a single idea in my head about the next line. The backing track kept playing as I mumbled unintelligibly. The producers had to cut away from me with the cameras.

Afterwards I sat in the dressing room, staring at myself in the mirror. People were very quiet around me. Nobody was knocking on the door and telling me how well the show had gone. The adventure was over.

Chapter Thirteen

LET'S BUILD A NIGHTCLUB

THE BBC DIDN'T COMMISSION ANOTHER SERIES OF *THE ROLF Harris Show*. I felt a mixture of relief and sadness. Although I had never felt as if I *owned* the show, or had a monopoly on Saturday night's TV, I knew that I'd miss the limelight.

Rather than dwell on the setback, I began looking ahead. I had my father's work ethic, which meant I could never relax unless I was doing something.

The 1970 World Expo was hosted by Osaka in Japan and I agreed to take part in the Australian week. Alwen and Bindi came along and we found ourselves looking at a landscape of high rise apartments as we took a taxi from the airport.

Japan had always been a mystery to me. I had grown up hearing terrible stories about the POW camps in Burma where so many soldiers had perished. My dad had a real horror of the Japanese as an enemy. Yet all of this seemed totally removed from Osaka, which had been polished and preened to within an inch of its life. Japanese people had been bowing to us ever since we stepped off the plane. They were so polite that it became quite tiring having to constantly return the bows.

Expo was bristling with high-tech gadgetry, special effects and mechanical stage props. The arena was rectangular and seemed at first sight to be about half a mile long, with seats on three sides and a fourth side that opened out onto sky and green fields. At one end was a huge robot with movable arms – one of which held a small circular stage, big enough for one person, which could be raised almost to the roof of the arena.

Seated in the head of the robot a controller guided all the robotic limbs and moved the various stages around the arena. The lighting could be pre-programmed for the whole show, along with the film and slides that could be projected onto huge screens above the arena.

Stefan Haag, our Australian producer, had been given the enormous task of filling out all the requirements of the various artists months in advance. Most Aussies lack any sense of urgency until the last possible moment, but Stefan managed to send off the paperwork and it came back signed, stamped and approved. We had the green light.

Our huge Australian team turned up for two days of rehearsals and immediately struck trouble. Whenever Stefan made a request, the Japanese interpreter replied 'Fkano', meaning 'Impossible'.

There followed a blazing row. Well, it was blazing from Stefan's side, but the Japanese technicians were incredibly, if coldly, polite. Stefan kept waving his bits of paper showing that everything had been approved.

'Fkano,' said the interpreter.

At one point the thirty-strong Australian Navy Band was seated in raised tiers on the biggest of the moving stages. The platform was supposed to move them gently around the arena as they played their music.

'Fkano!' said the interpreter.

Stefan waved the piece of paper under her nose.

'Fkano!'

No amount of shouting or slapping of his forehead made any difference. Eventually Stefan tried to physically push the stage, laden with musicians, single-handedly into position. Almost horizontal and purple with effort and anger, he managed to move it about three feet.

Finally the interpreter relented. 'We will try,' she said. Instructions were given and the stage moved off smoothly under mechanical power and manoeuvred beautifully.

Every argument took this long to resolve. After we had waited to rehearse for eight hours, Stefan sent us all back to our hotels until he sorted out the technical problems.

The first show was at 7.15 p.m. the following day. That morning we arrived at rehearsals to discover that the massive projection screens suspended high above the arena had been torn to shreds by a mini-typhoon during the night. Months spent editing film and colour slides to go with large sections of the show now went for nothing. Gritting his teeth, Stefan made new plans.

To our surprise, the stands were almost full by midday. The seats for the show couldn't be booked, so people had turned up early. It was totally unnerving going through a rehearsal knowing the same people were going to be watching the show proper in a few hours' time.

At five minutes to seven that evening Stefan reluctantly stopped the rehearsal. 'You've got twenty minutes,' he said. 'Have a shower, get changed and I'll see you back here. Good luck.' I could sense that he wanted to add, 'We're going to need it.'

Ten minutes later, Stefan made his way down to the underground control room, which looked like an American baseball dugout. A smiling man he'd never seen before greeted him. Stefan looked past him and didn't recognize any of the technicians.

'Who are you?' he asked.

'So sorry . . . We night shift.'

Stefan was thunderstruck. After two days of difficult rehearsal he now discovered that nobody in the control room had seen *any* of the show.

In total disbelief, he flung his huge script in the air. At that very moment he realized there was nothing holding the sheets together.

Typewritten papers fluttered all around him. By the time he'd put them back in order, it was show time.

Because the rehearsals had been in daylight, the lighting for the show had never been tried. Given that it had all been pre-programmed, Stefan presumed nothing could go wrong.

'Lighting. Cue one,' said Stefan.

The head technician shouted, 'Cue-go one.'

Next to him a man shouted, 'Cue-go one.'

Alongside him, the next man shouted, 'Cue-go one.'

Eight voices later down the pecking order, somebody shouted 'Cue-go one' into a microphone.

The man sitting up in the head of the robot heard this on his headphones and activated the computer program. Stefan watched all this in stunned amazement. It had taken so long for the message to be relayed that the lighting was now three cues too late.

'*Cue four!*' he shouted.

The head man looked at him quizzically. 'You not go cue two?'

'Forget about cue two and cue three. Go to cue four.'

The instruction went laboriously down the line again. By the time it was acted upon, it was already time for cue six. Stefan jumped ahead and demanded cue nine. It worked. From then on he kept making calls three cues in advance.

To understand the audience reaction to the show, you need to understand a little about the type of people who had come to see the Expo. Many were simple farming folk and villagers from rural Japan who had been drawn by publicity about the greatest show on earth – a once in a lifetime experience.

Each morning, the crush of people at the gates stretched for hundreds of yards. On the first day hundreds were injured when the crowd surged forward unchecked and people fell down three broad steps inside the gate and were trampled. From then on the organizers employed a dozen Sumo wrestler-types to link arms every morning and stop people surging down those steps.

Some of these farming folk had never visited a city before. Parties from individual villages roped themselves together like mountaineers so they wouldn't get separated and lost in the crowd. They queued for up to four hours to see the most popular exhibits (the American and Soviet displays). Once inside, they raced through in their eagerness to get out again and queue for the next exhibit.

My first number was 'Jake the Peg' which had always been a showstopper. The 'oom-chuck, oom-chuck' march-on music started and I entered the arena in my three-legged persona. There was a universal intake of breath from the audience. I could see people turning to each other and talking in hushed tones, nodding their heads sympathetically.

They thought the leg was *real*! They were saying to each other, 'What a brave man to make mockery of his affliction in honour of his country.'

I went through the whole song without raising a smile, let alone a laugh. It was a disaster!

I finished the song and did a quick change round the back of the mobile stage. My overcoat and trousers had Velcro seams, so I could rip them off and be back on stage within seven seconds, wearing a completely new outfit. Again I expected the audience to be amazed by this, but the effect was totally lost because the arena was so vast that nobody realized I was the same person.

I could imagine them whispering to each other, 'He looks very similar to previous Australian, but then, all Australians look alike!'

In the aftermath of the mini-typhoon, a fine, almost imperceptible rain began drifting in from the open side of the arena, almost like a Scotch mist. Normally, this wouldn't have been a problem, but all of my music had been copied out by hand in ordinary ink.

The four musicians accompanying me watched powerlessly as the ink began gently washing off the lines and collecting in a black puddle at the bottom of their music stands. They finished up 'busking', trying to remember their parts. But what worried them most was the fear of electrocution. They were standing in wet shoes on a stage covered in a slick of water. Two of them were playing electrical instruments and power leads were curling through puddles.

I had taken a lot of time and effort learning particular Japanese phrases and perfecting the accent. I wanted to be able to tell the audience about certain songs and translate the lyrics. I also wanted to tell a few jokes in Japanese during my painting spot.

After three months of practising the lines, my pronunciations were convincing, but I still struggled to remember everything in the right sequence. I realized that I needed someone to prompt me with key words at particular times.

The solution was for me to wear an earpiece. I had a young Japanese interpreter, standing off stage, reading my lines of Japanese dialogue into a radio microphone. I listened out for key words or repeated the lines parrot fashion. Some of the jokes worked perfectly and raised a good laugh.

At the very end of the show we were going to finish by singing 'Waltzing Matilda', with the entire cast up on stage with the Navy Band. I launched into my final bit of Japanese. As far as I knew, I was saying, 'We have all come from Australia to see *your* country. We invite you all to come and see *our* country.' As I finished I made a 'come hither' waving movement with both my arms to emphasize the invitation.

To this day I'm positive I repeated, sound for sound, exactly what my interpreter said in my ear. Yet somehow the message got mixed up in delivery. En masse, 25,000 people leaped to their feet and surged down onto the floor of the arena. They were running with the speed of an express train, heading straight for us.

'Oh shit!'

All around me panic-stricken musicians were lurching to their feet, looking for an escape route. Seeing none, they clutched their instruments above their heads and sat down again, waiting to be hit by the wave of humanity coming at us from three sides.

The stage rocked on its wheels. People stumbled and fell. Just when I imagined us being swept away, the surge flattened out and equilibrium was restored. I opened my eyes to see a smiling horde, grinning inanely at me, all happy to have been invited closer.

All of these disasters had visited one performance, but new calamities became a daily feature of the show. The worst of them was a sudden fault in the ceiling speakers. I had just finished 'Jake the Peg' to the usual sympathetic sighs and sad murmurs. I moved across to the personal stage area to do the rest of my songs. That's when I realized most of the ceiling speakers had stopped working. I could only hear my voice coming from a lone sound source at the far end of the arena, echoing back to me with about a second delay.

At that moment, the moving stage with my four backing musicians set off from the far side of the arena to join me. Unbeknown to anyone, the technician who had disconnected the power supply from their stage had forgotten to close the cover protecting the power points. One of the wheels of their moving stage drove straight into the hollow and the stage shuddered to a halt, toppling slightly sideways. The guys in the band had difficulty standing on the angle. They also had no electricity feeding the bass and electric guitars, or their microphones.

I had to carry on. I could just hear the acoustic instruments reaching me half a second late; and another half a second after that my voice arrived from the far-off speaker. What a nightmare!

Ignoring the evidence of my ears, while the band did the same, we made exaggerated beating movements with our feet on the first beat of every bar, trying to stay in time.

I thought we managed to keep things together, although later an Aussie radio commentator sent a recorded despatch home saying, 'Typical Australian cock-up.' If I'd known his name I would have happily murdered him.

Osaka was fascinating despite the continuous rain. I went sightseeing with Alwen, Bindi and Phyl Rounce, trying to learn more about the city. Strangely, the footpaths were deserted, yet traffic choked the streets. Where did everybody go?

Eventually, we used a subway underpass to cross a road. As we descended, a subterranean world opened up. Row after row of smart shops stretched as far as the eye could see. People moved in two orderly lines, passing each other like motor traffic, all walking on the left.

It seemed as though an entirely new city had been built underground to escape the rain. The brightly lit shops stretched for miles, linked by footpaths that paralleled the sopping wet pavements over our heads.

The food shops were amazing. Plastic replica meals were beautifully modelled and set out on plates. They were so realistic that the freshly cut tomato glistened wetly all day and night. You simply pointed out what meal you wanted and the real thing was delivered within minutes.

When the rain finally stopped, people emerged above ground again, promenading along the streets. We must have looked like a bizarre group. Phyl and I were head and shoulders above everybody, Alwen had a short fuzz of pure white hair and Bindi, aged six, had blond hair which was a real oddity to the Japanese.

As I walked along, I started to recognize people I thought I'd seen before. Maybe it was true – they *did* all look alike! No, I was definitely seeing the same people over and over again. Then I realized what they were doing.

As foreigners, we were fascinating to the locals, but the Japanese believe it is very rude to stare. To satisfy their curiosity, people were casually walking past us and then doubling back for another fleeting look.

Don and Anne Charles had remained friends from our days living in Regent's Park Road. Don had a few minor chart hits as a singer and regularly worked in the clubs. In the early seventies he did a season out in Malta and came back full of enthusiasm for the island.

'The place is crying out for a fantastic club,' he said. 'It's full of British servicemen and their families. There's nowhere for them to go. It's all honky tonk stuff. We could clean up.'

Don had it all worked out. If we had a nightclub all my showbiz friends could bring their families out for a holiday and do a cabaret in the club each night.

Deciding to have a look for myself, I took Alwen and Bindi to Malta for a holiday. The islands, hanging beneath Sicily in the Mediterranean, were stunning, with soaring limestone cliffs and sparkling waters. Temples, churches and hilltop citadels dotted the landscape. We had a wonderful time wandering the streets and staying in ancient limestone buildings. I taught Bindi how to snorkel and we spent hours in the water.

Everything Don said about Malta seemed to be true. As well as the British military base, NATO had a large presence and the servicemen were starved of good entertainment.

The more I thought about it, the more I liked the idea of owning my own club. I could picture myself wandering between the tables, chatting to the regulars and shaking hands with newcomers. We could spend most of the summer out there and close down during the winter months.

Phyl Rounce was also excited by the idea and she came in as a third partner with Don and myself. Our roles were never defined although Don had offered to live in Malta and manage the club. As it turned out, I provided almost all of the finance.

We built the place from scratch – choosing the location and hiring local builders, plumbers, plasterers and electricians. We had to import the lights, china, bathroom fittings, refrigerators and bottles of spirits, as well as a huge Japanese air-conditioning unit that took up a whole room. A dear friend, Jason Monet (the grand-nephew of impressionist Claude Monet), came out and carved statues in Malta stone as decorations. I painted the murals inside.

The club took a year to build and cost more than £30,000 – a small fortune in 1972. Alwen and Bindi spent months in Malta while I was overseeing the building. I didn't do a business plan. It didn't even enter my head. And my English accountant never said, 'Do you know how much this is going to cost?' I simply went ahead.

We called the club Caesar's, which was unfortunate because the locals pronounced it Scissors. It didn't matter because we figured the majority of our clientele was going to be British. Even so, I imagined that the locals were quite looking forward to having this slice of glamour on their doorsteps.

We printed flyers and stuck up posters publicizing our opening night. The place looked amazing and even the napkins had the Caesar's logo. Don had spent weeks training the staff, teaching them how to wait at tables, take orders and mix drinks.

On the big night the place was packed with 200 servicemen and their wives, along with a smattering of wealthy locals. I welcomed everyone, wandering between tables and playing the role of owner of a brand new club.

At about nine o'clock, a chap came up to me and said, 'Look, I don't want to upset you or anything, but I think you should know that nobody has been served any meals yet.'

'What?'

'I've just been into the kitchen. There's no staff.'

I slipped round the back and found Don sitting at a kitchen bench with his head in his hands. The chef was sitting on the back step puffing on a cigarette. All the meals had been cooked, but we had no waiters.

Don looked ready to slit his wrists. 'I don't know what happened. They just didn't show up.'

It turned out that when Don hired our staff he had put a few noses out of joint. In particular, he had poached a band from a rival club run by a Maltese family. They, in turn, regarded this as a declaration of war. The weeks we spent hiring and training staff had been a con trick – the perfect act of sabotage. They were all friends of the rival club owner who had planned to make sure our opening night was a disaster.

I didn't know whether to laugh or cry.

'We can still do it,' said the chap who had brought the bad news to me.

I looked at him as if he was mad.

'I've got some mates. We can do the serving. But you have to get up there and say something. You have to let people know what's happening.'

I stood on the dance floor and announced that virtually all our staff had failed to appear. 'We were conned,' I said. 'I'm sorry. But if you bear with us, we'll try to put food on the table very soon.'

There were murmurs of 'Typical Maltese' and nods of agreement. What happened next amazed me. Everyone pitched in, setting tables, serving meals and clearing things away. Afterwards, I did the cabaret. It turned into a wonderful night and I think everybody felt they knew each other a little better afterwards.

At dawn the next morning, a convoy of twenty cars turned up and drove round and round the square tooting their horns. Locals hung out of the windows cheering and laughing. Our bar and kitchen staff had come to rub our noses in it. But they hadn't succeeded. If anything the attempted sabotage made us even more determined. We recruited more staff and made very sure they were heavily vetted. Within a week we had the restaurant and bar operating smoothly.

Two weeks later there was a general election. In June 1971 the Labour leader Dom Mintoff won office by the narrowest of margins – a single seat. As Mintoff took his oath of office in front of the British Governor General Sir Maurice Dorman, he handed him an order for the British to leave Malta. He did the same to NATO.

Mintoff had come to power promising to deliver Malta its independence, regardless of the cost. The result was an economic disaster. Thousands of local civilians lost their jobs as the British families living in Malta began leaving.

Initially, it looked as though the new Prime Minister might be holding out for rent of £20 million a year for use of the military base. But when the talks stalled at the end of 1971 he issued an ultimatum to the British government, ordering all British personnel to leave.

Within a matter of days the British had dismantled all their facilities and evacuated the servicemen and their families. Six months after the opening of the club, our audience had disappeared.

The club might still have worked if the locals had embraced the idea. Instead, everybody from the government down to the local suppliers tried to screw more money out of us because we were foreigners. Almost every week a new notice was pinned to the door saying the club had been closed. Some new building ordinance had been enacted, or we failed to comply with fire and safety regulations.

'But we've never heard of this permit,' we'd argue.

'It's a new one.'

'How much does it cost?'

'Four hundred pounds.'

'That's ridiculous.'

'OK. Your club must stay closed.'

The money was paid, of course. They must have been laughing at us.

At every turn we encountered more problems. Some were ludicrously small but just as irritating. For example, on the opening night a woman had complained that there was no toilet paper, soap or towel in the washrooms. Initially, we thought it might be more evidence of sabotage, but it continued happening, night after night. Then we discovered that Maltese women had a liking for foreign 'luxuries' and would strip the toilets of anything that wasn't screwed down.

Food was regularly disappearing from the kitchen. Don finally caught the chef. He'd been wrapping fillets of beef in cling film and putting them in the bottom of the garbage bin every night. At three in the morning he'd creep back, burrow through the rubbish and retrieve his booty.

I was back in England and Don had to deal with the day to day hassles. I tried to get to Malta as often as possible. Whenever I did the cabaret we did good business, but when I was away Don did the show and he didn't have the same pulling power.

'Can't you get Val Doonican to come out?' he'd say.

That had always been the plan . . . for me to offer my showbiz friends a free family holiday in exchange for doing some shows. Unfortunately, when it came to the crunch I couldn't do it. These people were professionals. They performed for a living. I had too much pride to ask them to come out and basically save my bacon. It was like asking for charity.

Years later, I recounted the sorry story to Ken Stauffer, who had been so successful at running nightclubs in Canada. 'I wish you'd spoken to me first,' he said. 'I'd have told you straight away not to get involved. If you were going to do it, I'd have told you to forget about having a band and a cabaret. Get a young chap in with some records and have him run a disco. Forget about meals and just have a bar. That way you cut down on all your big overheads. Then you've got a chance of making it pay.'

I also wish that I'd spoken to Ken first. That was my big trouble. I never went looking for advice from anyone who might know.

The final straw came when Mintoff passed a law decreeing that no business in Malta could be foreign-owned. Local interests had to control at least 51 per cent. We immediately had to sell 51 per cent of our shares or close down. Of course, nobody wanted them.

Our Maltese accountant (another prerequisite) suggested a way round the problem. We could gift 51 per cent of the shares to his son who would nominally hold them on our behalf. He would *appear* to be the majority shareholder and satisfy the new law. This seemed to solve the problem so we signed the papers. In the meantime we carried on, trying to make the club a success, as the audiences dried up.

After four years we ran out of patience and money. Although sad about selling the club I was also relieved. It had been a burden from the very beginning. After the deal had gone through, I surveyed the pitiful amount of cash we had to show for all our work. At that moment, our Maltese accountant waved a piece of paper under Don's nose. 'Haven't you forgotten something? My son owns fifty-one per cent.'

We had been screwed. Then again, we were screwed from day

one. The whole idea seemed to be 'fleece the foreigners'. It taught me a huge lesson. Never try to run a business in someone else's country.

I don't know what I lost on the whole deal. At least £50,000 – a lot of money in 1974. Most of what I'd earned from *The Rolf Harris Show* and the success of 'Two Little Boys' had probably disappeared. Again, I don't know for sure, because IAR still collected my money and I drew cash as I needed it.

Sadly, I was forced to sell a wonderful investment property at the fledgling resort town of Noosa in Queensland. My Australian accountant and friend, Tony Clune, had bought it for me a few years earlier. We made only a few thousand dollars' profit on the double block, which overlooked the ocean. According to Tony, it would now be worth between nine and ten million dollars. We live and learn, although I don't seem to do a lot of the 'learning' bit.

Chapter Fourteen

CLUBS, PUBS AND CHINESE TAKEAWAYS

O
N A TYPICAL AUSTRALIAN WINTER'S MORNING IN 1968, I
walked around a building site on the edge of Sydney
Harbour, accompanied by Jack Neary, an entrepreneur and good
friend. We were looking at the beginnings of the Sydney Opera
House – a building that would eventually capture the imagination
of the world.

'I'd love to see you do the first show in the concert hall,' said
Jack.

'It'd be fantastic,' I echoed.

'Well, let's make it happen!'

Neither of us expected to have to wait six years, but the end result
was worth it. When I first set eyes on the finished Opera House it
looked as though it had been moored against the shore and would
set sail in the first strong breeze. A lot of modern architecture
leaves me cold, but this had a magic that was instantly timeless.

I was enormously honoured to be doing the first concert. It was
going to be videoed, edited and broadcast around Australia. As
part of my contract, I was given the colour video footage rights.

This meant I could have it edited the way I wanted and then sell the finished product anywhere in the world as 'Rolf Harris live in concert from the Sydney Opera House'.

I spent weeks planning routines and arranged to arrive in Sydney with plenty of time to rehearse. That's when I discovered that Australian Equity was making waves.

'Rolf Harris can't do this show because he's not Australian,' declared the president.

'What do you mean he's not Australian?' scoffed Jack, jumping to my defence. 'He's an Australian Equity member!'

'Yeah, but he works overseas. He's not really Australian, is he?'

The logic of this was a mystery to everyone except Equity. They were adamant and threatened to pull every other Equity member out of the show if I appeared. This was unionism gone mad.

My show included sixteen young Australian singers and dancers on stage with me, as well as a band of Australian musicians. On top of this, I had two full blood Aboriginals coming down from the Northern Territory to perform. And they were saying the show wasn't Australian!

All of this was pointed out to Equity, but they chose to ignore it.

'Our members have rights,' we were told. 'Unless we get a full representation of real union members, we're pulling the plug.'

It felt like a slap in the face. I loved Australia. It was my birthplace and had been my home for twenty-one years. Since then I had travelled the world and had never stopped talking about Australia, or painting pictures of its landscapes, or singing songs about its people and its animals. It was my spiritual home, if not my physical one.

After hours of heated discussions, Equity issued Jack with an ultimatum. The only way that I would be allowed to perform at the Opera House was if there was another show on the same night, of identical length, using 'genuine' Australian artists. It was either that or nothing at all. I had no choice but to agree.

For the opening of the show I planned to do a painting of the

Opera House as seen from the top of the south pylon of the Harbour Bridge. As I finished, the studio camera shot of my painting would gently merge into the real scene – the Opera House as seen from a camera high up on that same pylon. Then this camera would zoom in closer and closer to finally reveal me, standing on the highest sail of the roof in front of what looked like a real piano.

'They're all down there,' I'd say, waving at the crowds around the Opera House. 'And they're all coming here for this amazing night.'

I needed a really good colour photograph taken from the south pylon, so my painting of it would exactly match the later camera shot.

'Why would you want a photograph in colour?' asked the producer.

'What do you mean?'

'Won't a black and white one do the same job?'

'But the show's in colour, isn't it?'

'Good God no! There isn't enough light in here for colour. We don't even *own* any colour cameras.'

'But it's in my contract.'

'Ah, don't take any notice of that, mate.'

I spoke to my old friend Roger Henning and he made a few phone calls. He suggested that we fly colour cameras from Queensland, but the cost was prohibitive. By then the heart was going out of me.

Equity had demanded that their show go on before mine, which was another kick in the teeth. Both were to be recorded and edited to be broadcast at a later date.

On the opening night there was a real buzz of expectation. This was the hottest ticket in town and seats were snapped up weeks in advance. The first show was due to start at 7.30 p.m. but by eight nothing had happened. I asked a stage manager what was wrong.

'Don't tell anyone,' he whispered, 'but somebody has cut right through the coaxial cable to the outside broadcast van.'

'Why?'

He shrugged. 'Sabotage. They reckon some of the workmen are pissed off. They spent twenty odd years putting this building up. Now they're out of a job and this is their spiteful farewell present.'

Television technicians were scrambling to find a replacement cable, but only a few of them existed and each cost $32,000.

'Shouldn't I go out and tell the audience?' I asked the producer.

'No, for God's sake don't say anything. We don't want any copycat vandalism.'

'But you can't leave them sitting there.'

The show was fifty minutes late and the slow handclapping had started. It took another forty minutes before a new cable could be hooked up.

When the first show started, I listened from the side of the stage. The sound problems were appalling, with so much high-pitched squealing feedback that I could almost hear the audience grinding its collective teeth. At last here was a reason to be thankful for being put second.

After a half-hour interval, I began my show. The opening sequence worked like a dream, but I noticed that people had started glancing at their watches. It was now 10.30 p.m. and the last trains and buses would leave at eleven. All through my show people were getting up and leaving. I didn't blame them. They had to get home. By the time I finished, the cameras couldn't cut to any audience shots because they would have shown empty seats.

When the concert was finally edited and transmitted, they used virtually none of the second half of my show. They concentrated on the first half when I still had an audience of sorts. It meant that all my old favourites were included, like 'Jake the Peg' and 'Sun Arise', but none of the new things I wanted to show off.

Anybody watching would have said, 'Same old stuff from Rolf.'

The video footage also proved to be absolutely useless. It was in black and white, with hardly any applause and no audience interaction.

I thought opening the Opera House was going to be the greatest moment of my career to date. Instead, it proved to be a damp squib. At the time I was absolutely devastated, but I didn't let myself get too downhearted. Being Australian gives you a fatalistic sort of attitude.

'She'll be right, mate,' is the catchcry. You make the best of a bad job and get on with life.

On Christmas morning that same year – 1974 – I turned on the radio to catch the weather report. I wondered if it was going to snow. A very sombre newsreader announced that Darwin had been flattened by a cyclone as people went to bed on Christmas Eve. The early reports spoke of absolute devastation, with 90 per cent of the city destroyed and sixty-five people confirmed dead.

I kept thinking of all the friends I'd made in Darwin. I could also picture the fibro houses collapsing like cards and roofing iron flying through the air. The winds had been clocked at 135 mph before the anemometer stopped working.

As the first eyewitness accounts emerged, people described how they had braced themselves against refrigerators while sheets of tin smashed walls and shattered windows. The suction of the wind tearing past the broken windows stripped houses of anything that wasn't bolted down, even sofas and beds. Houses shifted on their foundations. Doors popped open as frames buckled. Cars were wrapped round trees and steel lampposts were bent double, touching the ground.

I called Phyl Rounce and cancelled any upcoming concerts in England. Then I talked to Bruce in Sydney who said that several charity events were being arranged to raise money for the survivors. I volunteered my services and flew to Australia within days of the disaster.

A host of entertainers put on a big show at the Entertainment Centre in Sydney on Saturday night, with everyone donating their services free. Paul Hogan stole the show, with a brilliantly funny routine. The following week we did the same fund-raiser in Melbourne. Unfortunately, someone from the TV brains trust decided to air the Sydney special on the same night as the fund-raising show in Melbourne. Of course, people stayed at home to watch the show on TV and the theatre was half empty.

Darwin had a population of about 45,000 when Cyclone Tracy struck. In the mass evacuation afterwards, three-quarters of the residents were moved. Many of the Darwin evacuees were being billeted with families in Sydney and Melbourne who donated their spare beds and floor space.

After the show in Melbourne I found a phone message waiting from Colleen Leonard. She and her husband Clive were great friends of Ted Egan and we had stayed with them briefly while filming *Rolf's Walkabout*. In the short note Colleen mentioned that Clive had stayed in Darwin to help with the clean-up and the beginning of any rebuilding, while she and the children had been evacuated to Melbourne. There were four kids – two older girls and a twin girl and boy. The message mentioned all of them by name except one.

Oh my God, I thought. What's happened?

Colleen had left a phone number. I called but was too scared to ask about the kids. Instead I caught a taxi from the theatre and drove for nearly an hour through the outer suburbs of Melbourne. When I arrived, I did a head count. All the kids were OK. Whoever had taken the message had missed out a name.

Colleen told me the story of their Christmas Eve. The family had sheltered under beds and the kitchen table, as wind-borne chunks of wood and debris punched holes through the walls and water poured in. They had lost most of their belongings to water damage, or the wind.

The Director-General of the National Disasters Organization, Major-General Stretton, had been inspirational, according to Colleen. With all other communications destroyed, he broadcast on the radio every day.

'If you stick with me, we will do it together,' he told them. 'I'll get more planes in tomorrow. And more the next day. We'll get everybody out of Darwin.'

Colleen had tears in her eyes as she described the moment that Clive put them all on a military plane. As he said goodbye, he told his son Peter, 'You're the man now. Look after the girls.' The boy was nine years old.

Two weeks later, I flew north and witnessed the devastation at first hand. From the air it looked as though a giant hand had turned the city into confetti and scattered it across the landscape. In some places it wasn't possible to distinguish the streets from the remains of the houses. Bulldozers had cleared the road from the airport leaving debris simply piled up on each side. Cars lay upside down and the wreckage of light planes and bicycles lay twisted amid the rubble.

I managed to find Mike Pfizner, a local musician I'd worked with before. He gathered all his musician mates together and we put on a big open-air concert in the Darwin amphitheatre. There wasn't a single leaf left on any tree in the park surrounding us, but everyone who could walk turned up and loved the show.

I also did separate shows in school halls and gymnasiums and on one of the navy ships anchored in the bay. Thousands of emergency workers, most of them soldiers, worked in Darwin during the day and returned to the ships at night to sleep. The shows were a bit of light relief that took their minds off the devastation.

I stayed at the Travelodge, which had an open house for anyone who was in Darwin to help. The carpets were sopping wet, the windows were boarded up, and the dining room had serve yourself meals because most of the kitchen staff had been evacuated.

Colleen's story and the courage of people like her inspired me to write a song called 'Northern Territorian'. Here is just a taste of it:

I'm a Northern Territorian, I'm a refugee from Tracy,
And I can't wait to get back home, I belong in the town I know,
Can't wait to get back home to Darwin.

Stood in line in the searing heat, kids all clustered round your
   feet,
Precious little left to eat, waitin' for a plane.
The men all felt they had to stay, workin' eighteen hours a day,
Only barely time to say, 'Goodbye . . .
Goodbye love, look after the kids love,
I'll see you again.'

A man is not supposed to cry, but, when he tried to say goodbye,
Thought that I was gonna die, leavin' him behind.
He looked across the plane to Pete, strapped securely in his seat,
I had to strain to hear him speak, 'Goodbye son,
Look after your mum son, you're a man now,
You're the man now, son,
See you soon.'

In the years since *The Rolf Harris Show* had ended, I had slipped into the comfy world of summer seasons and children's television in the UK. Once or twice I tried to repeat the success of 'Two Little Boys', but none of the new songs troubled the charts.

Mums and dads, grannies and youngsters seemed to love me, but older teenagers and young adults had moved on. They were listening to punk, glamour rock and disco. I must have seemed like a relic.

In 1974 the BBC launched a new series called *Rolf on Saturday, OK!* It was a massive undertaking, involving a team of about 180 people, filming at a new location each fortnight. The idea was to present a show from different schools around the country, letting the schoolkids perform on their own and alongside me.

Two shows were filmed at each location, with different children from two different schools, performing. This took weeks to plan and rehearse. We began by organizing the music and songs. Barry Booth did the research and found hundreds of old music hall numbers and folk songs. He wrote simple piano arrangements and recorded the songs on tape for the kids to learn. While they were practising, Barry set about doing the orchestral arrangements and getting music together for the big band to record.

In the week before shooting, Barry would visit the schools to make sure the choirs and music teachers were up to speed. Then he'd come back to London and conduct the big band as they pre-recorded the backing tracks for every song.

Every second Thursday the circus rolled into a new town. We had cameras, lights, recording equipment, make-up, wardrobe and props. The logistics were a nightmare.

We stayed overnight in a hotel and on Friday morning began pre-recording each of the school choirs onto the backing tracks. It was normally pandemonium and the biggest problem was keeping the kids' energy levels at fever pitch for the strenuous dancing and singing routines.

It was hard physical work and we gave them all a good breakfast before we started. Jim Moir, the producer, was wonderful at keeping the kids enthused. In his best sergeant-major voice he would bellow, 'ARE YOU STATUES OR ARE YOU MOVERS?'

'MOVERS,' the kids would shout back.

'Good, well let's see it.'

I performed 'live' on the show each Saturday, while the kids sang along to their own pre-recorded voices. Having them on tape gave us the extra security we needed to be able to concentrate on getting the action and TV pictures just right.

On top of this we had a resident animator, Mic Rolfe, who visited schools beforehand and showed the kids how to animate their artwork. They came up with some amazing pieces – beautifully drawn and coloured cartoon characters, with moving parts and huge painted backgrounds.

At the end of each series we had a wind-up party which nobody in the enormous crew ever missed. Barry invented a cocktail – equal parts brandy and crème de menthe – which he called the Parrot. It was a potent green colour and was made by the bucket load. The bucket was then carried around the party by two strong men and a large cupful measured into each person's glass for the toasts. That was usually enough, according to Jim. Then I'd get out the accordion and we'd all sing until we were exhausted.

Although I normally managed to see Mum and Dad at least once a year when I toured Australia, I was still very aware of living so far away. When things happened like Dad retiring from his job at the power plant after forty years, I was on the other side of the world.

I had a dream one night that I was down at the riverbank in Bassendean and I saw Dad dive into the water. He didn't come up again but instead stayed under, trying to drown himself. I dived in after him and found him sitting on the bottom of the river.

'What are you doing?'

'Just leave me alone. My time has come.'

'Dad, don't do it,' I pleaded.

'No, just leave me. This is the best way to go.'

'I can't let you.'

I fought with him and dragged him up to the surface. I managed to get him breathing again. It was such an awful dream that I woke drenched in perspiration. I went straight out that day and booked Mum and Dad a trip round the world. They took a cruise ship across the Pacific to Canada and travelled through the Rockies by train before flying to the UK and staying with us.

I told Dad about the dream and he laughed. 'Nothing is further from my thoughts. Is that why you did all this?'

I nodded. 'I didn't want to lose you without seeing you again.'

He laughed once more and ruffled my hair, just like he did when I was a kid.

My television career had spanned nearly twenty years, although I didn't feel as though I'd been around that long. Hang around long enough and you become an 'institution' in show business. The first sign of this is when comedians begin telling jokes about you, or impersonators start to mimic you perfectly.

For impersonators like Phil Cool I was a godsend. Apart from having a distinctive voice, I had all the sound effects and catchphrases. After seeing his impersonation of me on television, Bindi wrote him a letter saying, 'Your show was hysterically funny. You captured every element of my dad. It was perfect.' Phil was knocked out and sent us tickets to see him perform at a theatre in Reading.

I don't know if he was nervous, knowing we were in the audience. I laughed so loudly I felt embarrassed. I kept saying to Alwen, 'I do that. I do.'

'Sshhhshshshsh.'

'Look. I do that.'

Afterwards I went backstage. Phil was slightly anxious when he saw me. He was probably thinking, 'Oh, no, who have I offended this time?'

I told him how much I loved the show and we all went out for a curry together.

Even earlier still, in March 1975, my phone began running hot as friends called up asking if I'd seen *The Goodies*.

'No.'

'Didn't they tell you?'

'Tell me what?'

'The show . . . it was all about you. Little Rolfs, running loose . . . a plague . . .'

The Goodies – Tim Brooke-Taylor, Graham Garden and Bill Oddie – were in their fifth series and their mixture of slapstick, lunacy and vaudeville had a lot in common with *Monty Python's Flying Circus*, which was around at the same time. They loved poking fun at showbiz figures. Max Bygraves, Des O'Connor, Tony Blackburn and Nicholas Parsons had all been 'targets'. Now it was my turn.

The episode was called 'Scatty Safari' – a satire about zoos. The Goodies had created a Celebrity Safari Park and journeyed to Australia to catch a Rolf Harris in the wild. It proved to be a big crowd puller in the park, especially when they mated it with the Russian Rolf Harris (mirroring the London Zoo story of pandas

Chi Chi and An An). Much to their shock, these Rolfs bred like rabbits and soon escaped, plunging the whole of Britain into its darkest days – 'the Rolf Harris Plague'.

The episode ended with a Pied Piper of Hamelin routine, where they all followed one another in through the gates of ATV, with the narrator announcing, '. . . and they were never seen again!'

People asked me if I was offended. The answer was no. When I saw a tape of it I *loved* the show. It was brilliantly funny. I was also very flattered. A part of me felt as though I had truly arrived, because they wouldn't bother doing a show about me if nobody knew who I was.

My only regret is that *The Goodies* didn't contact me first. I would have loved to have played myself in it.

Since the mid-sixties I'd been touring Australia, New Zealand and Canada, doing two-month stints, twice a year. I don't know how many concerts I did in how many towns. I've never tried to count them. There was nothing glamorous about the lifestyle. I travelled thousands of bum-numbing miles, stayed in motel rooms, ate Chinese takeaways and signed autographs until my fingers seized up. Alwen says I'm an applause junkie. Maybe that explains why I did it for so long.

When Bindi started school it became more difficult for the family to tour with me. It was desperately hard being away from them but I had bills to pay. The itineraries were arranged in advance by an Australian or Canadian agent, who booked the venues, hired musicians and arranged transport. I couldn't afford to fly the same band all round Australia with me, so it meant hiring locals and rehearsing new bands for different legs of the tour.

The only person who stayed with me throughout was Barry Booth, my musical director. Barry is a quietly spoken Yorkshire-man, whom I first worked with on commercial TV in Britain. He is a terrific musician and arranger, with a wonderfully dry sense of humour.

A typical week might see us in Rockhampton. The show would

finish well after eleven at night and the only place open for a meal was invariably a Chinese restaurant or, if we were less lucky, we might have to make do with a plate of sandwiches left out for us in our hotel rooms.

At seven the next morning we'd be loading the station wagons for the seven-hour drive to Mackay. As soon as we arrived, the band would set up and do a sound check, while I was interviewed on local radio. Then I'd try to catch an hour and a half's sleep before the show. At 8 p.m. I was back on stage.

This whole routine was repeated the next day and the day after. I can tell you the names of hundreds of small towns, but I saw nothing of them except the local theatre, club or dance hall. Some of the touring venues were pretty ropy and I met some real 'cowboy' organizers along the way.

One night at the Manly League's Club in Sydney, the secretary-manager asked me how I'd like to be introduced.

'Just make sure that my name is the last thing you say,' I said. 'You know the sort of thing . . . "He's come all the way from England to be here. You all know him. Give a big welcome to *Rolf Harris*!" Then I'll go straight into "Jake the Peg".'

The secretary-manager nodded and gave me the thumbs up.

A few minutes later he got on the central mike, cleared his throat and motioned for a bit of quiet. I waited in the wings, dressed in my 'Jake the Peg' gear. The band was ready.

'Now, ah, um, we've got Rolf Harris here for you tonight,' he mumbled.

My heart sank. The band looked at me and I looked back at them, mouth turned down and eyebrows raised.

'He's come a long way . . . ah . . . um . . . from . . . ah . . . England. So youse should all give him a welcome clap . . .'

There was some sporadic applause and the band launched into the music. I had one leg through the curtain when suddenly the secretary-manager shouted into the microphone, 'But before he starts we oughta draw the raffle for the chook. Have youse all got your tickets?'

I shook my head in disbelief as the band crumbled to a halt. There had to be an easier way to make a living.

At the end of each concert, back in my hotel room, I called Alwen and Bindi. Down echoing phone lines, from the far side of the world, I heard about the day to day things that I missed the most. Bindi would breathlessly tell me about the latest gossip at school, what friends she'd made and which teachers she liked best.

'When are you coming home?' she'd ask.

'Soon.'

'How many sleeps?'

'Not too many.'

One day she grew frustrated and said, 'Listen. Daddy, next time you ring up, I'll ask when you're coming home and you say, now.'

I could hear my heart breaking.

When I think of all the big events in her childhood that I missed I feel tremendously guilty. I wasn't there when Bindi had the mumps or the measles or when she broke her arm. I missed birthdays, school concerts, swimming carnivals, speech days and just being around when she wanted a cuddle on her dad's lap.

Great periods of separation put pressure on marriages. Alwen was left to cope on her own, while I went in search of applause. She rarely complained, even when the gaps grew longer and the venues smaller.

Many of the tours barely broke even, after the musicians had been paid and the transport costs covered. Bruce used to say to me, 'It's crazy, Rolf. The only person making any money is Barry. You fly him around first class with you and guarantee him a wage as your musical director, but you finish up with nothing yourself.'

If the tours coincided with school holidays, Alwen and Bindi came with me. Alwen rarely watched my shows any more. She had heard the songs so often. Instead, she carried a stock of paperback novels and looked after Bindi.

I can't blame her for getting bored. I did hundreds of gigs sometimes in places that were barely more than a main street with nothing behind it. Once you had walked up and down, there was nothing left to do. The cinema, if the town had one, was boarded up long ago and the swimming pool was closed for the winter. The TV in the hotel room had only one channel showing twenty-year-old sitcoms like *I Love Lucy* and *Mr Ed*.

Invariably, Alwen would be handed over to the mayor's wife, or a local stalwart from the Country Women's Association, who would take her around to see the local points of interest, like the water ski-ing facilities at the dam, or the arts and crafts fair. She had endless cups of tea and scones, on tin-roofed verandas, where she struggled to think of things to say to numerous well meaning and lovely people.

On my rare days off, we had a great time going bush together, exploring nature trails and hunting for interesting rocks. Harry Butler had helped Alwen to really appreciate the beauty of the Australian bush. Up until then it had seemed too messy to her and the colours too washed out. The greens are less vibrant than those in Britain and the heat haze makes the landscape shimmer, I think, like an impressionist painting.

Bindi was never very comfortable when we ventured too far off the beaten track. She was always getting prickles in her feet and had a fear of ants that bordered on a phobia. But she loved trying to catch little scurrying lizards.

In the early 1970s I was approached by a company in Australia called British Paints who wanted me to help promote their new product range.

I'd become well known for my big paintings on television using house painting brushes, which made me a pretty obvious choice to sell paints on TV. When I signed the contract I made it very clear that I wouldn't tell lies, or say things I didn't believe. The company agreed.

One of the early TV commercials was for 'Glossmaster' – a high gloss oil-based paint. The plan was for me to say straight to camera 'I can't see myself using any other paint' and then the camera would pull back to reveal that it was my mirror image, seen in the gloss of a painted door. It was a nice line and a clever idea.

When I arrived on the set the director said, 'Right, we'll just put a mirror on the door—'

I stopped him. 'I won't do it.'

'What?'

'We have to use a painted door.'

'But I'm just trying to get a really clear image—'

'I know exactly what you're trying to do. You're trying to make people think the door is painted in this high gloss paint, when really you're using a mirror. You're telling lies.'

'Don't be ridiculous.'

'Well, what do you call it?'

He went away in a huff and spoke to Norman Tonge, the senior British Paints man on set. Norman, to his undying credit, backed me completely. 'If the paint is that good, let's paint the door.'

After putting several coats of dark red gloss on the door we shot the commercial. It worked wonderfully and set the scene for an association with British Paints that lasted more than seventeen years. I did new TV ads every year and toured the country promoting the products. The catchphrase – 'Trust British Paints, sure can!' with my little hand-drumming effect on the lid of the paint tin – is still one of the most recognizable and remembered advertising slogans in Australia.

Our house in Sydenham seemed to grow smaller as Bindi grew older. We wondered if we could buy the house next door and knock the two of them together. Our neighbours weren't planning to move, but we saw an opportunity when the people next door to them put their house on the market.

What happened next was the conveyancing equivalent of musical chairs. We bought the house two doors down and did a swap with our neighbours, so that we had two houses together. Then we put steel joists in the ceilings and knocked through the walls, creating one large home. I had a swimming pool built in the back garden – a long-held dream – although we soon realized it was so cold that nobody would swim in it.

When Mum came to visit, more work had to be done. She had bad arthritis in her ankles and couldn't get up and down stairs without help. I had a lift installed so that she could move between the three floors.

All of this proved to be ludicrously expensive. Again, I had no advice from my accountant warning me about over-capitalizing. In the end I had spent so much money that I was never going to be able to sell the house – not in an area like Sydenham. Buyers with that sort of money chose different neighbourhoods.

Bindi was eleven years old and growing up fast. One moment she seemed to be all ribbons and curls and the next she was trying make-up and playing Elvis Presley records non-stop.

Although mine was one of the most recognizable faces on children's TV, I had never stopped to think how my celebrity might affect Bindi. All her friends felt as though they knew me because they watched me every Saturday afternoon on TV.

Bindi came home from primary school one day and said, 'What does it mean when kids say, "You lucky pig. Your dad's rich"?'

'I'm not rich.'

'But why do they say that?'

'Because I'm on television.'

Bindi didn't understand this. She had grown up watching me on TV and stage, and a lot of it seemed very boring. To her my job was no different from any other job. Yet she had to endure snide remarks, petty jealousies and comments behind her back. 'Just because you're Rolf Harris's daughter . . .' people would say, or '*You* have a famous dad.' She had no way to deal with this and it made her feel very separate, isolated and alone.

I tried to help her. I went along to her school and gave a talk and did a painting for the annual fête. I wanted the kids to see I was an ordinary bloke, no different from the other dads. I don't know if it helped. There were many times when Bindi began to wish I was someone else entirely; someone she didn't have to share with every other child. I didn't know the full extent of her feelings of isolation until much later. She didn't want to upset me or appear disloyal. She felt it was just *her* problem but she didn't have any clever words to deal with it.

She was fiercely loyal to those who proved themselves to be real friends. At the same time she could be very unforgiving if someone let her down. One day she walked into the classroom and it was obvious all the kids had been talking about her because of the terrible guilty silence that followed. Bindi's best friend was in the group, and though they remained friends Bindi never felt she could trust her fully after that.

Although the teasing was hard, the loss of identity was perhaps worse. Instead of being accepted for herself, Bindi was always 'Rolf Harris's daughter'. And she began to question whether people liked her for who she was, or because of me.

Because I was away so often, I tried to make up for things when I got home. I'd take her swimming at Crystal Palace just up the road, or we'd all go to the movies in the West End. In restaurants we used to scribble on the paper tablecloths, drawing wonderful cartoons and coming up with adventures. Bindi did the narrating and we both did the artwork. We also drew wonderful adventure stories on great sheets of cartridge paper using coloured felt pens. The stories were full of giants, wizards and fairy tale characters, with a normal group of youngsters caught up in this fantasy world.

One of my favourite photographs of Bindi and me was taken when she was three and a half or four years old. I'm standing in front of a huge roll of rehearsal paper doing a big painting of her, and she has her own little paint brush and is working next to me.

Sadly, the extra attention I gave Bindi lasted only a day or two before I threw myself into the next project.

I expected a lot of Bindi. Perhaps that's a legacy of her being an only child. I wanted her to be happy, of course, but often I tried to teach her to do things my way, rather than letting her explore and find her own path.

Chapter Fifteen

'THE GENDARMES' DUET'

AFTER A CONCERT IN CANADA MANY YEARS AGO I WAS approached by Eunice Sidwell, a schoolteacher who wanted to get her children singing some of my songs.

Eunice explained that she couldn't find any of my sheet music, so I offered to write out the songs for her. I used my own musical shorthand, hoping the kids would find it easier to relate to. A few days later, Eunice contacted me again. She had been amazed by how easily her students were able to pick up on my simplified music writing and play the tunes.

That chance meeting led to the creation of 'Instant Music' – a wonderful system for teaching children to play songs. Instead of getting bogged down in the theory early on, they could almost immediately be playing things that normally would take them weeks to learn. They could also gradually pick up the theory while playing and enjoying songs they knew.

Thanks to Eunice, the new method won tremendous support in Canada. Unfortunately, when I tried to introduce it into Britain, the howls of protest and ridicule were almost deafening. The word 'instant' was a total anathema to the music purists, who were horrified by the idea of making something easier or giving it broader appeal.

As a thank you, Eunice gave me a copy of a book which she said had changed her life. *Try Giving Yourself Away* was written by David Dunn in the 1930s and recounted the story of how he'd been travelling in a sleeper berth on a famous train called the Twentieth Century, en route from Chicago to New York.

He was woken in the middle of the night by the roar of the twin train going in the opposite direction. As he lay awake in the darkness, he began wondering where the eastbound and westbound Centuries had passed. Unable to get back to sleep, he put on a dressing gown and wandered down to the club car. He said to himself, 'What a good advertising slogan that would be – "Where the Centuries Pass".'

On a piece of paper, he began sketching a picture of two trains passing each other in the night. In the background he portrayed the lights of a little town. Across the top he wrote: 'Where the Centuries Pass'. He also thought of all the different promotional ideas, such as interviews with the train drivers and the mayor of the little town nearest the passing point. There could be articles in the *Saturday Evening Post* and *Life*.

In the morning, when the train pulled into New York, he had five pages of ideas. He put them all in an envelope and wrote a note to the railroad company which basically said, 'I've had a wonderful trip on your train. I came up with these ideas. By all means use them, with no strings attached. I'm not looking for payment or recognition.'

A few days later he received a thank you letter from the company informing him that the two Centuries normally passed each other near the little town of Athol Springs, New York, nine miles west of Buffalo.

A year later, as David Dunn walked down the steps of Pennsylvania station, he looked up to see a poster bearing the slogan 'Where the Centuries Pass'. It had a wonderful piece of artwork, just as he'd suggested, showing an oncoming locomotive and the lighted observation platform of the other train passing on a curve, with the lights of a little town glimpsed in the background. The poster finished up in railway stations and hotel lobbies all over America and each time David Dunn caught sight of 'his' handiwork, it gave him enormous pleasure.

When he tried to work out why he gained so much joy from what he'd done, he realized it was because he had done it with no desire for reward. He had *given* the idea away, rather than trying to make money from it.

From then on, he began looking for other opportunities to make himself feel that good again, to 'give himself away'. He started going out of his way to compliment people. If he saw a window display that was eye-catching, he praised the store and asked them to pass on his compliments to the person responsible. If he read an article that he liked, he would send a postcard to the author saying how much he had enjoyed it.

Try Giving Yourself Away had a profound impact upon me. In particular it crystallized my philosophy of being nice to people and giving them my time. The world didn't have to be dog eat dog.

I also learned, as David Dunn had discovered, that it takes courage to compliment total strangers because they suspect some ulterior motive or that you're trying to con them. When you say to a woman in a lift, 'Gosh, don't you look stunning,' or, 'What a wonderful dress. It's the colour of the sun rising,' you have to be prepared to be snubbed, or misunderstood, or treated with suspicion. But if someone can accept the compliment in the spirit in which it's been given, they go away walking on air. At the same time you feel great for making them feel good. Everybody benefits.

At times I've given myself away and got back more than I expected. In Sydney one morning, I was coming down in the hotel lift and was joined on the fourth floor by a big American wearing a bright floral shirt in red and white.

'What a stunning shirt!' I said.

'You like it?'

'Yeah.'

Me and Bruce: he's still my big brother, but now he's my manager as well.

FAMILY PORTRAITS

(Above) My portraits of Mum and Dad.
(Below) Bindi's wonderful portrait of my mum.

OPPOSITE (Top) Revisiting the Harrises' old home in Sully in Wales. Dad hadn't been back since he was 15. Check the painting trousers. *(Below left)* With Mum and Dad during their world tour in 1977. *(Below right)* Opening a family exhibition, 'Art in the Lives of Alwen, Bindi and Rolf Harris', at the Halcyon Gallery, Birmingham, December 2000. © Zoë Jelley

WORKING WITH CHILDREN AND ANIMALS

From humble beginnings *Animal Hospital* kept coming up with new ideas, such as 'going west' with Tippi Hedren *(left)* and Bo Derek *(below right)*. BBC

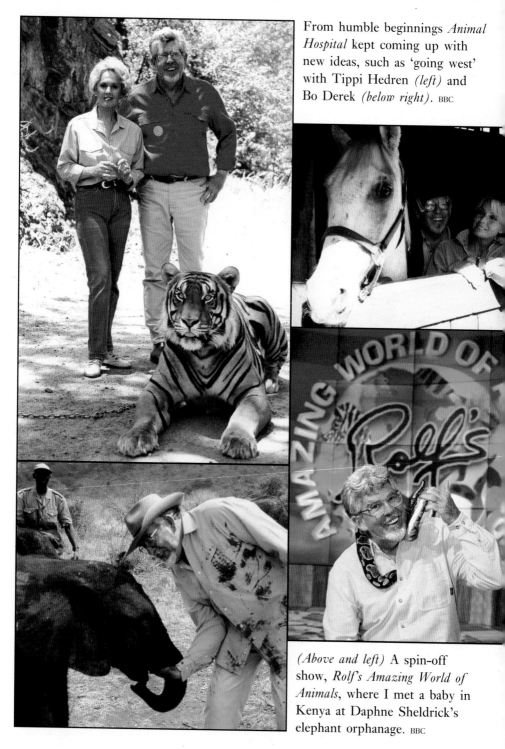

(Above and left) A spin-off show, *Rolf's Amazing World of Animals*, where I met a baby in Kenya at Daphne Sheldrick's elephant orphanage. BBC

(Right) Boxing a kangaroo down under.

(Below) Working with the Prince's Trust in 1995. © Alpha *Rolf's Cartoon Club* with Andy Crane. HTV

(Above and right) Whale-watching in Canada for *Rolf's Amazing World of Animals.*

REDISCOVERED

AUSSIE WOBBLES HIS WAY INTO MERCURY'S SHOES

SUNDAY MIRROR

MAGAZINE

APRIL 21, 1996

Rock 'n' Rolf
A BOHEMIAN IN RHAPSODY

'Rock's Renaissance Man'. © Syndication International

What a buzz! Glastonbury in 1998 *(above left)* and in 2000 *(below right)*.

(Above right) One man and his didge.

(Left) Doing 'Stairway' at Gawsworth Hall, Macclesfield, in 1998.

OVERLEAF No worries, mate: the boy from Bassendean comes home, 70 years young.

'It's yours.'

He began taking it off and wouldn't take no for an answer. By the time we reached the ground floor he was bare-chested. The doors opened and an elderly couple in the foyer stared in disbelief at me clutching a floral shirt next to a half-naked man.

Since then I've done exactly the same thing once or twice when someone has admired a shirt of mine. It's a great feeling, although I try to make sure that I'm never far away from another shirt.

Religion has never been a big part of my life and I've never regarded myself as a particularly spiritual person. Mum's dad had been a lay preacher but Dad was very anti the Church. He thought that religion caused more problems than it solved, including most of the wars in the world.

When I was about ten years old, I spent a couple of months telling myself, 'Don't worry about anything, God is in charge.'

In particular, I remember leaving my only pair of sandals in the grass on a vacant block of land after I'd been climbing trees. I didn't realize until three days later and I set off on my bike to find them.

'Don't worry,' I said to myself as I cycled up the track in the dark, 'God will have sorted it out. He'll look after me.'

According to my limited knowledge of God, He would have known I was going to lose my sandals because He knows everything. He would also have known that I was going to call on His help and, given that I was a pretty good kid, He would have made sure my sandals were still there for me.

This is exactly what happened. I found the sandals, put them on and cycled home again. I thanked God in a matter-of-fact way because, once again, I was only telling Him the obvious.

My newfound religious bent was relatively short lived. Faced with Dad's total scepticism, I found it difficult to answer his arguments about why God would let terrible things happen to good people – even those who believed in Him.

The only time I ever saw my father rude to anybody – and it

came as a real shock – was when two Seventh Day Adventists came down the path to the door.

'Have you read your Bible?' they asked.

'Get off my property!'

I turned and looked. Dad was normally the most charming man you could ever meet.

'We just wanted to ask—'

'Get off my property. Now! Go!'

His face was set in stone and his fists were clenched. I had never seen him so angry.

I can't remember exactly when in my life I started to get interested in spiritual things. In many ways I began questioning why I had been so lucky. I can count at least twenty times in my life when, according to the law of averages, I should have been dead. Some of them were childhood incidents, like when I fell in the river before I could swim, but managed to survive. If I'd fallen into shallower water I could easily have been stuck in thick mud with my head under water. Teddy Merritt's baby brother died this way ten years later.

Sometimes I was too reckless for my own good. When I was about eleven, I tried to climb the tallest gum tree in the neighbourhood, showing off to all my mates. Using a rope, I threw one end over the nearest branch, which was horizontal and about twenty-five feet up. Then I tied a slipknot that I could sit inside (potentially lethal in itself). Bouncing my bottom up off the rope and pulling like crazy with both hands, I managed to inch myself upwards.

After fifteen minutes, I reached a point where my chin was level with the branch. I let go of the rope and reached out with both hands to grab hold of the smooth wood. Of course, in that split second the branch had disappeared and gravity was hurtling me downwards. The next thing I remember is having a wonderful dream. I looked up through the mist at all these tall tree trunks. Only they weren't trees, they were the legs of my mates. They were standing over me, sure that I was dead.

A year later, after swimming practice one evening, I went

running across a road to get the trolley bus. It was drizzling with rain and Mum was coming behind me. I saw two cars approaching from the right, with their lights glinting off the wet road. I waited until they passed and set off like a rabbit without glancing to my left. I was running flat out when I heard Mum's scream. It was like no other sound I'd ever heard her make. The urgency froze me dead in my tracks.

At that precise moment, the trolley bus barrelled past me at top speed. Its wheels made a *wish, wish, wish, wish* sound on the wet roadway. If I had leaned forward an inch it would have clipped the buttons of my shirt and taken off my glasses.

Mum had made a split-second decision. Her scream would either stop me, or make me jump forward in surprise. It saved my life. For months afterwards, she and I both had dreams where my bones were crunched under the wheels of the bus.

Of course, everybody has near misses. It might be a road accident or a late change in travel plans that put you on a different train or plane from the one that crashed. But when I add up how often it has happened to me, I start to wonder whether there isn't somebody up there protecting me. Maybe He or She has a plan.

If I do have a higher purpose, I think it's to bring a little happiness and make people smile. I might not change the world, but hopefully just a tiny piece of it.

When people stop me in the street, or ask for an autograph, I happily give them my time. I stop and chat and ask where they're from. Normally we find something in common. Complete strangers feel as though they know me. They tell me jokes and hard luck stories in equal measure.

Wearing your heart on your sleeve is not seen as a very Australian trait. Blokes are supposed to be tough and dispassionate. That's rubbish! There's a sensitive side to all of us. Maybe by showing my emotions, I can encourage other men to do the same.

My most dramatic near-death experience came on a sunny afternoon in Berkshire where I was opening a factory as a favour for the

Aussie owner, Ken Mackintosh. A photo opportunity had been set up with horses and a coach.

'Any chance you could ride up top with the driver?' Ken asked me. 'It's better for the photographs.'

'Yeah, sure.'

Phyl Rounce climbed inside the coach along with Ken's wife who was recuperating from a recent operation and had her forehead swathed in bandages. The under-coachman also rode inside because I had taken his seat.

I clambered up on the driving bench next to the coachman who wore a top hat and carried a long coachman's whip.

'Alright in there, ladies?' I asked.

'Fine, thank you,' said Phyl.

We set off up the hill towards Windsor Castle. Ken followed us in his Mini with a photographer friend. The plan was to pick up the Mayor of Windsor at the gates of Windsor Castle and then drive to the factory for the opening ceremony.

It was a great view from the top of the coach and I loved the sound of horses' hooves on the hard surface.

Halfway up the hill, the lead horse started to lean into it. He bunched his shoulders, put his head down and wanted to run. The horse on the right went with him and they broke into a gallop. The driver pulled back on the reins but this seemed to make them more determined. The harder he tugged, the faster they galloped.

We were now racing up the hill and I could hear the metal-rimmed wheels bouncing crazily over the asphalt. White-faced and sweating, the coachman handed me his long whip and top hat. He tightly wound the reins round both hands for better purchase and then pulled back with all his weight. It made no difference at all.

A lone cameraman had set up his tripod on the grass verge to get a shot of the coach as we made the sharp left turn towards Windsor Castle. Instead we kept going straight ahead. He looked up, his mouth wide open in amazement. His camera was facing the other way and the index finger of his left hand pointed in the direction that we were supposed to go. It hung in the air like a question mark.

Ahead of us, parked at the kerb, was a gleaming new grey Jaguar. We were heading straight towards it. I pushed my hips sideways, as if my bodyweight could somehow move the coach to the right. It didn't work. The left wheel ripped off the mudguard of the car with a sickening crunch.

It was quite a jolt and I wondered if we had lost a wheel. I turned to ask the coachman but found an empty seat. Spinning around, I was in time to see our driver land flat on his back on the road behind us. It sounded like a watermelon being dropped from a great height. Surely he was dead.

The reins were still wrapped around his hands and were slowly unravelling as he was dragged along the road on his back. His hands came free at the last possible moment before he would have hit a concrete traffic island. I was just able to see him struggling to get to his feet before the coach blocked my view.

Lathered in sweat and with their hooves pounding, the horses went thundering down the centre of the road between cars parked on either side. I sat transfixed on the driver's bench, clutching the long whip and the top hat. I couldn't imagine two more useless things. Ahead the road was getting narrower. Beneath me the asphalt blurred with the speed. It seemed as though I was thirty feet above it.

What to do?

John Wayne would have leaped onto the back of the nearside horse, pulled back on the bit and ridden him to a halt. That's what all the cowboys used to do on those runaway stagecoaches in the Saturday afternoon matinees in Bassendean.

Looking up, I realized it would soon be over. Straight ahead was a huge stone wall. The road turned slightly left at the wall and then straightened up to go through two tall iron gates. Only one of them was open.

It's true what they say about your life passing before your eyes when you're about to die, but in my case, everything went into slow motion. It was as though someone flipped a switch and the whole scene was being shown one frame at a time. I began to make my farewells to everyone I knew and held dear. To Alwen and Bindi, Mum and Dad . . .

The sound also slowed down. The flashing hooves and clattering wheels became a dull buzz rather than a deafening roar. My knuckles were white as I clutched the top hat and whip against the driver's bench. I couldn't move.

The wall approached but the horses showed no signs of slowing. Surely they must stop. Suddenly, back to real time again, they jinked to the left at breakneck speed and straightened up. The coach flashed through the space left by the one open gate. Ken Mackintosh in the chasing Mini told me afterwards that he clocked our speed at 38 mph as we shot through the opening with what seemed like a quarter of an inch to spare on either side.

I had no time to be relieved. We were now racing across grass, heading for an iron fence with spikes along the top. The horses saw the fence at the same moment I did and turned instantly 90 degrees to the right. At that speed the laws of physics took charge. The right wheels of the coach left the ground. For a brief moment the whole rig seemed to balance on a 45-degree angle. Then it tipped over, still going flat out.

A photograph exists somewhere, taken by the man in the passenger seat of the Mini. It shows a very blurred coach with its right wheels off the ground and an equally blurry image of me, with my backside about a foot above the driver's bench, still clutching the whip and the top hat.

I don't remember hitting the ground, but my legs must have bent and tucked one behind the other. I looked up to see the black mass of the coach falling towards me, inch by inch, in slow motion once again. Very dispassionately I reasoned that I was going to die or be seriously injured. If the coach landed on my legs, bones would be broken. If it landed across my hips I'd never walk again. Across my chest or head and it was 'Goodnight Irene'.

I said goodbye to loved ones once again as the sky disappeared. The black mass kept falling.

Bang! My left knee.

Suddenly everything went into real time again. The coach skated away on its side at thirty miles an hour. I lay on the ground, blinking up at the blue sky.

Slowly I stood up and moved my arms and legs, trying to work out if anything had been broken. An amazing thing had happened. The weight of the coach had punched my left leg into the moist earth down to the level of the grass. There was a perfect imprint, like the mould for a plaster cast. Only a foot away was a solid gravel path. If I had fallen there, the coach would probably have crushed my leg to a pulp. I held both hands out in front of me – not a sign of a tremor.

I looked across to see what had happened to the others. The coach had come to rest on its side a couple of hundred yards away. Phyl and Ken's wife were climbing out of the door, which was now technically the roof. The horses were standing nearby, lathered in sweat and snorting.

Then I noticed Ken's car. The roof of the Mini had been crushed. In a bid to stop the runaway coach, he had cut diagonally across the grass from the gate and driven directly in front of the horses. The frightened animals reared up and smashed the roof with their front hooves, while Ken and the photographer jumped clear.

We all stood there in shock and amazement, surveying the devastation. A little old lady walking a pair of long-haired dachshunds wandered by.

'You doing this for a film, are you?' she asked. We all stood and stared at her, slack-mouthed. After a long wait, she tried again. 'Doing this for a film?'

Nobody could think of an answer.

At the age of fifty, I'd spent roughly half my life in Australia and half in Britain, or travelling in between. People often asked me where I felt most at home. I couldn't honestly tell them.

I had never shaken the feeling of uneasiness because of the way I spoke. No matter that I'd been honoured by the Queen, or won various awards, all it took was someone to murmur, 'I say, old boy,' with that well-known accent, and I immediately felt second-rate somehow.

I had seen a number of Australians tackle this sort of thing in their own way. Some became more aggressively Australian, pouring beer over people's heads in pubs to show they weren't affected by it, while others lost their suntans, adopted the accent and sank into the background by becoming 'English'.

I wasn't about to do the latter. The success that I had enjoyed had come because I had been myself – unashamedly Australian. Nineteen million people speak with my accent. Why should I be ashamed of it?

With hindsight it seems ridiculous to have spent half my life believing that people with upper crust accents were trying to make me feel inferior or to put me in my place. It was simply the way they spoke. This might seem pretty obvious, but I had neither the insight nor the powers of observation to realize it sooner. Instead, I was weighed down with preconceived prejudices.

For example, it wasn't until the late seventies that I heard a symphony orchestra for the first time. I was in Canada and the Vancouver Symphony approached me and asked if I would do a series of children's concerts with them.

'Oh, gosh, my stuff isn't for you,' I said, being very honest.

'Why not?'

'Well, it isn't . . . you know . . . suitable. You're used to doing Bach and Mozart and stuff.'

'Children love your songs. We want to show them that a symphony orchestra isn't daunting, or unattainable. Everyone can enjoy it.'

I still wasn't entirely convinced, but I agreed to give it a go.

Barry Booth wrote all the orchestrations and symphony charts for my material. At our first rehearsal, I was incredibly nervous. I was used to having a little four-piece band, or at most a ten-piece. Now I had eighty musicians and a conductor. They were tuning up and chatting to themselves. I somehow imagined these brilliant musicians would look down on my songs as beneath them.

The orchestra took up such a large space it created an immediate problem with the sound. The percussionists were right at the back and the sound reached me fractionally late. I found myself slowing down to keep in time with them. Eventually the conductor stopped and Barry took me aside.

'It's not working,' he said.

'I know. It's getting slower and slower.'

'You're listening to the music.'

'Yeah . . . and?'

'Well, you can't do that with a symphony orchestra. You have to ignore the evidence of your ears. Watch the man with the baton. Watch his hands. Stick to his down beat.'

Apart from that disastrous day at Expo in Japan I had never had to ignore what I was hearing during a concert. I found it incredibly hard to switch off and simply go with the conductor. After a few false starts, however, things came together. The sound was amazing. Suddenly my songs had a whole new depth and seemed to resonate through every corner of the concert hall. I began to realize what I had been missing all those years. And I wished that someone had given *me* the opportunity as a child to see a symphony concert. Maybe then I wouldn't have grown up with the notion that such music belonged only to the privileged few.

In 1979 I had another chance to work with a symphony orchestra. It was the 150th anniversary of the founding of West Australia and I was back in Perth for a special anniversary concert. Barry still had all the orchestral charts from Vancouver and we began rehearsing at the brand new entertainment centre. The concert was to be filmed for an ABC television special.

Barry and I came up with the idea of getting my dad up on stage. I knew that he'd never agree voluntarily. Dad was such a shy person he would have caught the first bus to Kalgoorlie, four hundred miles in the other direction, if he knew what I had in mind.

There was a great song that we used to sing together when I was a kid, once my voice had broken. 'The Gendarmes' Duet' was our party piece and I knew Dad would remember the words. We added it to our rehearsals with the West Australian Symphony Orchestra but kept it in reserve, leaving the decision until the last minute.

Dad was eighty-three years old but he didn't seem to have changed in my eyes. He was the same strong, silent and gentle soul who had cycled to work at the power station for forty years. That's why it came as such a shock when he'd suffered a fall a few years previously. He'd been up at the top of the bank where the sixteen steps went down to the river. He and I had fashioned those steps when I was a youngster. They were cut into the earth and the edges were supported by planks held in place by wooden stakes. One of the stakes had come loose and Dad decided to pull it out and drive it back in again more firmly.

As he leaned forward to remove the stake, he overbalanced and fell heavily, rolling down the bank and into the water. He collided with a post sticking out of the mud and bruised his rib cage. Winded and out of breath, he dragged himself out.

Later, when I talked to him on the phone, I told him to be more careful.

'You're no spring chicken any more.'

He agreed and tried to laugh it off, but I could tell he sounded less sure of himself. It didn't sound like Dad at all.

On the night of the concert in Perth, the new entertainment centre was the focus of the city. It was wonderful to see the reaction to my songs all written up for a symphony orchestra. I had a bunch of flowers that I was going to present to Mum. Because of her arthritis, I asked Dad to come on stage and collect the bouquet for her.

'What a marvellous man,' I announced to the audience.

He blushed.

'Do you know he came out to Australia as a young bloke from Cardiff – he and his brother. And when the First World War broke out, both of them enlisted . . .' I told the whole story, how Dad and Mum had been childhood sweethearts. How they lost touch and then met each other again during the war . . .

Dad stood nervously on stage beside me, wearing a suit and tie. I knew how much he hated wearing ties, so Mum must have insisted.

'You remember that song we used to sing when my voice broke?' I asked him.

'Yes.' Suddenly he twigged. 'Oh no.'

Barry had started playing the rousing introduction on the piano and the orchestra joined in. Dad looked left and right and I thought for a moment he might try to run.

'You remember the words, don't you? Do you feel like doing it with me now?'

He shook his head.

'You're among friends. What do you reckon?' I turned to the audience. 'Shall we do it?'

They chorused, 'Yeaaaaah!'

Not good enough, I thought. 'Shall we do it?' I shouted. This time they nearly raised the roof. I put my arm round Dad's shoulders. 'I'll start, so you'll be alright. Let's do it.'

All this time the orchestra had been vamping away, waiting for the song to start. I picked my moment. 'We're public guardians bold yet wary . . .'

Dad came in at the right spot, a bit shaky, but OK. 'And of ourselves we take good care.'

We each took alternate lines and did the harmonies on the chorus lines.

To risk our precious lives we're chary,
When danger looms we're never there.
But when we meet a helpless woman,
Or little boys that do no harm,

We run them in,
We run them in,
We run them in,
We run them in,
We show them we're the bold gendarmes.
We run them in,
We run them in,
We run them in,
We run them in,
We show them we're the bold gendarmes.

Dad tried to slow down, thinking I'd end the song there, but the music kept going. He looked at me as if to say, 'Oh, no, we're not doing another verse.'

We did the whole song. It was one of the best moments of my life to be up there with this man I loved so much, showing his sense of joy and fun to everyone. The crowd gave him a stunning ovation.

The videotape of the concert and the 45 rpm recording of that song are two of my most prized possessions. I had never thanked Dad for all he had done for me. I couldn't have found the words. But I wanted everybody to know how much I loved him. I hope he understood that.

Chapter Sixteen

'WHO AM I DOING ALL THIS FOR?'

O N A SCORCHING DAY EARLY IN THE NEW YEAR, I STEPPED OFF a plane at Sydney Airport and found Jack Neary waiting for me. Jack and I had been friends for years and he still kept an eye on my career.

'We have to talk.' He looked pale and careworn.

Feeling a sense of dread, I followed him into an office that had been set aside in the terminal.

'I'm afraid that I have some bad news. It's your dear old dad. He's very sick.'

I watched his lips moving, but the sound arrived a few seconds later.

'He's been diagnosed with cancer . . .'

Cancer! Was that what he said?

'. . . it's in his lungs . . .'

I had to sit down. Not *my* dad. He'd always been so fit. There had to be some mistake. He didn't smoke. Only smokers got lung cancer – didn't they?

'They think it's asbestosis,' said Jack. 'We've cancelled your shows. I've arranged a flight to Perth.'

We were standing in silence. Jack put his arm round my shoulders. 'I don't know what to say. I'm really sorry.'

The flight to Perth passed in a daze. The bottom had dropped out of my world. Mum met me at the airport. She looked smaller and stooped, as though weighed down with worry. Dad had always been so fit and healthy that Mum imagined she would go first and he would look after *her*, not the other way round.

We drove to Hollywood Hospital, near the university. When I walked into Dad's room, I could see the shock register on his face. Mum had kept my arrival a secret, thinking it would cheer him up, but it seemed to do the opposite. It gave him an inkling of how ill he really was. The doctors had told him, of course, but Dad didn't always believe the medical profession. Now he realized that I'd cancelled concerts and flown across the country. This *was* serious.

He wore a dressing gown and sat in a wheelchair. Periodically, he had to cough and clear his throat. He wiped the blood and phlegm from his lips with a handkerchief. For a man who had been active all his life, being out of breath all the time really brought him down.

Over the years he had grown to look more like his father, without the moustache. I once found a photograph of my grandfather in one of the art magazines that Dad used to have sent to him from England. I must have been sixteen at the time. From the photo, I painted a black and white portrait of George F. Harris as a secret birthday present for Dad. When I gave it to him, he spun on his heel and walked out of the room. He didn't say a word and the subject was never brought up again.

'It's funny,' said Dad, in between coughs. 'You remember when the main turbine broke down at the power station?'

I remembered it well, but I let him tell me the story again.

'You were just a teenager. The main turbine went down so they switched to the stand-by turbine which was running ragged. It was so out of alignment that it shook the whole place. All the pipes carrying hot water from the turbine were lagged with asbestos cloth. As the turbine shook, all the dust started drifting down. It was like working in a blue fog.'

It had taken them a month to fix the main turbine. Meanwhile, Dad had worked a daily eight-hour shift, breathing in this lethal fog. The tiny fibres of asbestos had become embedded in his lungs and forty years later they were killing him.

The doctors couldn't give us any idea how long he had left, so I spent as much time as I could with him over the next four days. Then I flew back to the east coast for the rest of my concerts. I was due back in England straight afterwards to start a new series of *Rolf on Saturday, OK!*

Dad was eventually allowed to leave hospital and go home. I talked to him on the telephone a few times and we had a laugh.

As soon as we could fit it in between work, Alwen and Bindi and I flew back to Perth to spend a bit of quality time with Marge and Crom.

We had two weeks and we booked into a hotel, hired a car and spent every minute we could with them at my old home in Bassendean. Dad was coughing a lot and was very embarrassed to have to carry a handkerchief with him at every moment to wipe away the stuff that he kept coughing up. He loved to sit on the shady side of the veranda where there might be a bit of cool breeze to make his laboured breathing easier.

As the days of our visit grew shorter, we were all dreading the farewell. We instinctively knew it would be the last time we'd see dear Crom. On the final day, Dad told Bindi how much he loved her and what a ray of sunshine she had been in their lives. Try as she might, Bindi was too choked up to say anything. 'I understand, I understand,' he said, patting her shoulder. 'I love you very much.' I was able to tell him how much I loved him and we exchanged a huge bear hug, although it still felt a bit strange to him. He made the effort to stand up to hug Alwen, who inadvertently stood on his toe, which gave him the chance to make a joke to avoid the awkwardness of the goodbye.

I was relieved we'd hired a chauffeured car to run us to the airport. I certainly couldn't have seen to drive. We were all of us in tears as we went slowly up the drive between the jacarandas and box trees Dad had planted and lovingly nurtured for nearly fifty years.

For my fiftieth birthday, with the help of the local television station in Perth, Mum and Dad made a video message. I had a party at the Hyde Park Hotel, inviting friends from all round the world. On the night we had a video machine set up to show the video messages. For some reason they couldn't get it to work. Afterwards, when Alwen and I managed to watch the video from Mum and Dad, I was glad we hadn't seen it on the night. Dad looked so frail and cadaverous that I would probably have cried in public.

He didn't last long after that. He collapsed in the middle of the night when he got up to go to the bathroom. Mum heard the thump and she found him sprawled unconscious on the floor. She couldn't move him – not even to make him more comfortable.

She phoned an ambulance and knelt on the floor beside Dad until the paramedics arrived. Mum's mind was in such a mess that she stood at the front door and watched the ambulance drive away. She should have gone with him. Somebody should have seen this frail old lady, totally lost without her husband, and said, 'Lock up the house, love. Bring your handbag. Come with us.' Nobody did.

Afterwards, she kept saying, 'I should have gone with him. I should have been with my Crom.'

He didn't regain consciousness and she never saw him again.

We all three happened to be in the bedroom when the call came from Bruce in Sydney. I put the phone down, stunned. My shoulders slumped and I said, 'Dad's dead'. We were instantly in a big sobbing hugging mess on the bed – it was an awful moment.

I had to drive to Chichester that night to be ready for a two-day shoot on *Hey Presto, It's Rolf!* the next day.

Early the next morning I phoned Jim Moir, the producer, in his room and asked him to come and see me. I broke the news to him, and I think that was the first time it really sank in. I don't think I heard anything Jim said. I stood by the window, a picture of grief, and the memories flooded over me. I thought of the faded box Brownie photograph of my dad looking lovingly down at the tiny baby in his arms. I was only a few weeks old when it was taken. And I remembered him silhouetted against the sun on the cross struts of the house, while I scaled the upright with a bag of nails between my teeth.

Once when I was very ill, he came home from his shift work in the middle of the night. I can still remember hearing his anguished cry of 'Rolf!' as he felt my icy cold forehead and for a split second thought I was dead.

There were so many wonderful moments. It seemed like only yesterday that I was coming home at night on the pillion seat of his old Matchless motorbike. I had one arm around his waist and my head pressed against his broad back. I'd press my right hand down hard over my right ear and lift it on and off, creating lovely rhythms with the sound of the engine and the rushing air.

Dad was always so gentle and just. As long as we told the truth, he always forgave us when things were carelessly broken or lost. I once dropped his favourite chisel into the mud and lost it while trying to cut footholds into a tall tree by the river. I dreaded what he would do and say, but he simply told me that I should have tied a piece of string round the chisel and looped it over my wrist.

Year after year he kept our bikes roadworthy, without ever complaining. He let us use his tools and then stood back and allowed us to learn from our mistakes.

He played our favourite games – the pretend egg in the eggcup and the mouth full of small change from the Christmas pudding. My favourite was when he'd get dressed up as an old Gypsy fortune-teller with awful lipstick and a shawl wrapped round his head. He'd come knocking at the door with his silly put-on voice and I would giggle until I nearly wet my pants.

Jim came back into my consciousness. 'What do you want to do, Rolf?' he said. 'We can cancel the shows.'

When I thought of all the people involved and how much preparation had been done I knew that we had to go ahead. The schoolkids had been rehearsing for weeks. I didn't want to disappoint them.

'I want you to make me a promise, Jim. Don't tell anybody about this. Please.'

Jim kept his word and we recorded the shows. It felt very strange to be singing and painting with all these kids, when behind every smile was the knowledge that Dad was gone.

A big crowd turned up for the funeral. Dad had always been a popular figure in Bassendean. Bruce gave a wonderful eulogy.

He spoke of how gentle, thoughtful and kindly our dad was. 'In my fifty-odd years I have met many men, but not one has been so kind, so self-effacing, so patient, thoughtful, cheerful, good-humoured – so good, really good – as Crom,' he said.

He told the story of how, at the age of ten, Crom plighted his troth to another ten-year-old, Agnes Margaret Robbins, with a sixpenny ring, bought with pennies saved over many weeks. And how in 1915 he joined the Australian Military Forces with his brother Carl, who died in the mud of Flanders.

'When I learned of his death in Sydney on Thursday at ten a.m., I wept,' admitted Bruce. 'Then I realized I was weeping for me – selfishly – because I had lost such a good, wise friend. I know his wishes were that not one of us should grieve. You knew him too – and you know I am right. He wanted us all to remember him the way he was – with his bright blue eyes, his shock of white hair, his fresh face, even in his eighties, and his quick quirky smile, his inner strength . . .'

Dad's ashes were returned to the land by the river that he loved. Meanwhile, on the other side of the world I spent that day in a daze. The very work ethic that I had inherited from Dad kept me toiling away, filling the hours between when I woke up and when I went to bed. Yet I couldn't get away from the question, 'Who am I doing this for now?'

All through my life, it was Dad's opinion I had valued most – his praise I sought above anyone else's. Mum had been my biggest fan, often boring people silly with stories and photographs of my latest doings, while Dad sat quietly in the background, proud of his sons in his own way. What was I going to do without him?

This sense of loss didn't go away. It was as though a storm had torn off my rudder and I was drifting aimlessly. It wasn't just Dad's death. I began to question a lot of things. The long periods away from home. The merry-go-round of clubs and theatres, singing the same songs and telling the same jokes. It had become a treadmill.

Although I still enjoyed performing live, I had lost touch with what I wanted to do and where I wanted to go. The idea of 'giving myself away' had been taken too literally. I couldn't say no to people. I said yes to everyone – charities, schools, hospitals, fêtes. It was first come first served.

Alwen could see me floundering. She tried to get me to slow down, but I didn't know how. I was the most disorganized person she had ever met. My office was like the Australian bush – messy and all over the place. I lost track of things and double-booked myself. On my rare days off, I'd be exhausted and spend most of my time sleeping.

Alwen, too, was struggling, although for different reasons. It had been sixteen years since she sacrificed her art to look after her family. With no creative outlet, she went through a very bleak time. Arthritis had been diagnosed in her shoulders – a legacy of lifting heavy sculptures. Meanwhile, some of the friends she had made at art college had forged successful careers. Alwen felt she had been left behind.

Bruce was the person who turned our lives around. I had never really known him when I was growing up. We were at daggers drawn most of the time and he left home and joined the army just when I reached an age when I might have become interesting to him.

We had seen each other regularly enough over the years – on my tours to Sydney, or when he came to London on business. Even so, we were very different people. Bruce didn't let his heart rule his head. He had a mind for business and weighing up options. He planned things carefully and rarely took risks unless they were calculated ones.

Not long after the funeral, he came to London. Straight away he could see that I was struggling. Perhaps he and Alwen had talked. I don't know.

In the kitchen one morning, we sat at the table drinking mugs of tea.

'How are you off financially?' he asked.

'I don't know.'

'How much money have you got in the bank?'

'I don't know.'

He looked at me in disbelief. 'What happens to the money you make?'

'Well, my agent banks it all. If I want anything I just ask. Then they give me fifty quid, or whatever I need.'

'So you're telling me that your money is in *their* bank account?'

'Yeah, I guess.'

'And *they're* earning interest on it.'

'Are they?'

'Too right. What do you get paid for a job?'

'I don't know.'

'What do you mean, you don't know?' Bruce leaned closer and pushed his cup to one side. I tried to explain that I didn't like discussing money.

'You remember what Dad used to say? "Money is the last thing you worry about."'

'But that doesn't mean that you let people rip you off,' said Bruce. 'Friends don't argue about money, but this is business.'

He couldn't believe that I didn't discuss fees until after a job was over and then just accepted the first figure I was offered.

'It means your bargaining power is absolutely nil,' he said. 'How do you know if you're getting what you're worth?'

I shrugged.

He asked if he could research my finances. I gave him the go ahead and he uncovered the extent of my earnings and expenses. Then he drew up some balance sheets. The results shocked me.

'You're going down the tubes,' he said. 'You're getting less money now than you were two years ago for the same job. Costs are going up because of inflation, but your fees haven't changed. Look at that tour last year. Everybody made money except you. By the time you paid Barry and the musicians and the agents' commissions you might have just broken even. That's three months of slogging your guts out for nothing.'

Even with the rough figures in front of me, I couldn't see what changes I could make. I didn't know how to do things any differently.

That's when Bruce suggested that *he* could manage me.

'But what about *your* career?' I asked.

'I'm taking early retirement next year. I'm giving them a year's notice.'

'But you're in Australia and I'm here.'

'That doesn't matter. We've got telephones.' Bruce convinced me it could work and a year later he retired from advertising. Immediately, he negotiated the end of my management contract with IAR. Phyl Rounce and the other senior agents were unhappy, but Bruce pushed it through anyway.

Afterwards we sat down at the same kitchen table in Sydenham and he insisted that I make some tough decisions. He put a notebook and pen on the table between us. 'I want to work out a five-year plan.'

'But Phyl used to always tell me that in show business it wasn't possible to plan ahead,' I said.

'Rubbish! You might not be able to plan your next job, but you can decide what direction you want to take.'

He drew a column down the centre of the page. 'OK. Where do you want to be financially and professionally five years from now?'

'Well, I want to be financially secure. I want enough money to send Bindi to art college, if that's where she wants to go . . .'

Bruce wrote this on one side of the page.

'Where do you want to be professionally?'

'Well, I'd like to get back into mainstream television. I don't want to be for ever associated with kids' shows.'

'OK.' He wrote this down on the other side.

He kept adding to each column until I'd exhausted my ideas. It finished up looking like a wish-list and I couldn't see how it was supposed to help me.

'From now on you pick and choose the jobs you do,' Bruce explained. 'At the moment you use a scattergun approach of shooting everything that moves and hoping some of them fall into your lap.'

'OK, but which ones do I choose?'

'Well, for a start you must stop doing all these charity shows for nothing.'

'But they're good causes.'

'Yes, but you're doing twelve charity gigs to every paid gig. You're so busy working for nothing that you have no time for paid jobs.'

It was true. I'd been 'giving myself away' to the point where I had nothing left over.

Bruce also argued that I was losing my value to charities because I wasn't appearing on television regularly enough. 'Keep this up and the charities will eventually stop calling. They'll drop you like a hot cake and go for somebody else. They don't care about *your* future.'

In the past I had always taken the view that charity work was far nobler than paid jobs. Fees were never discussed. It wasn't an issue. Bruce wanted to change this.

'I'm not saying that you don't do charities,' he said. 'But only do the ones you really want to do. And if you're going to do a charity gig, you must charge them your full fee. Let them know what you're worth. If you want to donate your fee back to them, then write them a cheque afterwards.'

According to Bruce, when people get something for nothing, they think it's worth nothing.

'That's when you turn up and find there's nobody there to meet you,' he said. 'People wander by and say, "Who are you again?" Instead of a dressing room you have to change in the kitchen, or behind a screen. And if you're lucky they might scrounge up a sandwich for you to eat.'

All of this rang true because it *had* happened to me. I also remembered Bob Harbin telling me exactly the same things.

From that day onward I began to charge a full fee for charity jobs, even though I normally handed the fee back. The difference it made was dramatic. Suddenly, I had charities offering to send cars for me. Dressing rooms were provided, with bowls of fruit and offers of meals. They began asking how I wanted to be introduced and what sort of lighting I liked.

It's true what they say – people don't appreciate things they get for nothing. If something is free then it must therefore be cheap, or second-rate.

Having drawn up a five-year plan, we worked out exactly what I wanted to achieve by the end of each year. The result was quite amazing. Three months after Bruce took over managing my career, I had reached my financial target for the whole year. I couldn't believe it! I had more time to do things on mainstream TV. This didn't mean turning my back on children's programmes, but I didn't limit myself.

The bond between Bruce and me grew to be incredibly strong. Yes, we still argued like mad. We had different opinions and attitudes about most things. But he turned my life and career around just when I had started to question who I was doing it all for. It hadn't just been for Dad. I had Alwen and Bindi and a legion of wonderful friends. And I also had a *need* inside me.

Part of what used to drive me was the thrill of trying new material. I had lost that. Maybe I'd grown too comfortable, or become complacent.

As a result I'd missed a string of opportunities. For example in 1976 at the American Bicentennial celebrations I performed at the United Nations building in New York to stunning applause. Afterwards, an American agent wanted to book me on a college circuit around the States, but Phyl Rounce had told me not to do it. She said it was beneath my dignity to play to college kids.

I should have put my foot down and insisted that I go, but I lacked the courage. Bruce and Jack Neary were furious when I told them. Here was an opportunity to break into a hugely lucrative market with a whole new audience that had never heard most of my stuff. It could have been great.

Mistakes like that made Bruce even more determined to get my career on track. He arranged for me to sign with Billy Marsh at London Management, to handle my UK bookings. Billy represented a lot of big names and was a real gentleman.

For the first time in my life I felt as though I was in *real* 'showbiz'. Every contract was spelled out and I received a copy. Cheques were banked in my account within two days and I got a statement through the post. I felt like a respected and successful entertainer.

When it came to touring and my concerts, Bruce was brutally frank. 'Your act hasn't changed in twenty years,' he said. 'People have seen and heard it all before. It's old hat.'

'It seems to be working alright to me,' I said defensively. 'People love hearing old favourites.'

'Yeah. That's fine, but what are you giving them that's new? When you go back to a town that you haven't visited for two years, what are you doing that they haven't heard before?'

I didn't answer.

'Nothing. Absolutely nothing.'

Phyl Rounce had been telling me this for years and I hadn't listened to her. It was even harder hearing it from Bruce.

But where did I get new material from? I had lost confidence. I'd forgotten how to find new songs and create new routines. In the past this sort of thing had come naturally. I bumped into people who gave me songs or I came up with my own ideas.

'I can't find songs for you,' said Bruce, 'But you have to start trying new things. Be adventurous.'

Maybe he was right. For a start, I agreed to do pantomime. For years people had been asking me, but I always said no. Australians have no tradition of panto and I didn't think I had anything to offer. The person who convinced me otherwise was Paul Elliott, one of the biggest producers of pantomimes in the country. A former actor and star of the long running *Dixon of Dock Green*, Paul was responsible for bringing back the traditional style of pantomime which had been replaced by loose variety shows where pop stars plugged their records.

Paul had tried to get me to do panto for years because he said that I'd be perfect for it. 'Everything you do in your own stage shows is exactly the sort of thing that happens in pantomime,' he told me. 'The way you interact with the audience and get them involved – the lovely little asides and improvisations. You're able to break through that imaginary fourth wall in a theatre and stroll forward and talk to people as if they're all old friends. That's what panto is all about.'

My first panto was *Cinderella* at Lewisham Town Hall. Lorraine Chase played the lead role and the radio personality Pete Murray was Baron Hardup, Cinderella's father. I played Buttons, the Baron's bellboy, who is secretly in love with Cinderella.

Paul had been right. Panto was perfect for me and I kicked myself for not having done it sooner. I loved being able to step out of the role, walk to the front of the stage as myself and say, 'G'day. Now let me tell you what happens next . . .'

Although panto often seems off-the-cuff and spontaneous, in reality it's very tightly structured. That's what makes it work so well. Everybody in the cast is aware of ad-libbing opportunities, but for the most part there is a very strict running order to give people time to prepare. Backstage, everybody keeps one ear on the tannoy system, calculating how many seconds or minutes they have before making their next entrance.

Being a newcomer, I had a lot to learn. During one performance

I was about to sing my Australian Christmas song 'Six White Boomers' when someone in the audience shouted, 'Sing "Two Little Boys".'

I faltered and somebody else echoed the request. More cries went up. Barry Booth was there on the piano. We knew it backwards. Why not?

I launched into 'Two Little Boys', completely unaware that I was throwing everybody backstage out of kilter. They all assumed that I'd do 'Six White Boomers' next, so no one rushed to get changed or in position. Instead of doing the Christmas song, I finished 'Two Little Boys' and said, 'Right, let's go to the ball.'

The curtain went up and nobody was on stage. I had to ad lib. 'Ah, well. I don't know where everyone is. They're supposed to be at the ball. Perhaps they're running late.' I made lots of silly sound effects and mucked around. Meanwhile, it was absolute pandemonium backstage as people pulled on costumes and wigs. Afterwards I apologized to the whole cast over the tannoy system.

I didn't make the same mistake again.

After living in Sydenham for sixteen years, I didn't really see us ever moving. Alwen had a different view of the future. Her idea of a perfect address is either right in the heart of the city, or out in the countryside, where she can ride or go for long walks.

The possibility of moving didn't come up until we visited some long time friends, Vince and Annie Hill, at their home on the Thames in Wargrave, near Henley. Alwen loved the house and so did I, especially because it reminded me of growing up beside the river in Bassendean.

Annie offered to send us the bumf from all the local estate agents and we began looking for riverfront properties. There were some lovely places in Bray near Maidenhead, but I was sure they were too expensive.

Mum had been staying with us and we took her for a drive to Bray one weekend. I remembered that Laurie Holloway and his wife Marion Montgomery lived in the area, so we dropped in and had a cup of tea.

'There's a place for sale just up the road,' said Marion. 'Let's go and have a look.'

The house had been empty for eighteen months according to Marion. It looked beautiful from the outside, with the Thames meandering past the garden and a big willow tree dipping its branches into the water. Colourful barges and rowers slipped by.

We can't afford this, I thought, but Mum convinced me to arrange an inspection. A few days later we drove back to Bray with an estate agent and walked through the house. The lounge was forty feet long with floor-to-ceiling glass down one side, bringing the river inside. The leaves were starting to turn and the skeletal shapes of trees were becoming visible beneath a riot of oranges and browns.

Mum took one look and said, 'It doesn't matter what it costs. You have to get this house.'

Bruce had only just taken over my affairs and I didn't know if the five-year plan was going to work, or how much we could afford. We started negotiations and managed to get the price lowered a little. The owner had been trying to sell it for so long, he was willing to compromise. Finally we agreed a price and I felt a mixture of elation and fear. Two days later another buyer emerged who offered the owner £10,000 more, but to his credit, he stuck by our agreement.

Within months, thanks to Bruce, I felt more relaxed. I also discovered that moving to Bray had a strange effect on the people booking me. I suddenly had more standing. I looked more successful and therefore *became* successful. The jobs started getting better and the money improved. Oddly enough I think Ronnie Corbett and Val Doonican had the same thing happen to them when they moved out of their south London homes.

Bindi didn't want to move to Bray. All her friends were in London and she loved her school and the teachers. There were arguments and tears as we packed our things. We sold her on the idea that she could live in the little cottage in the garden, away from the main house. At the age of sixteen, she was ready for the responsibility and freedom.

Parents aren't supposed to understand their adolescent children and I was no exception. I couldn't fathom Bindi's unhappiness and solitude. It went beyond normal teenage angst. She seemed to be struggling over where she fitted in and what she wanted to do with her life. At school she felt as though she was sharing her dad with every other child in the country. She didn't see any special place for herself – not even in *my* life.

I had no idea that she felt like this and it came as a bombshell when she told me. We were walking along the banks of the river, taking the dog for a run. As always, I made eye contact with people, smiling and waving. I love that moment of connection when I catch someone's eye, or the wonderful double take when they recognize me.

A father with two young children stopped me and asked for an autograph. I chatted away to the kids, making them laugh, while Bindi waited nearby, throwing pebbles into the river. Further down the path, I stopped to chat with an elderly Scottish couple and their grandchild. We had a long discussion about the scenery around Loch Lomond.

When I said goodbye, Bindi fell into step beside me. After a few minutes she said in a matter-of-fact voice, 'Do you know that you pay more attention to any child who stops you in the street than you pay to me? You will give them more of your time and your total attention. Why didn't I ever have that?'

It felt as if she had driven a dagger into my chest. I tried to think of something to say in my defence, but I couldn't because what she said was true. We walked home in silence. I wanted to cry.

At home I told Alwen what Bindi had said.

'Why do you sound so surprised?' she said. 'You've always been like that. You seem to think members of the public have some prior claim on you. You forget that we're your family.'

'Oh, come on, that's not fair.'

'Isn't it? Well, look at what happens whenever we go out to a restaurant, or shopping, or for a walk. You can't go twenty yards without somebody stopping you. You smile and chat and sign autographs. But what about us? When do we get to have you? It's as if you have time for all the world but no time for us.'

I shuddered. I suddenly had a glimpse of why Bindi had grown up feeling so isolated and insecure. She must have had these thoughts for years, but it was only now that she was old enough to put them into words and tell me what was wrong. I wished that I could turn back the clock. I wanted to relive that part of life . . . to change things . . . to be a better father . . . but it was too late.

I remembered finding Alwen's diary after we came back from Australia and discovering how lonely and bored she'd been – to the point of absolute despair. Yet I'd been so blinkered and self-centred, I hadn't realized. Now I'd been guilty of the same thing. It is like the old story of the shoemaker's kids who never have decent shoes. Their father is so busy repairing other people's shoes that he forgets about his own children.

When I was young I used to go looking for somebody new to impress, grabbing kids and taking them home to see our place. But once I impressed each new kid I dropped him and went looking for somebody else. Nothing had changed. I was still trying to impress new people. It was like an addiction.

Alwen and Bindi were always telling me, 'You don't have to impress us. We *know* who you are.' Maybe that was half the problem.

Bindi had spent her childhood looking for ways to let me know that she existed. I could see that now. I should have seen it sooner. I should have made more time for her, but I was always away working. Even when I came home, I was up and out again. I just assumed that Bindi would get on without me; that she didn't care.

I was wrong.

How could I make up to her?

I made a resolution that from then on she and Alwen would get my undivided attention when I was with them. There had to be a public me and a private me. Instead of always stopping and chatting to people, I had to erect a sort of 'privacy' bubble round myself and avoid eye contact. Perhaps then we could find some space to be a normal family doing everyday things.

For the sake of Bindi and Alwen I had to change. It was a hard lesson to learn and I'm not there yet.

Chapter Seventeen

WHAT'S UP, DOC?

AFTER DAD'S DEATH THE LOCAL COUNCIL HAD CONTACTED ME. They passed on their condolences and said how much they'd admired my father.

'It's because we liked him so much that we haven't said anything about this before,' said the building inspector.

'About what?'

'The house. It doesn't comply with a lot of the rules and regulations. It isn't safe.'

I knew that a lot of Dad's work had been pretty makeshift. He had done the wiring himself and there were double adaptor plugs on top of double adaptor plugs all over the house.

'You'll have to completely redo the wiring and plumbing,' the building inspector said. 'And we'll have to look at the structural integrity.'

He sent me a long list of all the regulations that were contravened. Bruce and I had to make some terribly hard decisions. Dad had built the house with his bare hands. He had straightened every second-hand nail and added one room at a time when he'd had the money.

Much as we loved the old house, neither Bruce nor I had any desire to go back and live there. Yet both of us had so many memories locked up in those walls we hated to see it pulled down. One of the toughest decisions of our lives was to demolish our childhood home. It felt as though Dad was dying all over again.

The bulldozers moved in and we arranged to have a new house built for Mum. It was hard, being so far away, to keep any sort of control over the building. Mum didn't really like the new place. It wasn't the same without her beloved Crom. To make matters worse, she went out one day and a burglar broke in and stole the television and personal things. After that she was too frightened to stay in the house by herself.

Bruce and I tried to find a lodger or companion for her, but it wasn't easy. Her arthritis had grown worse and she normally needed a wheelchair to get around. The best option was a nursing home and we found a lovely place. Mum seemed to be happy.

Hazel, my first girlfriend, had stayed in touch and she used to visit Mum, bringing her gifts of books, fruit and flowers. Hazel had never forgotten the kindness Mum showed her when we were going out together. She was treated like the daughter that Mum never had. Deep down I think Mum wished that Hazel and I had stayed together and perhaps married, although at the same time she knew we weren't suited at all.

When Mum's health deteriorated she moved to another home which offered more intensive care. Bruce and I bought her a little electric wheelchair and she would scoot around the place, leaving black marks on the walls.

I tried to see her at least once or twice a year, whenever I was touring Australia. I was still doing my annual tours, which sometimes included New Zealand, Canada and South Africa. The anti-apartheid protests were reaching their peak and pressure was mounting to isolate South Africa.

I hated apartheid just as much as anybody else, but I didn't believe that I should stop touring South Africa. I'm an entertainer. My shows are a bit of fun and escapism. I'm not a protest singer and I don't make political statements. In my experience, protest songs only appeal to people who already believe in the cause. It's like preaching to the converted.

Rather than boycott South Africa, I demanded that all my shows be open to multi-racial audiences. As a result, on my previous tour, five theatres that were previously 'whites only' were opened to blacks and coloureds for the first time. One of them was in Bloemfontein, the heart of Afrikaner territory. I thought I was making a difference, but soon realized that only a few coloureds were turning up at the shows. It is one thing to create the opportunity, but another to break down a century of fear and distrust.

On that same tour I also insisted on doing some shows in the black townships. Ronny Quibell, the promoter of the tour, had tried to talk me out of it, but I held firm. I did two concerts in the townships – both open-air venues at dusty soccer grounds with scaffolding stands. The places were empty long before I finished. Ronny had been right.

If I'd been a rock 'n' roller, with gutsy chord changes and lots of decibels, it might have been OK. But so much of my show relied upon clever wordplays and comedy songs. The black audiences didn't understand most of what I did.

My last attempt to tour South Africa with Ronny caused a fearful ruckus. My visa permission hadn't come through by the time I was due to leave London, but Ronny told me to come anyway. He was confident that permission would be granted by the time I arrived and rehearsed with the band.

When I reached Johannesburg, several local journalists were waiting to interview me. Very few international acts were going to South Africa, which apparently made me newsworthy. Unbeknown to me, one of these journalists had rung the anti-apartheid campaign headquarters in Melbourne, Australia.

'What do you think about Rolf Harris touring in South Africa?' he asked.

'We didn't know he was going to,' was the honest reply.

'He's here now. He starts his concert tour on Saturday.'

Having admitted they had no idea I was touring, the spokesman, with his next breath, said, 'We *warned* Mr Harris not to go and we will have his Australian passport revoked if he ever appears on stage in South Africa.'

. The story, printed as fact in South Africa, was picked up and sent around the world. 'Rolf to Lose Aussie Passport' declared the headlines in Britain. Nobody bothered to find out if there was any truth in the story.

The snowball had started rolling. Members of Parliament in Australia attacked me for flouting international sanctions. I was accused of being an apologist for the apartheid regime. One MP from South Australia demanded that my passport be revoked. The Prime Minister, Bob Hawke, to his undying credit, stood up and said, 'It is not the policy of the Australian government to interfere with anybody legitimately making his or her living.'

All these stories were reprinted in the South African papers. I had journalists waiting in front of my hotel and following my every move. Meanwhile, I still hadn't received permission from the Ministry of the Interior to perform in South Africa.

'What are you going to do if you don't get the permit?' asked a journalist.

'I've made my stand quite clear on previous trips,' I said. 'I don't perform unless the venue is multi-racial. If I don't get permission, then obviously I go home.'

This resulted in a huge headline: 'Rolf Harris's Threat to the Minister of the Interior.'

I shook my head in disbelief. What threat?

My fate was sealed, of course. The Minister refused my visa and I flew all the way home again. On the flight, I kept trying to work out why the media in South African had sabotaged the tour. They were crying out for entertainers to visit their shores. As far as I could see, by manufacturing the controversy they had simply deprived people – of all colours – of the chance to spend a few hours being entertained by a bearded bloke who sang some funny songs and told a few stories.

*

My relationship with the media had always been very good. I didn't court controversy and I kept my opinions to myself. Entertainers aren't naturally political animals. We normally depend on making friends with everybody rather than risking alienating sections of the audience by making political statements or moralizing.

I had a small taste of what politicians must face in 1975 when I was elected King of Moomba in Melbourne. Moomba is a big cultural festival held every year, featuring a parade through the city's streets in which the king, or queen, rides on a float and wears a crown.

It's all good fun, except in 1975 there was a distinct whiff in the air. The city garbage collectors – better known as 'garbos' – had gone on strike for more money. The streets were piled high with garbage just as thousands of interstate and international visitors arrived for the festival. One Sydney newspaper wrote: 'Now It's Official: Melbourne Stinks.'

The union, of course, insisted the timing of the strike was purely a coincidence. The Mayor of Melbourne, Ron Walker, contemplated calling in contractors, but knew all hell would break loose. Instead, he convinced me to issue a 'royal edict'. At the next televised news conference, I blithely told all my loyal subjects to grab a broom and report to the town hall at 5 a.m. on Saturday.

Within hours telegrams began arriving from all over the country. Union leaders attacked me for trying to break the strike with 'scab' labour. I was interfering with a working man's right to strike to get a better deal for his family.

One of the telegrams declared, 'Call yourself King of Moomba? More like King Rat.'

I had never intended to disparage workers or unions. I didn't want to get involved.

A journalist found me the next day, sitting in the hotel coffee shop, with my head in my hands. 'How do I get out of this one?' I asked.

'Apologize.'

'But that's just going to upset a lot of other people . . . all those people who don't agree with the strike.'

'True.'

I withdrew the edict and apologized. As it turned out, hundreds of local scouts cleaned up the city for Moomba and nobody complained.

The whole episode had given me an inkling of how politicians must feel. I'm amazed they can do their job knowing half the people out there hate them.

I didn't often get caught out saying the wrong thing at the wrong time, although I had my moments. I once caused a major blue on a Qantas flight from the UK, when Barry Booth and I were sitting together in the first class compartment. I was wearing headsets with the music blaring in my ears. A steward came down the aisle carrying a tray of canapés. He was very effeminate, with a mincing walk, and he wore the most appalling wig.

Thinking I was speaking in a whisper, I turned to Barry and said, 'Get a load of the Irish jig on the poof.'

Because I couldn't hear myself, the comment came out at ten decibels. Every person in the compartment heard, including the poor steward, who almost dropped his tray. He went straight past us and didn't serve us another thing for the entire trip. Barry was so mortified he wanted to crawl out the window.

I've always been prone to putting my foot in it. When we were first married, Alwen agreed to kick me under the table if I started saying something inappropriate during a dinner party. The first time it happened, she kicked me so hard that I let out a yelp, having totally forgotten our arrangement.

At a party once we came face to face with a hugely pregnant woman. 'How yer goin'?' I said. 'Full o' beans?'

The lady very graciously said, 'I sincerely hope not.' She and Alwen burst into laughter and I went scarlet.

As well as saying the wrong thing, I was also accident-prone. On one tour of Canada with Alwen and Bindi, we stayed with Ken Stauffer in Vancouver. I got up early on Sunday morning to find Ken's youngsters and Bindi all watching some mindless children's TV show. Outside in the garden it was brilliantly sunny.

'This is ridiculous,' I said enthusiastically. 'Let's do something really interesting on this glorious day.'

I switched off the TV and mustered the bemused youngsters into a group. 'Right, follow me.'

I marched straight through a huge glass sliding door. I only realized my mistake as the glass began to bow outwards, but it was too late to stop.

With a bell-like ringing sound in a perfectly pitched A, the glass door exploded outwards. The lawn and rose bed were showered with minute shards of glass and I was lucky to get away with just a small cut to my knee.

The kids stood dumbstruck at first and then dissolved into uncontrollable laughter. Our gloriously sunny day was then spent picking up minute pieces of glass. Bindi and Alwen never let me forget. Even today they burst into laughter whenever I mention doing something 'really interesting'.

Perhaps my most embarrassing professional moment came when I met the folk singer Alan Mills on a TV show in Toronto. Alan and I were going to sing some songs together and I suggested 'The Old Woman who Swallowed a Fly'. I launched into singing it and Alan interrupted. 'You've got the wrong tune. It goes like this.'

He sang a bit, but I cut him off. 'No! That's the Burl Ives version. Dreadful tune! *This* is how it goes.'

I started singing the other melody again, but Alan stopped me. Very politely, he said, 'I should know what the tune is, Rolf. I wrote the song.'

End of discussion.

Rolf on Saturday, OK! had been running very successfully for six years but it had run its course. The BBC didn't renew the contract. Instead, they offered me a new show.

'We've got all these cartoons,' said the producer. 'Ninety-four of them to be exact.'

We were sitting in a small office at the Television Centre at Shepherd's Bush. I felt totally comfortable at the Beeb. It had been like a home from home for more years than I cared to remember.

'What sort of cartoons?' I asked.

'Bugs Bunny, Daffy Duck, Tom and Jerry. Warner Brothers stuff. They're part of a job lot. We've got a year to show them – one time only. After that we have to send them back.'

'And what do you see me doing?'

'Well, at the moment we're just slotting the occasional cartoon into the schedule when we have a gap. But we thought of you doing a half-hour show with them. You could introduce the cartoons and do drawings. Maybe you could draw a scene from each of them.'

It was a pretty simple brief. I had to watch the cartoons beforehand, choose particular scenes and then draw them on air before introducing the relevant cartoons. We filmed four shows on a single day, starting at nine in the morning. Each was exactly the same format and the only things that seemed to change were the cartoons and the shirts I wore. Oh yes, and the drawings.

From a programming point of view, it was cheap TV – one small studio, two cameras and a bunch of cartoons could fill half an hour of children's programming, but I found it nowhere near as challenging or interesting as past shows that I'd worked on. I loved doing the drawings and pointing out the odd mistake made by the animators, but the sameness of the show and lack of feedback from the kids watching made me question the format.

At the same time, on the other side of the world, my old mate Jack Neary had come up with a new vehicle for me. Jack was a founding shareholder of the newly built Sydney Entertainment Centre – the biggest concert venue in the city. A huge school choir had tested the acoustics of the venue and everybody marvelled at how much talent they showed.

This gave Jack an idea. If he could pull together a thousand performers from schools up and down the country, he could put on a stunning show. He would also guarantee himself an audience of nearly two thousand parents, even before he started counting grandparents, aunts, uncles, brothers and sisters and friends.

'We just need to base the show around a personality,' said Jack, as he kicked the idea around. 'Someone like you, Rolf.'

Bruce and I agreed to come on board and we got permission from the NSW Education Department to begin approaching schools. A remarkable woman came to the fore. Mary Lopez was a high school teacher and choir mistress from Sydney. She had a passion for music and the sort of electrifying personality that got kids off their sofas, away from their TV sets and singing songs. At her school, Epping Boys High, she did a deal with the sports master. Unless the boys turned up for choir practice they couldn't train for football. She convinced them that singing wasn't for sissies and created one of the best school choirs in the country.

Mary was asked to produce the first 'Schools Spectacular' and did an amazing job. She pulled together creative teachers from all over the State and they in turn inspired the children. The parents made the costumes and did the make-up. The only professionals on hand were the sound and lighting technicians and a few of the musicians who worked with the school bands. I did the introductions and sang the occasional song, but the show belonged to the kids. More than 8,000 people gave them a standing ovation at the end of the show.

It had been such a stunning success that the Schools Spectacular became an annual event. Some wonderful young singers emerged, including Human Nature, who later performed at the opening of the Sydney Olympics.

While the schoolchildren rarely put a foot wrong, I wasn't so lucky. One year I arrived for the Spectacular on the red-eye flight from Perth to Sydney. The plane landed at 6 a.m. having crossed the country during the night. Having had very little sleep, I tried to catch a few hours' shut-eye at a hotel before going to rehearsals.

Even after several coffees, I felt dizzy with exhaustion. All the scripts were waiting for me, but the type was too small for me to read properly. In the dressing room, I wrote it out again in long-hand, making it bigger.

We did a 'walk through' rehearsal and then full dress rehearsal, finishing only an hour before the show was due to start at 7.30 p.m.

I sat in my dressing room, totally exhausted, trying to remember everything I had to say and do. I cursed myself for cutting things so fine. I should have given myself a day to recover in Sydney.

'Five minutes, Rolf,' called the stage manager. I picked up the script to have a final read.

A very strange thing happened. I couldn't recognize the writing, or understand a single word on any of the three handwritten pages. I knew that I was definitely holding *my* script in *my* hand-writing, but I didn't believe it. It might just as well have been written in a different language.

There was a knock on the door. 'It's time, Rolf.'

I tried to shake off the sense of panic in my chest. I walked to the wings and heard voices wishing me luck. A host of children, all in costume, looked at me with expectancy. This was the biggest night of their lives.

I managed to get through the opening part of the show until we reached a point where I had to sing 'Send in the Clowns'. I sang the first line and my mind went blank. It was as though someone had wiped a duster across my memory. A hundred children were dancing in the arena dressed as clowns and two young solo dancers were performing an exquisite ballet up on stage.

I stopped and held my hand up. 'I'm sorry . . . I'll have to stop you. Can we stop the music?'

Everything slowed and the music died. The kids on stage and down on the arena floor were staring at me, unsure of what to do. This hadn't been rehearsed.

'I'm sorry, but I've had a complete blank. I can't remember a single word of this song.'

Eight thousand people in the audience let out a slight gasp of surprise. A handful laughed nervously, thinking I must be joking.

'If you'll just bear with me for a moment, I have to go to the dressing room where I have the sheet music. Just chat among yourselves for a minute. I'll be right back.'

I went sprinting out, past the backstage staff, whose mouths were hanging open. Grabbing the sheet music, I came running back. Nobody had moved. There was absolute silence.

'Please forgive me. I didn't have a single word in my head. Let's start again.'

This time, reading from the music, I managed to get through the song, and subsequently through the rest of the concert.

How could I fail to recognize my own handwriting? It was bizarre. With no other explanation, I put it down to exhaustion.

Alwen had been urging me to slow down for years. Occasionally, I made noises about cutting back on my commitments and spending more time with Alwen and Bindi, but something always came up. It was almost as though I had to keep moving because I knew no other way.

When the Commonwealth Games came to Edinburgh in 1986 I finally had the chance to make amends for my embarrassing first appearance on a Royal Variety Show.

This time I chose a comic routine that had been given to me by a young Australian bloke I met by chance at Australia House in London. He had come up to me during a function and suggested that I do a British version of 'Tie Me Kangaroo Down, Sport'. Then he launched into the tune to show what he meant.

'Yeah, what a great idea,' I told him, thinking he was a complete nutter.

Only later did I realize what an inspired idea it was. To this day, it is probably the best bit of material ever suggested to me and I wish I knew the young chap's name so I could thank him.

The Queen and the Duke of Edinburgh had travelled to Scotland for the show. Shirley Bassey was singing directly before me on the programme. With the big orchestra and her powerful voice, she had the audience in raptures. I wandered on stage looking bemused. 'How can I follow that?' I said, in a thick Scottish accent. It got a great laugh.

I grabbed the wobble board and the orchestra joined me in the first bars of 'Kangaroo'.

'Hang on a minute,' I said, stopping the music. 'Here's an idea. Let's do the *British* version of "Kangaroo". What do you reckon? We haven't rehearsed this, but let's give it a go.'

I walked to the orchestra pit. 'What's a good key?'

'Eh?' said the musical director, giving a perfect impression of somebody who hadn't quite heard the question.

'OK, that'll do. Key of A. Can you give us a sort of bolero rhythm on the piano in A? Yeah, perfect.'

I turned to the audience. 'Can you sit up straight? It looks a bit sloppy for the British version. That's it.' The bolero rhythm was playing away behind me. 'OK. Here we go . . . the British version.'

I took a big breath and began singing 'Tie Me Kangaroo Down, Sport' to the tune of 'Land of Hope and Glory'. The lyrics fitted the music perfectly. After the initial laughter had died down, everybody began singing. They were waving their hands in the air, like the Last Night of the Proms.

Belting out the song, I yelled, 'COME ON!' straight at the Royal Box, and then 'Oops!' covering my mouth in an embarrassed way.

The whole routine worked wonderfully and afterwards, in the traditional line-up backstage, the Queen and the Duke both said how much they enjoyed it. I felt as though I had made amends for the past.

Although I was never happier than when drawing, *Cartoon Time* became a real chore. The format of the show didn't change and week after week I did the same thing, except that eventually all the good cartoons had been used and I was trying to enthuse about second-rate material. Kids deserved better than this.

In 1986 I had a call from television producer Peter Murphy while I was doing a pantomime season in Hull. Peter was interested in making really good creative children's television – where the kids were encouraged to be original and imaginative, rather than vegetating in front of the box.

Peter came to see me in Hull and over lunch we tossed around some ideas. In particular I told him how much I disliked programmes that used children as an unpaid moving backdrop, while the presenter stands with his back to them working directly to camera. The kids are totally ignored until a floor manager tells them to cheer or to shut up.

Peter listened to my thoughts and said, 'You've told me what you *don't* like. What *do* you like?'

'I want to see kids given a chance to shine,' I said, 'instead of just being in the background. I want to use fewer children, with each of them given a spot in the limelight.'

'What would the show be about?'

I didn't hesitate. 'Animation. We should take their drawings and, stage by stage, show them how to animate their work.'

Peter got very excited. The idea fitted perfectly with the new technology becoming available. He'd just been offered exclusive use of a computerized line tester that could scan drawings and then be programmed to run them in sequence, testing the animation.

I didn't renew my contract with the BBC after the next series of *Cartoon Time*. The producer of the show was very upset. He'd imagined it going on for ever.

Rolf's Cartoon Club was launched in 1987 and became an instant hit. I loved the idea of making it a 'club' and getting kids to become members. It reminded me of the Argonauts Club on radio when I was a youngster.

Thousands of kids joined Rolf's Cartoon Club, each of them receiving a newsletter, badges and a poster. The administration was a nightmare, of course, with extra staff having to be employed to answer letters and run the membership list. But the new show was everything I'd hoped – creative, imaginative and hands on. We began by showing kids the principles of animation. I made all sorts of 'Rolf's Rollers' – simple two part animations on folded paper that my dad had shown me how to do when I was eight years old.

As the series progressed, as well as showing a lot of great cartoons, we delved into the history of animation and showed examples of the latest innovations. Different animators like Nick Park (Wallace and Grommit), John Lassiter (American Academy Award winner for his computer animation) and the legendary Chuck Jones came in each week. Only six children were featured in each episode and our 'resident' animators, led by Wendy Keay-Bright, showed them how to use all sorts of different materials and styles to create animations of their own.

The appeal of the show was seeing all these animations develop from a simple idea in somebody's head to the finished thing. It's the same reason my big paintings had been so popular. Perhaps for the first time, many people were seeing the creative process take place, from a blank surface to a finished picture, right before their eyes. Art galleries only show the finished product – not the process.

Nowadays, even on a show like *Blue Peter*, the craft segments are truncated and the presenter says, 'Here's one I made earlier.' They don't understand that a lot of the joy is in watching something emerge. The only shows that are doing it right are the cooking programmes and make-over shows like *Ground Force* and *Changing Rooms*. Viewers get to see things develop.

Working on *Cartoon Club* was like being back in Perth again. It was a full-time job and I spent most of my weekends in my studio making props and animations. Then early on Monday morning I drove down to Bristol and went straight into the studio to get dressed and made up. We started filming at 9.30 a.m. and didn't finish until after six. Then I stayed back shooting the animations that I'd prepared over the weekend, or creating new ones with modelling clay, filming them shot by shot.

The director, Doug Matthews, was a brilliant guy, who worked even harder than I did, spending his weekends editing the show for transmission.

During the week we often didn't finish in the studio until ten at night. Then it was back to the hotel where we grabbed the last possible meal in the dining room. As we ate we'd talk through plans for the next day and kick around ideas for future shows. At seven the next morning, I was back in the TV studio, spending another two hours making animations before we started filming.

This routine continued all week until I drove back to Bray late on Friday night.

Our efforts didn't go unrewarded. Over the next six years *Cartoon Club* won a string of accolades, including a silver award in America for the best children's programme. I doubt if there was another show on television that had such creative spark and the sheer number of ideas.

Chapter Eighteen

ROCK'S RENAISSANCE MAN

THE NINETIES MARKED MY THIRD DECADE OF TOURING AND I was still spending at least four months away from home each year. In Australia in 1990, my local PR guy, Stuart White, was also working for a TV show called *The Money or the Gun*.

It was a comedy talk show hosted by Andrew Denton, who had a razor sharp wit and such innocent looks that he could ask the most awkward questions on taboo subjects and get away with it. The show featured a musical item each week and my name had been suggested. The producer came to Stuart White's office for a meeting.

'We want you to do "Stairway to Heaven",' he said.

'I don't know it.'

'You're kidding.'

'Never heard of it.'

He looked at me in disbelief. 'It's a Led Zeppelin rock classic!'

'Oh, well, nothing to do with me then. Couldn't I do one of my songs?'

'No, we only do the one song. It's a policy of the show.'

'Why?'

'Well, it's like an ongoing joke. Each week we do a different version of "Stairway". We've had an Elvis Presley impersonator, an
opera singer, a country version, heavy metal, reggae . . . We even had
actor Leonard Teale read it as a poem. Now we want the definitive
Rolf Harris version, with everything that says "Rolf Harris" –
wobble board, didgeridoo and an "All together now" type chorus.'

I still wasn't sure so I rang Bruce.

'Go for it,' he said. 'It's something different. Something new.'

The producer offered to send me the original recording, but I
told him not to bother. 'Just send me the sheet music. I don't want
to hear how anyone else has done the song.'

The music arrived at my hotel and I couldn't make head or tail
of the lyrics. The bit about fairies bustling in the hedgerow went
right over my head so I decided to leave that verse out.

My touring band thought it was hilarious when I handed them
the song, but they were really good about letting me do it my way.
There was a line: 'Sometimes all of our thoughts are misgiven . . .'
I wanted to have some fun so I rang the producer and asked him
to hire a glamorous young lady.

'What for?'

'She'll be playing Miss Given.'

I didn't say anything more – it was going to be a surprise.

I was really looking forward to doing the song in front of a live
audience, but sadly we had a gig on the same night as *The Money
or the Gun*. This meant we had to pre-record on a Sunday afternoon in an empty studio. Even without an audience, we had a ball
stamping 'Rolf Harris' all over 'Stairway to Heaven', with the
wobble board giving the basic rhythm, a didgeridoo solo, and of
course the chorus with all the band joining in.

When the show went to air, I was already away touring and the
song was never mentioned again until eighteen months later. I was
back in the UK when Bruce called from Sydney to say *The Money
or the Gun* wanted to put out an album of all the different versions
of 'Stairway'. There were twenty-six of them by then.

'There won't be any money in it,' said Bruce. 'The royalties'll be worth about a farthing a record, because there are so many musicians involved. But they really want you on board.'

No skin off my nose, I thought. 'Yeah, go ahead.'

Again I didn't give the album another thought. I had too many other things on my mind. In particular, a new controller of children's programming had been appointed at ITV. She had been somebody's secretary but was now suddenly in charge.

Doug Matthews broke the news to me. 'You know how it is, Rolf. New broom sweeps clean. They're cancelling *Rolf's Cartoon Club*.'

'No! Why?'

'They're saying it costs too much money and it's run its course.'

'But that's crazy! We've got enough material and creativity for another ten years.'

I kept telling myself that it had to be a mistake. It wasn't until people began calling me to commiserate that the reality sank in.

The axing of *Cartoon Club* depressed me more than any other setback I had ever endured in my TV career. It was particularly bad when I saw what replaced the show – two puppets who introduced the cartoons and mainly talked about farting. Was this what ITV regarded as quality programming?

The demise of *Cartoon Club* typified how television had changed and how accountants often held sway over content.

Nowadays, children are underestimated by programme makers, who seem to think that any segment lasting more than half a minute won't work, because kids don't have the attention span. It's not true. The knack is knowing how to keep something *interesting*. And there's also a tendency to choose presenters because they're young and loud and because they speak the language really badly. Children are already turning off in favour of computer games. One day I think there'll be a backlash against this cheap television. Perhaps then producers will get back to making programmes that have our children's interests at heart.

I was sixty-three years old and my television career was over as far as I was concerned. I couldn't see what else I could do now.

Cartoon Club had dominated my life like no other show since my days working on the children's half-hour in Perth.

For six years, I had done almost nothing else but *Cartoon Club* and before that *Cartoon Time*. Nobody had seen me doing any singing or musical work in the UK for twelve years, apart from pantomime. I did a few theatre shows, but the only brave souls who bothered turning up were mainly mothers with little children. I think they expected two hours of cartoons or animations.

A lot of people might have said, 'OK, you're sixty-three. It's time to give it away. Retire.' Secretly, I think Alwen would have agreed. But I couldn't do that. To me, retirement means giving up . . . lying down . . . dying.

I had a million things I could do. I could polish stones, carve wood, learn how to make furniture, paint, or collate a lifetime's worth of photographs . . .

But being out there in the public eye is like a drug. I was hooked on the buzz. I just didn't know what to do with myself when I wasn't working.

All I had left was pantomime. That year I had done a season in Bath, playing Baron Hardup, Cinderella's father. Lesley Joseph was the fairy godmother.

'I heard your song on the radio this morning,' she said one afternoon.

'My song?'

'Yes. "Stairway to Heaven". Why didn't you tell us?'

In truth, I'd all but forgotten about the album. It turned out that people in Australia had bombarded radio stations asking to hear the Rolf Harris version of 'Stairway', so the record company released it as a single. Somehow a copy found its way to the UK and Simon Bates, the morning show host at Radio One, had been playing it every day for a fortnight. He kept telling listeners, 'When is a record company going to put this out in the UK?'

Mercury Records, a part of Polydor, did just that. A few weeks later, while I was on stage in *Cinderella*, an announcement was made that Baron Hardup had just had a song enter the charts. 'Stairway' had been picked up by radio stations everywhere and the single was galloping out of music shops.

However, not everyone appreciated my version. How dare I do this to a classic song! It was sacrilegious. One commentator suggested Led Zeppelin should sue. Another asked whether blasphemy laws could apply.

Every journalist and talkback programme in the country wanted to interview me. I had reporters chasing me up at the hotel in Bath and phone calls from around the world. The question was always the same. 'How could you have done such a thing?'

'I did it for a television show,' I said, slightly bemused. 'I didn't mean to upset anyone. "Stairway" is a cracking good tune, but people normally just sit and listen to it. I've given everybody the chance to join in and sing along with it.'

I wasn't trying to poke fun at the song. And I freely admitted that I'd never heard of the original version.

'Never heard of it? What on earth were you doing through the sixties?' I was asked.

'To be honest I was recording my own things like "Jake the Peg" and "Big Dog" and heading in a completely different direction.'

I could also have pointed out that people had lampooned me over the years and *I* didn't get upset. I was quite flattered. Where was their sense of humour?

As the song climbed the charts I had invitations to appear on shows like *The Word* and *Top of the Pops*. They wanted me to perform the song, but I didn't have a band.

'Well, you have three days to get one,' said Bob Clifford, a music publisher at EMI.

With Bob's help, we pulled together a scratch band, made up of his muso mates. We had Bernard O'Neill on double bass, Alan Dunn on the accordion, Mick Gaffey on drums and Bob himself played guitar. This left me free to wobble the board and blow the didge.

We came together on 2 February 1993 at a small rehearsal room at Wigmore Hall in London. I'd written out rough chord charts for the guys and we spent an hour rehearsing. Three days later, in the early afternoon, we arrived at a TV studio in Wembley to appear on *The Word*. As I walked into the studio, the production crew dropped to their knees and began wailing, 'We are not worthy, we are not worthy.' Talk about embarrassing! (But nice!)

We had a run through and then went for a curry before the show. This was more like it – being back performing live on TV. Once the adrenalin started pumping it all came together. The audience in the studio that night was mainly youngsters who had grown up watching me draw cartoons. They loved the performance.

The following Thursday we were to film *Top of the Pops*. There was a charity dinner in London on the Wednesday night and, arriving early, Alwen and I wandered up Bond Street to Oxford Street looking at the window displays. I suddenly noticed a colourful jacket in one of the windows. It was bright blue, with big white clouds all over it. Instantly, I thought, ' "Stairway to Heaven".'

It was late opening, so we went inside. The jacket was a one-of-a-kind and fitted me in the shoulders but not in the sleeves.

'Just get it,' said Alwen. 'Don't worry about the fit.'

The next morning I painted a set of turquoise stairs on the front of a white T-shirt. I wanted to wear this under my 'cloud' jacket.

Twenty-three years after 'Two Little Boys' I was back on *Top of the Pops*. We performed live, without a backing track, which made the studio staff rather nervous. They had to hunt around to find enough microphones and monitors.

What did it feel like to be a pop star again? A little sweeter this time round because it was so unexpected. A little daunting because it happened so quickly. I didn't feel as though I was sixty-three years old. I felt I was still twenty-two – the same age I was when I arrived in Britain. And I kept thinking of all the things that still lay ahead of me. I had an autobiography to write and more books to illustrate. Another tour of Australia beckoned. Life was good.

'Stairway to Heaven' continued climbing and reached No.4 on the UK charts. It would have gone even higher, according to the experts, but the success had taken everybody by surprise, including the record company, which didn't have enough stock on hand. It's a shame. Although not a betting man, I had laid a little wager with a bookmaker and stood to win £32,000 for charity if I reached the top spot.

When all the fuss died down, Bindi took me aside one day. 'It's about time you heard this,' she said, putting the CD in the stereo. It was Led Zeppelin's original recording of 'Stairway to Heaven'. It was magic!

'My God, what have I done?' I said, feeling a mixture of embarrassment and disbelief.

I'm very glad I didn't ask to hear the Led Zeppelin recording before I agreed to do the song. Otherwise, I would have said, 'No way. You can't muck around with a song like that.'

Bruce was the first person to realize that 'Stairway to Heaven' could be more than a one-off. On my next visit to Australia he suggested that I do my version of all sorts of rock 'n' roll songs.

'Imagine singing "Wild Thing",' he said. 'You could do all the eefing and eyefing, like a dog panting. And what about "I Can't Get No Satisfaction"?'

'The Rolling Stones?'

'Yeah . . . It'll be hilarious. You can do them live.'

I wasn't sure. Over the years I'd learned that lightning didn't strike twice.

My musical director in Australia, Clive Lendich, had already worked out the keys for a whole list of songs. They included classics like 'Honky Tonk Woman', 'Smoke on the Water', 'Walk on the Wild Side', 'Roadhouse Blues', 'Great Balls of Fire' and 'Satisfaction'.

I saw the list and thought he was crazy. 'I can't sing those in a million years.'

Then I thought back to the old church hall in Sydenham when

I first heard the Rolling Stones. I was convinced they had no future. What did I know?

We set to work at the Megaphon Studios in Sydney, laying down the tracks with all the typical Rolf-like touches. Bands and session musicians from other studios kept wandering into the control room to listen. There was lots of laughter and I think they appreciated our sense of fun and irreverence.

The songs were eventually put on a CD called *Rolf Rules OK* and we made plans to tour. Back in England I hooked up with the same scratch band that had backed me on *Top of the Pops*. I could so easily have felt out of my depth, but these guys gave me enormous confidence. They were listening to my ideas and saying, 'Yeah. Sounds great. Let's do it.'

The first real test came when the students union at Birmingham University asked me to do a concert. When the invitation first arrived I suddenly felt a twinge of self-doubt. What did they expect? I still wasn't entirely sure about my new material. 'Stairway' had been a one-off . . . a novelty song. Did people really want to hear me singing rock 'n' roll classics?

Just when I was beginning to panic, the organizers sent a letter listing some requests. They wanted to hear 'Stairway', of course, and any other rock songs I wanted to do, but all my old favourites were also on the list – 'Sun Arise', 'Caractacus', 'Kangaroo', 'Two Little Boys', 'Jake the Peg' . . . What a relief!

The band travelled up separately to Birmingham and I drove myself from Bray, with a map spread on my knees. We arrived at 5.30 p.m., unloaded our stuff and did our sound check before they opened the doors. A big table had been set up backstage and they had promised to bring us a curry before the show, which wasn't due to start until eleven.

The union building had a permit for 733 people. By nine o'clock a crowd of over a thousand had gathered, with more arriving all the time. They were jammed in, nose to nose, with people passing drinks over people's heads from the bar. The guy running the disco was struggling because there was no room for anybody to dance.

At about 9.30 they started chanting, 'We want Rolf! We want Rolf!' We were sitting behind the curtain eating poppadams and chicken kormas. The chanting grew louder.

'We have to go on,' I said to the student organizer, shouting to be heard.

'No! You can't! What's going to happen at eleven? Who'll go on *then*?'

The noise grew worse. My mouth went dry and sweat poured down my forehead. The band shuffled around nervously. After an hour of this, I couldn't stand the tension.

'There's going to be a riot if we don't go on.'

'We can't. Not yet.'

'This is crazy. They'll tear the place apart.'

Finally, at about half past ten, he agreed. I nodded to the band and the music started. I was all dressed up for 'Jake the Peg'. A roar went up that almost lifted the roof. I walked on stage and turned, balancing on my middle leg and swinging the other two in unison. Every face was focused on mine.

Even before the end of the first verse they were singing with me. They knew every word of every song and belted them out at the tops of their voices like a football crowd. I could barely hear myself singing.

I had a whole routine worked out, with lots of jokes interspersed between the songs. After 'Jake the Peg' I started telling a joke. Before I reached the punch-line someone shouted, 'Just get on with the fuuucking singing.'

I stopped dead. 'Oh! Aah, right then.'

So I did. I ignored all the jokes and we just did one song after another. I did everything we knew – 'Honky Tonk Woman', 'Smoke on the Water', 'Walk on the Wild Side', 'Roadhouse Blues', plus all the old favourites. We didn't get off stage until half past one. What a buzz!

I signed autographs for an hour on stage. By then all the band guys had packed up and gone. When I finally headed out to my car, half a dozen students helped me carry my accordion, didgeridoo and painting easel. We reached the car park and I turned to thank them. One of the young blokes came up to me. He was only about five foot tall.

'Can I give you a hug?' he said.

'What?'

'Can I give you a hug?'

I said, 'Yeah, sure.'

He wrapped his arms round me in a bear hug. 'I've loved you all my life,' he whispered. He had tears in his eyes. So did I.

I drove home feeling absolutely euphoric. I couldn't remember the last time I had felt that sort of magic from an audience.

Word spread quickly along the university grapevine and I had invitations from all over the country. 'Stairway' had turned my whole career around. Up until then, most of these university age youngsters wouldn't have been caught dead listening to me, but this one song had given them permission to say, 'Hey, I like Rolf. I grew up with him.'

I was singing songs they remembered from their childhood, as well as classic rock 'n' roll numbers. They knew every word to every song. At times I felt like I was back at the Down Under Club, playing to a raucous crowd, who would yell out requests.

At some of the gigs, students would get dressed up in 'Rolf' glasses and 'Rolf' beards. An hour before the concert they'd start chanting, 'One Rolfie Harris . . . there's only one Rolfie Harris,' to the tune of *Guantanamera*.

I knew that partly they were having a laugh at my expense, but it was more than that. They came along and sang the songs. They relived part of their childhood. And if the lines were blurred between irony, parody and genuine affection, I hoped the latter was the most powerful motivation. They weren't laughing *at* me, they were laughing and singing *with* me.

'Maybe it could work at Glastonbury?' I said to the band at one of our rehearsals.

None of the guys laughed at the suggestion. They knew more about the rock festival than I did.

'Lenny Kravitz and Velvet Underground are headlining this year,' said Mick Gaffey.

'I haven't heard of either of them,' I said. They all laughed. 'So what do you reckon?'

'What have we got to lose?' said Alan.

I had Billy Marsh Associates contact the organizers of the festival. I would have loved to be a fly on the wall when they took the call. Rolf Harris at Glastonbury? They couldn't resist.

In truth, I'm convinced they booked me as a joke. That's why they rostered me to perform at ten thirty on a Sunday morning, when the crowd was still likely to be wrapped in sleeping bags.

Up before dawn, I arrived at Glastonbury at 8.30 a.m. My brother-in-law Hugh drove me through the gates and I looked out across a sea of brightly coloured tents. Wood smoke filled the air and rows of Portaloos stood like an army of soldiers on a battlefield.

'Dear oh dear,' I thought. 'Am I up for this?'

The butterflies were fluttering inside me as we unloaded the gear from the car. Backstage was a bit empty. There were a few lighting and sound guys moving around looking half asleep. A great big cockney bloke took a heavy suitcase and the piano accordion from Hugh and carried them round the back.

As he put the cases down, he said, 'You're the only one I'm interested in seeing 'ere today, Rolp.' (He called me Rolp with a p!) 'Ya gonna do that one about the three-legged geezer?'

'Yeah.'

'Good on yer, son.'

He clapped me so hard on the back I nearly went sprawling across the stage. It was wonderful. In that moment all my fears evaporated.

We set up our gear and cleared off to the dressing room cubicles away from the stage area. As I walked past one of the doors I noticed a sign had been pinned up. 'Robert Plant & Jimmy Page'. Wow!

Here were the rock legends who created 'Stairway to Heaven'. Maybe I'd get to meet them. What would I say? More importantly, what would they say to me? Would they mind about what I did with their song?

At that hour of the morning I had one act on before me – two fantastic guys who played bagpipes and drums. I sat in the dressing room growing more and more nervous. What had possessed me to think I could play Glastonbury? This was going to be a disaster.

I dressed in my 'Jake the Peg' gear and went to wait backstage. Sneaking a look outside, I could only see a portion of the crowd. It seemed enormous.

The band was on edge. They were all crack musicians, but this was a huge gig. The stage manager gave us the cue and the band walked on stage and picked up their instruments. I waited for the introduction.

'You all know who he is. He's come a long way to be here. Will you please welcome the one and only ROLF HARRIS!'

An amazing roar went up as I walked out as Jake the Peg. I blinked into the brilliant sunlight. As far as the eye could see there were people. They stretched to the horizon like a brightly coloured blanket covering the huge field. Women sat on shoulders, T-shirts waved in the air and the noise seemed to shake the stage.

'Can you believe this?' I shouted over the 'oom cha, oom cha' intro music, 'Jake the Peg at bloody Glastonbury!'

They gave me another huge roar.

The crowd was estimated at more than 80,000 and they sang every word of every song. At one stage, I began talking about the didgeridoo and a dozen didges were raised aloft in the audience. All sorts of people had brought them along.

There is nothing that can compete with performing live to a huge audience. When it's going well it's like the greatest drug in the world. The adrenalin will cure headaches at a hundred paces. You could have a sore leg, or a gut ache, or be dead on your feet with exhaustion, but Dr Adrenalin will fix it all.

It was wonderful. We did new songs and old stuff. When I sang 'Sun Arise' the crowd joined in and made so much noise that I couldn't hear myself or the music. I looked across and saw the band playing like mad. Even with the volume up to max, I couldn't hear my fold-back speakers on stage. I might as well have been miming.

When I reached the end of the song, we all stopped and I listened to the final notes of the guitar fading away. That's when I realized that I'd been a tone sharp throughout the whole song. Nobody had noticed.

We walked off stage to absolutely stunning applause which gradually gave way to chanting, 'We want Rolf! We want Rolf!'

I said to Bernard, 'We've got to go back out there and do something else.'

'What are you gonna do?' he said.

'I don't know. But shouldn't we go back?'

'No. You've got to leave them wanting more.'

For twenty minutes they kept chanting. It felt like I was king of the world.

I never did get to meet Robert Plant or Jimmy Page. I hung around for a few hours afterwards, hoping they might arrive, but they weren't due to play until later that night. In the meantime, we had another gig at Reading so I had to leave.

As a postscript to the whole adventure, a few months later I had a call from a national newspaper. The organizers of Glastonbury had just voted me the best entertainer they had ever had at the rock festival. Not bad for a young bloke!

In January 1994 I was back touring in Australia – showing off my new material. The tour started in Queensland and the third concert was in the Atherton Tablelands, west of Cairns.

On stage that night, I was just starting to demonstrate the

didgeridoo when my head began spinning. I could have sworn I was going to pitch forward and land flat on my face. In front of a packed audience, I clung to the didgeridoo with my left hand and the microphone with my right. Then I braced my legs wide apart like a drunk, fighting to stay upright.

I felt as though a cylinder of bone was inside my skull spinning round and round. It was as if someone had switched on a huge blender and my brain was being liquidized. Nobody in the audience guessed. I kept chatting away, while my stomach churned.

Somehow I managed to get through the show. Afterwards, I sat at a table signing autographs and CD covers. I should have gone straight back to the motel, but I thought it was important to make contact with the audience and let them into my life. Meanwhile, my head was casually spinning and then stopping again.

It was well after midnight before the tour manager, Ken Jeacle, drove me back to the motel. I set the alarm for 5 a.m. and collapsed into bed.

When I woke I felt no better. We had to be in Cairns at 7.30 a.m. for a flight to Sydney. The long drive from the Atherton Tablelands down to the coast is a nightmare of 196 switchback curves. I spent the journey trying not to be sick.

We boarded the plane and I managed to sleep a little during the flight. I knew that once we landed in Sydney I had to go directly to the Rooty Hill RSL Club in the western suburbs for three hours of rehearsal with the New South Wales band and then do a two-hour show that night.

The flight taxied to the gate and the passengers began to dis-embark. As I walked down the aisle to the door, something crashed into the plane and I was flung against the front bulkhead. I gave Ken a panicked look. 'What was that?'

'What was what?'

'That crash. Something hit the plane.'

'I didn't hear anything.' He looked at me strangely.

'You're kidding. What about the jolt? It knocked me over.'

'There wasn't any jolt.'

Suddenly, it happened again. I clung to the back of a seat to stop myself falling. 'There it goes again.'

Ken looked worried. 'Nothing happened, Rolf. I think it's all inside your head.'

I tried to stand and fell sideways across several empty seats. My head had started spinning again.

Ken grabbed my arm to help me up. I clung to his shoulder like a drowning man grabbing a lifeline. He kept talking to me gently as we staggered along the sky-walk. I struggled to walk because I had no sense of up or down. The world was spinning around me and going in and out of focus.

We reached a moving walkway and I felt enormous relief. I began to relax a little.

'We're going the wrong way,' said Ken. Sure enough, we had turned left instead of right and we were heading *away* from the baggage reclaim area.

Ken managed to negotiate the turn and we headed back to collect our luggage. I saw the gents' toilet looming and lurched away from Ken's arm. Stumbling inside, I fell to my knees, bracing both hands on the opposite walls of the cubicle to stop them falling in on me. The whole cubicle was swaying and spinning as I heaved my heart out.

I don't know how long I stayed there. Even with nothing left in my stomach, I kept dry-retching until my nose ran and eyes watered. The bile taste in my mouth was awful.

Climbing to my feet I washed my face and went back to Ken. Clearly, starting to get very worried, he had called to arrange for a doctor to meet us at the Rooty Hill RSL Club. I clung to his shoulder like a drunk as we made it to the baggage reclaim area. Ken put me on a seat and I fell sideways. I couldn't get up again without his help.

That was enough for Ken. He held my shoulders and straightened me up. 'Look, I'm going to cancel the rehearsal and the show. Then I'm going to find the car and get you to a hospital.'

I nodded and dry-retched into a handkerchief. He disappeared and it took all my powers of concentration to stay upright in the seat. In the back of my mind I kept worrying that people would recognize me and think I *was* drunk. Me, a non-drinker!

When Ken returned, he had to half carry me across the pavement to his car. We drove off and the balance mechanism in my head went haywire. I was convinced the car was plunging uncontrollably sideways down a 45-degree slope.

'We're going to crash! *Watch out!*'

I leaned across to Ken's side, hoping my weight could straighten us up.

He had to push me away. 'It's OK. It's OK. We're not going to crash.'

He drove me straight to St Vincent's Hospital and I was taken from the accident and emergency section to a private room. The only one available was the palatial Kerry Packer suite. Apparently the media mogul had made a major donation to the hospital after surviving a serious heart attack.

Ken waited for the diagnosis and spent his time on the phone cancelling arrangements. 'With your permission, Rolf, I want to cancel the rest of the tour,' he said. 'The doctors say you'll be here for at least ten days.'

I didn't argue. I just wanted my head to stop spinning.

The next day I woke with double vision – one image about an inch above the other. This was truly awful and it made me realize how much I relied on my eyes, more so than my other senses. Eventually, I became fed up with clenching one eye shut, so I used sticky tape to attach a piece of brown paper over one lens of my glasses.

I was diagnosed as having a virus that affected the balance mechanism in my inner ear. Because it was a virus, it couldn't be treated with antibiotics. Instead they gave me a course of mild steroid pills which would hopefully keep the arteries open and hasten the departure of the virus from my inner ear.

'But how did I get it?' I asked.

'It could have been lurking in your body for a long time,' the specialist said. 'Some viruses lie dormant and only hit when your body gets run down or exhausted.'

He asked about my schedule. In the previous fortnight I'd been filming two documentaries in Canada to promote the Commonwealth Games in the coming August. Up at 5.30 a.m. every day, filming often didn't finish until after midnight. Then I flew to Australia and went straight from the plane to a TV studio. I started the tour the next day.

The doctor shook his head in amazement. 'This is a serious warning,' he said. 'It's telling you to ease up.'

'But I have these concerts . . .'

'Yes, I know, but if you don't slow down you'll finish up being one of the richest corpses in the cemetery.'

I laughed along with him, but in reality he'd given me quite a fright. These crazy schedules hadn't been forced on me against my will. This was the sort of timetable I always maintained.

At times I'd talked of easing up. At one stage I told my booking agent that I wanted one day off between shows and in some cases four or five days off. I wanted to see a bit of Australia instead of rushing through it like a lunatic all the time. Yet despite my good intentions, I charged on. I couldn't shake the showbiz mentality of grabbing work when it presented itself. Who knew when it might dry up?

Now I was paying the price – lying in a hospital bed, with one eye blanked off with brown paper. Each time I turned my head, I had the sensation of plummeting down a 500-foot cliff at breakneck speed. I couldn't read, or write, or draw.

The steroids had the effect of keeping me wide awake on a constant high. I had to take a sleeping pill to get even half an hour's sleep at night. The rest of the time I spent staring at the ceiling. The telephone became my only salvation and I ran up ridiculous bills calling mates all around Australia and in the rest of the world.

When they finally released me from hospital, I went west and stayed near Fremantle with my dear mate Harry Butler and his wife Magi. I nearly drove them mad. I'd finished the course of steroids, but I was still on a constant high and quite manic. I couldn't sleep and spent all night on their telephone, calling people in different time zones.

Every day Harry drove me from Fremantle over to Midland Junction so that I could visit Mum in her nursing home. It was a very long haul and I appreciated his kindness. He would sit in the corridor outside the room while I chatted to Mum as she lay in her bed.

My reaction to sickness and infirmity had always been to crack jokes and clown around, trying to make light of things. I think it was a way of trying to hide my unease because I didn't know what to say to people who were sick or in distress.

On the last day before I had to catch the plane back to England, Harry sat outside and listened to me trying to say goodbye to Mum. I was making a real meal of it.

When I came out he said, 'For Christ's sake, tell her that you love her.'

I could feel my bottom lip beginning to tremble.

He put his arm round my shoulders. 'I know it's none of my business, sport. But you and I know that she's old and you might not see her again. Just tell her you love her. That's what you're trying to do, isn't it?'

I knew he was right, but I still found it so hard. Why couldn't I face up to the important issues? Why did I always have to skate around them?

I went back into her room. She was propped up on pillows. Her hair had turned white long ago. Her eyes still filled with pride when she looked at me.

'You know, I love you so much, Mum.'

Her face took on the most stunned expression. 'Do you *really*?'

It was as if she had never known. She looked at me in absolute amazement.

'Of course I do.'

'You never told me.'

I started crying.

She put her arms around me and we stayed like that for the longest time.

She died soon after that and went to join her beloved Crom.

Chapter Nineteen

NEVER WORK WITH
CHILDREN OR . . .

Back in England, I took a long while to recover from the virus and the side-effects of the steroid treatment. When I came down from the drugs it was like tumbling into a great black hole.

Until then I had never really understood depression. How could anybody feel so low as to consider suicide? Yet now I felt so awful that I couldn't see much reason for living. I had a suffocating black cloud around me that sucked the goodness out of life and left only the dregs. Killing myself didn't enter my head, but I know the family feared for me. I was a nightmare to be around, snarling and snapping people's heads off. It wasn't me at all.

The vacuum created by the cancellation of *Rolf's Cartoon Club* just made things worse. What was I going to do? I paced the house, fidgeting and fussing over minor irritations. Alwen started keeping out of my way and old friends avoided me.

I developed a fixation about the front steps. The bottom stair was only half the height of all the rest of them, which drove me crazy. Why would someone build steps like that? It had been bugging me for the best part of fifteen years – ever since we moved into the house. Now I decided to do something about it. I began drawing up plans and talking to builders.

Alwen could see that I was obsessing, but stayed out of my way. I only found out much later that she quietly went behind my back and told the builder not to bother with it. The stair is still the same today.

When the depression grew worse, I went to see my family GP who referred me to a specialist. As a result I was given some pills to lighten my mood. After two days, I threw them away. I didn't want to take *more* pills. The very reason I had become like this was from taking pills in the first place.

In the middle of this I had a call from Jan Kennedy, my UK manager since dear Billy Marsh had died.

'Listen, Rolf, the BBC is looking for a presenter.'

'What's the show?'

'It's a factual programme. Prime time. They want to talk to you.'

I should have been over the moon. Somebody had thrown me a lifeline. But instead I felt nothing at all. I was too depressed to care.

A few months earlier the BBC had produced a very popular programme called *Hospital Watch* – a 'fly on the wall' style of documentary following the progress of patients, doctors and nurses during a single week at a UK hospital. Each night an edited half-hour programme went to air and it proved to be compulsive viewing.

The logical next step was to do another *Hospital Watch*. It was pencilled into the BBC schedule and production personnel were assigned. Unfortunately, when they approached the hospital and asked if the August Bank Holiday week would suit, the answer was no. A new intake of junior doctors was due that week and the hospital management didn't want them put under the extra strain of coping with TV cameras.

Everything had been organized – staff, budget and equipment –

but the BBC had nothing to film and a gaping hole in the schedule. Then someone came up with the idea of doing an *Animal Hospital Watch*. The corporation had previously done a very successful one-off special about the RSPCA Wildlife Hospital in Norfolk.

Lorraine Heggessey had been given the task of producing the new series. She had only recently joined the Science and Features Department at the BBC and this was to be her first major project as series producer.

The first priority was finding an animal hospital willing to co-operate. The RSPCA's Sir Harold Harmsworth Hospital in Finsbury Park, North London, agreed to come on board.

Lorraine then needed to find a presenter. She had a researcher pull together a list of everybody in show business who had anything to do with animals. As she ran her finger down the names, she came to mine. I was a patron of the Cats Protection League.

'He's the one I want,' she said.

'You're kidding. He does children's cartoons and sings silly songs.'

'I've watched him all my life on television. He's been a part of my life ever since I was a child. I trust him. I believe him.'

I knew none of this when Jan Kennedy arranged for me to meet Lorraine for lunch, along with BBC producers Fiona Holmes and Sally Dickson. At a restaurant in Shepherd's Bush, they began telling me about the show. I don't remember any of what they said. I wasn't listening. Instead, I contemplated why the builder hadn't come back to me about fixing the steps.

These bright, talented women were pitching a wonderful idea to me, but it was all going past me. It had been months since I took joy in anything.

Jan did her very best to sell me and sing my praises. She told them how I loved animals. At home in Bray we had two Devon Rexes (Beetle and Toffee), a Bengal (Leopard) and a black standard poodle (Summer). She also mentioned that Alwen and I had recently collaborated on a book called *Personality Cats* about all the moggies we'd owned since we were married. It was full of my photographs and drawings and our recollections.

Jan was doing her best to get me a job, while I sat like a zombie, letting everything happen around me. As we walked out of the restaurant, she gave a huge sigh of disgust, 'Well, you've thrown that one away.'

'What?'

'You didn't say a word. You looked as if you were asleep.'

'Did I?'

'You could at least have *looked* interested.'

How could I explain? I was so depressed I didn't care whether I got the job or not. I wasn't in any shape to do anything.

Despite the lunch, Lorraine went in to bat for me. Most of the senior managers at the BBC regarded me as a poor choice, I heard later. They couldn't understand why Lorraine didn't find some bright young presenter.

'I think he's perfect,' she argued, sticking her neck out.

'Well, it's your neck,' she was told. I was given the job.

By the time we started filming *Animal Hospital Live* the side-effects of the steroids had worn off and I was feeling like my old self again. I was really excited about presenting a new show. At the same time, I knew this one would be very different from anything I had done before.

For the first time, I was involved in a project that wasn't all about *me*. I wasn't expected to entertain or amuse people. This time the limelight belonged to others. If I did my job properly, people would hardly know I was there. It was a major change, but in a way it took some of the pressure off me because I didn't feel as though the success or failure relied solely on me.

'You'll have to wear this ear-piece,' said Lorraine, as I arrived on my first day of filming. 'And you're also going to use Autoscript for your live pieces to air during the show.'

Most of this technology was fairly new to me, but I was reasonably confident this old dog could learn a few new tricks.

Harmsworth Hospital had to deal with a huge range of pets and injured wildlife and I was confident I could handle most things. Dogs and cats were fine and rats didn't bother me. Harry Butler had taught me to have a healthy respect for snakes, but I wasn't all that thrilled about spiders.

Because the concept was entirely new, the BBC wasn't sure about whether the content of the show would be interesting and varied enough to hold an audience's attention. Just in case, they had plans for me to do a six foot by four foot painting. The idea was that I'd paint the animal that most fascinated me from the day's filming, adding a new one to the painting each day.

The vets and nurses were brilliant although very nervous about having the cameras at the hospital. That's where I could help. By chatting to them and simply being myself, I showed them that they could do the same.

We filmed over five days at the Harmsworth – showing the day to day clinical consultations, operations and emergencies. I was quite unsure at first when I should make an observation, or ask a question. But as the clinics unfolded, I found I was naturally curious and amazed by the expertise of the vets, although I never lost sight of the fact that the main priority of these professionals was to look after the animals and therefore I had to make sure that I didn't distract them too much.

We filmed throughout the day and the usable footage was fever-ishly edited into a half-hour show for transmission at 8 p.m. that night. I did all the 'straight to camera' links live as the show went to air.

On the Monday and Tuesday we pulled in much bigger audiences than expected, but the real turning point came on the Wednesday night. A young chap had brought his father's dog in to Spanish vet Jon Vivanco's clinic. The big old Alsatian called Floss could only walk three or four steps before her back legs collapsed.

Jon ran a few tests and discovered that Floss's heart was so enlarged it was battling to get blood through her system.

'We have to look at the quality of her life,' he said, giving Floss a scratch behind the ears. I asked the young chap a few questions and he said that his dad and Floss were inseparable. They lived on the second floor of a block of flats.

'Dad has to carry her down the stairs. He's sixty years old and she's a heavy old dog. When she gets down she can normally only walk to the gate. Then she collapses.'

Jon very gently explained that he couldn't fix Floss's legs. 'I'm sorry, but there's nothing I can do to help her. Her quality of life at the moment is pretty non-existent.'

'So what do you think?'

'Well, to be honest, I think it would be kinder if we gently put her to sleep. It won't hurt her. I'll give her an anaesthetic and she'll drift off and won't come back.'

'I'll have to go and phone my dad,' he said. His hands were shaking.

'OK. We'll wait.'

Ten minutes later the young chap came back. I doubt if he had ever made a more difficult call. 'Dad agrees,' he said, looking sadly at Floss.

'Do you want to stay with her?' Jon asked.

'No, I couldn't bear that,' he said.

There was an awful silence. Nobody could think of anything to say. At that point I forgot Floss's name. For the sake of something to say, I asked, 'How long has your dad had the dog?'

He turned to me and just burst into tears, burying his head in my neck and shoulder. I put my arm round him and found that I was crying too. There was total silence except for his sobbing.

He finally pulled himself together and wiped his cheeks. Then he bent down and kissed the old dog on the nose. As he went out the door the camera stayed on Floss. Her eyes followed him, giving him a big, trusting loving look.

To their credit the BBC left all of these scenes in the final edit. It was probably the first time that viewers in England had seen two adult males unashamedly crying on TV. The show went out that night and caused a sensation. People were talking about it on tubes and buses, at work and over backyard fences.

The next evening nine and a half million people tuned in to watch the programme. By Friday we had ten million viewers. Nobody could believe it. The Science and Features Department had been expecting maybe one and a half million. Its other flagship programme, *Tomorrow's World*, regularly got two million.

Animal Hospital Live had been the television equivalent of striking gold. When our Christmas show that same year pulled in nine and a half million viewers, the BBC couldn't ignore the numbers. It commissioned a nine-part series called *Animal Hospital* which began in January 1995. Instead of running nightly, it went out each Thursday night. After three shows, they cleared the schedules and extended the series to thirteen weeks.

We started filming early each morning and my first job was to put the owners at ease. Already worried about a sick pet, they didn't need more stress. Obviously we needed their permission before we could film the consultation, so I took them to see the examination room first and explained what normally happened.

People felt as though they knew me because they had grown up watching me on TV. I'm sure this helped me reassure them that nobody was going to make them look foolish or ask them anything embarrassing. Of course they were nervous, but it's amazing how quickly they forgot about the cameras when they began talking about their sick animals.

Right from the outset, I laid down the law about how we should tackle the medical side. I told the producers that I didn't want to pussy-foot around by coming up with cute names for anatomical realities. 'Let's call a penis a penis and a vulva a vulva. This is a factual programme, so let's stick to the facts.'

In particular, I didn't want problems to be trivialized, or sensationalized. The staff at the Harmsworth did brilliant work and the owners of these animals were part of a real-life drama. They deserved to be treated with respect.

The first series was made even more demanding for me because I was already committed to doing pantomime at the Windmill Theatre in Wimbledon. The BBC arranged that I should finish my part of the filming every weekday at around midday. Then I had to dash from north London to south London, across the West End, to be on stage at 2.30 p.m.

Some days, due to the heavy traffic, I arrived so late that I had to smudge on make-up and get changed into costume while the music for the opening number was playing. I had a second show each evening and I didn't get home until after eleven. Then I was up before dawn to get to the Harmsworth.

My co-presenters in the first series were Shauna Lowry and Steve Knight, who were both very enthusiastic and professional. For me, a lot of the real magic came from the special demands of treating everything as being 'live'. We had only one chance to get it right. You can't say to a dog or cat, 'Can we do that again?'

We used three cameras for most of the filming. One was always on a wide shot that took in the whole scene, which included the owner, the animal, the vet and me. The other two cameras concentrated on getting close-ups and capturing reactions.

Once the owner and pet had left the clinic, I could re-ask my questions with the camera on a close-up instead of on a wide shot. I was amazed at how well I remembered how and where I'd been standing and what I'd been doing with my hands. I could make it look as though it had all happened in 'real time' during the actual consultation.

Having had pets around me all my life gave me an insight into how much these animals meant to their owners. I had experienced my share of grief. I once walked home in tears carrying a dog collar, having seen my dog run down and killed by a car. He was too heavy to carry and I had to leave him in the gutter.

Another time our cocker spaniel Ginger swallowed a poison bait on the far side of the river where Mum, Dad and I had gone looking for mushrooms. We were coming back in the rowboat when Ginger clenched his jaws and fell into the bottom of the boat. Dad tried to lever his jaws open to get some of the slightly salty river water down his throat to make him sick. But rictus from the poison caused him to lock up. He bit right through Dad's thumbnail. Dad gritted his teeth with the pain and Ginger slowly died in his arms. It was awful.

The same thing almost happened to Buster Fleabags. I heard a crash in the house one day and discovered Buster lying on his side, stiff and shuddering. I rushed to put a kettle on the stove, dissolved a load of salt in the hot water and lifted Buster onto the sink. Holding the side of his lips open, I made him swallow salt water and then massaged his stomach until he brought up the poison. Buster survived.

My life was full of animal stories. I had seen puppies and kittens born, rescued cats and had a dog as bridesmaid at our wedding. I might not have been able to talk to animals in the Doctor Dolittle sense, but I knew how to put them at ease and how to hold them and stroke them.

All of this stood me in good stead for *Animal Hospital*. I think being older also helped. A young presenter of twenty-four might not be able to put his arm round an old guy's shoulders and say, 'It's going to be alright.'

One of those early cases will haunt me for ever. We were packing up after a busy day when a call came through to the RSPCA from a local police station. Someone had dumped a brown paper carrier bag on the counter and left without anybody's noticing.

One of the officers became aware of the disgusting smell. He opened the bag and immediately drew back in horror. All he could see was a motionless ball of muddy fur, which he assumed was a dead animal of some sort. Suddenly it moved.

I was just leaving through the main doors when someone from the production team yelled for me to come back. The ambulance had arrived and Bairbre O'Malley, an Irish vet, opened the bag. I didn't know what I was looking at. The stench was unbelievable.

'It's a dog,' said Bairbre, who was clearly shocked. Filthy matted fur covered its back and head while its stomach and legs had no fur at all.

'It must have been standing in its own pee for a long time,' she said, examining the raw skin on its limbs and stomach. 'You can see where the acid in the urine has burnt off the fur.'

I felt physically sick.

Bairbre began to cut through the solid covering of matted fur with her scissors. As she lifted back the tangled two and a half inch thick covering, she revealed a pair of bright eyes. Up until then the dog had been totally unable to see. More fur was cut away to reveal a small emaciated female dog that was possibly a poodle of some sort. She looked pitiful and really ancient.

Bairbre prised open her mouth to check the teeth. 'Oh, my God,' she said. 'She's just a puppy. Can't be more than eighteen months old.'

It was outrageous. 'How could anybody do this?' I asked.

'I've seen worse,' said Bairbre, and then added, 'but not often.'

The poor little mite looked like a skinned rabbit, yet she was so pitifully happy to see people and desperate to make friends that she responded to any kindness with enormous affection by licking hands and fingers.

Gordon Cowie, who regularly fosters animals for the RSPCA, was asked to take the poodle until a proper home could be found for her. It was snowing on the day he took her home, so he called her Snowy. By then her white fur had started to grow back and she was turning into a pretty little thing, with a wonderful nature.

Snowy bonded with Gordon so totally that she followed him everywhere. Even when he had a shower, Snowy would stand and get soaking wet rather than let him out of her sight. She had decided that she wasn't going to lose him. He, too, realized that he didn't want to give her up.

The mailbag for this one story was enormous. Everybody wanted to know what happened to Snowy. She became a national celebrity and people recognized her in the street when Gordon took her walking.

Gordon and Snowy came on our Christmas show and also appeared on *Good Morning TV*. They wanted me to hold Snowy for the cameras, but the little dog only had eyes for Gordon. The only way she'd sit still was if he sat just out of camera range, letting her know that he wasn't going to leave her.

The expertise of the vets was quite incredible to see. On my first day, the chief vet David Grant said to me, 'Listen, we're going to have to do operations. If you're going to be sick, don't ask permission to leave, just get the hell out the door. And if you're going to faint, faint backwards, away from the table. Whatever you do don't faint forwards. This is a sterile environment. How are you with blood?'

'I think I'm OK.'

'The smell is quite unexpected.'

'Hopefully, I'll be alright.'

In one programme an elderly lady in a wheelchair brought in her little Pekingese pride and joy called Sushi. The dog kept whimpering and couldn't sit down properly. David Grant examined Sushi and felt two huge sausage-shaped masses in her stomach area. He knew straight away she had a diseased womb.

The old lady sensed that something was wrong and kept asking, 'She will be alright, won't she?'

I could tell from David's face that things looked dire. 'We have to operate,' he said. 'She's very close to death. Whether we can save her or not, I don't know.'

The woman was absolutely shocked. 'Can't you just give her penicillin or something?'

'No. That's treating the symptoms, not the cause. We have to remove the womb. Even if I do that, there is still a very strong possibility that Sushi will die.'

'Please, no. Please,' she sobbed.

Having changed into sterile theatre greens, I watched the operation. David made the initial cut right down the mid-line and then the blunt dissection, opening and closing the rounded ends of the scissors to separate layers of fat and muscle.

'Don't ask any questions during this,' said David, a study of concentration.

He uncovered the two infected arms of the womb. They were about nine inches long and bloated with pus and poison. If he accidentally nicked either of them, the poison would leak into Sushi's abdominal cavity and she would almost certainly die of peritonitis in her weakened condition. 'Not a word,' said David.

We all held a collective breath as he tied off each end of the infected arms of the womb and then cut through with a scalpel and removed both pieces. Then he flushed her entire system with saline solution and antibiotics, before sewing Sushi back up again. The operation took less than fourteen minutes. I had never felt tension like it.

Now it became a question of whether Sushi had enough strength to pull through. It was touch and go. David was so uptight that he woke at half past two in the morning and contemplated going back to the hospital to see how the dog was doing. He told himself he was being crazy; there were people in the intensive care section through the night.

Next morning he arrived and went straight to see Sushi. She wasn't there. His heart sank.

'What happened to the little Pekingese?' he asked, sounding desperate.

'Oh, we moved her to the recovery ward,' said a nurse. 'She did really well overnight.'

David had succeeded. Within a week Sushi's tail was wagging again. She bounced out full of rude health and jumped into the old lady's lap as she sat in her wheelchair. Tearfully, she kept hugging David and thanking him.

We finished filming *Animal Hospital* on 30 March 1995 – my sixty-fifth birthday. It seemed strangely appropriate. At an age when most people were considering retirement, or getting their gold watches, my career had suddenly been given a wonderful new lease of life.

And for the first time I had taken a step back from being the show-off trying to prove to everyone how clever I could be. The owners and their animals were the real stars of *Animal Hospital* and so were the vets, nurses and inspectors who looked after them.

All of the things that I put on my wish-list when I sat down with Bruce in 1980 had come true. I was financially secure, in demand for concerts, and I'd made it back to mainstream television.

Not everything had come so easily. My relationship with Bindi had been difficult for a long time. We didn't seem to understand each other and there were a lot of arguments. The silences were even worse.

Bindi has always had periods of intense self-doubt. It is like a great black shadow hanging over her. She had never lost her anxiety that people were only interested in her because she was my daughter. Now this included her boyfriends. She couldn't be sure of their motives. Were they only interested in telling their mates they were going out with Rolf Harris's daughter?

We had always told Bindi to feel free to do what she wanted with her life. This had seemed easy when all she ever wanted to be was an artist. She had talked of going to art college ever since we could remember. I was really proud of her.

She left school at eighteen and went to Kingston Polytechnic. It was a nightmare journey to get there and back from Bray so she eventually transferred to Maidenhead Art School, which was nearby. But instead of finding her place in the world, she became still more lost. She even began to doubt her own obvious talents as an artist.

She sat us down one day and announced that she wanted to leave art school. It came as a huge shock.

'I've been a student all my life,' she said. 'Now I really need to get out into the world and do something other than go to school.'

'Are you talking about dropping out?'

'Yes. I just can't cope with art college. I don't like it.'

We tried to talk Bindi round, but her mind was made up.

On the day she left college she walked into Our Price and got herself a job earning £25 a week selling CDs and tapes. She was happy as a sandboy. From there she moved on to a job selling cosmetics.

She made new friends – not all of them good influences – and she had a few disastrous relationships. Throughout this time, we struggled to relate to each other. Only later did I realize that she was desperate to find a place where she fitted in. Not as my daughter, but as her own person.

She'd spent years trying to tell me this, but either she didn't have the words or I didn't listen or know what to say to her. When she was growing up she'd come and talk to me, but I'd be on the phone, or answering a letter, or filling out a visa application.

She'd be saying, 'Are you listening, Dad?'

'Yeah, yeah. Of course I am.'

But I wasn't listening hard enough. She didn't have my full attention.

When you are a parent you don't find out until years later the mistakes you make. For example, we didn't discover until Bindi had grown up that we used to scare her stupid at night when she was small with a nursery rhyme.

> *'To bed to bed,' said Sleepy Head,*
> *'Tarry a while,' said Slow,*
> *'Put on the pan,' said Greedy Nan,*
> *'We'll sup before we go.'*

Bindi thought Greedy Nan was a witch who was going to eat her.

A far more painful discovery came even later. Bindi came to me one day with a painting and asked me what I thought. I told her, 'That's marvellous,' and then started suggesting ways that she might make it even better.

She stopped me. 'Why is it that I can never do anything that you don't start to criticize? You always say, "That's good, but . . ." The "but" is always there.'

'I'm just trying to help.'

'No you're not. You can't help it. I can't do anything that pleases you for its own sake.'

She looked at me and I felt my heart crumble. From the mouth of one so young had come a very big truth. I am forever trying to impose my sense of perfection onto anything anybody else does. It doesn't matter if they're taking photographs, or driving, or playing a song, I am always giving advice.

I wish now that I had told Bindi things were perfect. I wish I had said, 'I love what you've done. It's wonderful,' and just left it at that.

Bindi spent five years doing different jobs; making a living and standing on her own two feet. During that time she gained the confidence she lacked. Then, at the age of twenty-three, she asked if she could try art school again. Alwen and I were over the moon.

She did her foundation year at Amersham Art College and discovered the things she loved and the things she could do. Unlike me at art school, she didn't walk away from difficult aspects like figure drawing and anatomy.

She had a marvellous tutor, Romeo di Girolamo, an Italian who saw her potential and encouraged her to develop it. He boosted her confidence and gave her the grounding to go on and do a degree in fine art at Bristol Polytechnic.

Her degree exhibition was brilliant. She painted in bright, vibrant colours on huge canvases. More importantly, she painted from the heart.

That is one of the great differences between us. I try to portray things that I see, or have seen – landscapes, or reflections on water, or a girl reading a book in the park. I can paint all sorts of aspects of the Australian bush from memory. Bindi's paintings come entirely from her imagination.

I have always been fascinated by the tonal aspects of things – the different degrees of dark and light. That's why I love foggy and misty days. Bindi isn't interested in this. Her paintings are all about bright colours and portraying an emotion. I often do paintings from start to finish in one sitting, whereas Bindi will take her time and change things if she sees something new developing.

Having spent years trying to impose my way of thinking on Bindi, I could finally see that we were totally different artists. She has no obligation or duty to do things my way.

Her self-doubt has never entirely gone away. After her degree show in 1991, she went through another bad patch and was desperately unhappy. I had no idea until she told me. Again, I could have kicked myself for not being more attentive to those dearest to me.

Bindi began doing therapy courses to restore her confidence. She moved down to Devon where we helped her buy an old farmhouse with space for a studio. I desperately wanted to get close to her, but I seemed to have left it too late.

In 1993 I did the pantomime *Jack and the Beanstalk* in Plymouth and arranged to stay with Bindi. I found out afterwards that she was absolutely petrified that I was coming. She didn't know what we'd talk about, or whether we'd be able to find anything to say to each other.

It was a six-week season and we spent a lot of time together. There was nowhere to sit in the kitchen, so I bought a couple of high stools for the breakfast bar and we ate lunch together each day before I went to the theatre. I think we both discovered that we could talk about anything and swap ideas like fellow artists. We weren't competing with each other, or trying to show off, or win praise.

It was lovely to be in such close contact with Bindi. Maybe the bridges could be rebuilt.

Chapter Twenty

THREE SCORE YEARS AND TEN

WHEN THE FIRST SERIES OF *ANIMAL HOSPITAL* FINISHED I JUST assumed that all the possibilities had been exhausted. In thirteen weeks we had seen and done everything there was to see and do about the work of the RSPCA. It had been fun while it lasted, but now it was over.

The BBC had other ideas. Having regularly drawn audiences of eleven million, the show couldn't just fade into the sunset. Another thirteen-week series was commissioned to begin in the autumn of 1995.

The second series saw similar numbers and even challenged the previously invincible position of *The Bill* on ITV. By then we all knew that we were part of something very special.

All manner of animals emerged as stars – Jaffa, a colourful parrot, Murphy the eight stone Irish wolfhound puppy, Maureen the iguana and Pepe the python who had to change her name to Poppie when her sex was revealed. But the best bit for me was getting to meet people and have real conversations that weren't scripted or contrived. Each time we set up the cameras we uncovered new stories and watched real-life dramas unfold.

The plight of Lottie, a young German shepherd, caused outrage. She was discovered when somebody noticed water trickling through the front door of a derelict building. The fire brigade broke down the door to turn off the water supply and found two dogs locked inside. One had starved to death and the other had eaten its remains. Every bit of flesh had been picked clean from the bones. It was an appalling sight that moved me to tears. Many people wept with me.

Because *Animal Hospital* was a factual programme, we tried to make it as informative as possible – teaching people how to look after their animals and keep them safe.

I saw one of my tasks as translating the complicated medical terminology often used by vets into simple layman's terms. If I couldn't understand what the experts were saying, I'd ask a question and get them to give me a simpler answer.

The mailbag each week was enormous, with many of the letters from children. This new generation didn't remember me from *Cartoon Club*, or any of my earlier TV shows. Some wanted to know about particular animals or to how to convince their mum and dad to let them have a pet. They were also fascinated about whether I had ever been bitten. The answer was yes.

In one show a white cat with a sunburnt nose was brought to the clinic. It had developed a cancerous growth on the tip of its nose. As the vet tried to get a closer look, he asked me to hold its front legs. The moggie didn't fancy this idea. The top incisor teeth went into my hand, hit the bone leading to my index finger, slid over the top and met up with the two lower incisors coming up from underneath.

I had always been taught that when you get bitten you should never jump or pull away, or the animal will hang on, or bite harder. This might be very good advice, but keeping totally still isn't easy when you're in agony. When the cat let go I whipped my hand away and began shaking it like crazy. The hand blew up like a balloon and I needed a course of antibiotics.

In another show a cat called Brandy needed a blood test, but let it be known right from the outset that he didn't want to co-operate. Two attempts were made to get a blanket over him, but Brandy was a ball of spitting and snarling fury. He looked like the cartoon version of the Tasmanian devil. The poor owner retreated to the far wall with bad scratches on her arm, muttering, 'Oh my gawd!' over and over.

I looked at the camera and pulled a face. This was definitely beyond the call of duty.

In the end I put on a falconry glove with metal chain mail on the back and tried to hold Brandy down. Even with two blankets and the glove on top of him, there was no way a nurse could get anywhere near his leg. Eventually we gave up and Brandy was declared the winner. He never did get his blood test.

David Grant had always warned me about getting overly familiar with the dogs that came in. I was always getting down to their level and making matching panting sounds or doing doggie sound effects.

'When an animal is sick, you don't know how they're going to react,' David said. 'Don't be fooled by their friendly looks.'

In particular he wanted me to keep my face away. He had a horror of a dog turning around and biting off my nose.

Normally I was pretty careful, but one particular day I got carried away with a lovely-looking boxer, who had come into the clinic with a mystery illness. He was eating properly but losing weight and the tests didn't seem to indicate why.

David had just gone out to get something and I was left in charge of this skinny-looking dog, which was standing on the examination table. I made my usual attempt to befriend him, by sniffing and panting.

'Rrrrrummph!' In the blink of an eye, the dog had spun his head round and latched onto me. His top teeth were hooked over my nose, forcing my glasses out of the way, and his bottom teeth were under my chin.

With most of my face in his mouth, his eyes were less than an inch from mine. He looked at me. I looked at him. His expression seemed to say, 'Look, I'm sick, OK. Just leave me alone.'

I gave him a look that said, 'OK.'

He let go. I stood up, white as a sheet, as David came back into the room.

'What's wrong?' he said.

I looked at the cameramen. 'Did you get that?'

'Get what?'

I couldn't believe it. There hadn't been a camera on me. One of the close-up cameras had been on the door waiting for David to re-enter and the other on the owner. The wide shot camera had the boxer's body obscuring what happened. What a shame. It would have been a good warning lesson for people about what not to do around a sick dog.

With each new series we tried to come up with fresh ideas and angles. The reporters and vets changed, as did the locations. We did a series at a private veterinary establishment in Aylesbury, another back at the Harmsworth, and then moved to the Putney Animal Hospital in south London.

The decision to circulate the show took some of the pressure off the various hospitals. Our presence could be disruptive and sometimes slow down the treatment of animals. At least at a place like Putney they had three clinics and we could take over one without causing too much commotion.

Aside from changing locations, we tried to feature new segments, such as visiting equine hospitals and aviaries, and reporting on the lambing and calving on local farms. We also drew a lot of stories from the work of the RSPCA field officers and ambulance drivers, who rescued animals that had been neglected or become trapped.

Perhaps the greatest compliment *Animal Hospital* received was to be syndicated around the world and trigger a rash of copy-cat shows about animal rescues, celebrity pets and trainee vets.

Despite the long days of filming and promotional work for *Animal*

Hospital, I still managed to do panto up until 1996 – my sixteenth year of dressing up and treading the boards. In that time I worked with some wonderful people like Bill Owen, June Whitfield, Bonnie Langford, Sylvester McCoy and Lesley Joseph.

The last panto I did was at the New Victoria Theatre in Woking. *Animal Hospital* had just finished filming and I missed the first week of rehearsals. We were doing *Cinderella* and I was playing Baron Hardup. The cast included Gary Wilmot as Buttons, Robin Cousins as Dandini, and Judy Cornwell as the Fairy Godmother.

I went straight into the second week of rehearsals, when the rest of the cast knew all the words and were virtually on their final run-through. Clutching a script in one hand and getting measured for costumes during the breaks, I tried to catch up.

On the opening day we were due to do three full shows – a rehearsal for timing in the morning, a matinee for disadvantaged children and then the official opening for the public and critics at eight in the evening.

By the time I got to the last show I was almost dead on my feet. Exhausted and dizzy, I felt myself weaving about on the stage during the first few numbers. I tried to sit down when I was back-stage but that didn't help.

When it came time to do 'Two Little Boys' I could feel myself swaying. I had to stand with my legs wide apart to stop myself from toppling over. At the same time, I kept gasping for air as though running out of breath. I had visions of doing a Tommy Cooper and keeling over. Tommy had suffered a heart attack and died during a televised performance. He'd collapsed into the curtain and the audience thought it was part of the act.

Somehow I managed to hold on and get through the show. I drove myself home and crawled into bed. Alwen was already asleep.

In the morning I told her what had happened. I was still feeling awful.

'You're not going in,' she said.

'I have to. I'm one of the stars.'

'And what if a star collapses on stage and dies? How much good is that going to do them? Call them now. Tell them you can't do it.'

I had rarely seen Alwen so adamant about anything. She usually watched me wear myself out and said nothing. Now she looked genuinely frightened.

I rang Jan Kennedy at the office and she contacted Paul Elliott, the producer of the show. To his undying credit, Paul told Jan, 'No play is worth an artist's life. Tell Rolf to take as much time off as he needs. We'll work around him somehow.' He sent me a huge bouquet of flowers with the same message.

That evening they introduced a new scene into *Cinderella*. A telegram arrived from Baron Hardup in Australia. Gary Wilmot, as Buttons, read it aloud to the audience. The Baron had met a wonderful woman and was thinking he might marry her. In the meantime, her two lovely daughters were coming to England and he hoped they would be entertained in his absence. At that moment the ugly sisters came on stage.

I spent the next twelve days recuperating at home. Max, our family doctor, ran lots of tests. I knew the answer already. I was exhausted. *Animal Hospital* had been a punishing thirteen-week shoot, with other bits and pieces fitted into my days off. All my talk of slowing down and smelling the roses had come to nothing.

Once I felt rested, I went back into *Cinderella*. This time, they let me sit out the fast and furious dance routine at the beginning of the show. I gave what could be classed as a senior citizen's performance rather than me trying to pretend I was a teenager.

At the end of that season I retired from pantomime. I couldn't cope with six days a week, two shows a day and three on Saturdays. It was a sad old day, because I had rarely enjoyed anything more. I also cut back on my concert commitments, although I still managed the occasional one-off gig with the band at universities or festivals. I had a dodgy knee but I could leave my walking stick at the side of the stage and let Dr Adrenalin do the rest.

I seemed to be accepted everywhere I went – regardless of the age of the audience. And I made a point of doing things that had a local flavour. For instance at Newcastle University I played a few Geordie songs that I'd learned before most of the audience was born. They began chanting 'Rolf 's a Geordie. Rolf 's a Geordie.'

In Scotland I sang 'Flower of Scotland', in Wales I sang 'Calon Lan' and the Welsh National Anthem; and in Ireland I sang 'Mountains of Mourne' and 'The Wild Rover'. Some of these I had learned as a kid and others I collected over the years. Audiences were often amazed that I knew more of the words than they did.

The University of Warwick wrote and asked if they could name their student union bar after me. Apparently, it had previously been dedicated to a former student turned political activist. Unfortunately, she had fallen out of favour for some of her more extreme activities.

The students held a meeting and 95 per cent voted to rename the bar the Rolf Harris Room. The student union executive tried to stop the move but the students threatened to vote them out of office unless they agreed.

I went up to Warwick for the opening and did a big painting on the wall. Then I signed autographs for two and a half hours.

I was asked back to the Glastonbury rock festival twice. By then the band had been boosted by the presence of Shining Bear, a brilliant didgeridoo player who would do things with a didge that were beyond me. Alwen came to both of these shows and had a great time. She loved all my new stuff and the amazing atmosphere generated by such an enormous crowd.

I was still a bit of an odd choice for a rock festival, but I did my set to the best of my ability and we got a fantastic reaction from the thousands who jammed in to see us.

After my last show at Glastonbury, a long queue of people formed to get autographs. I signed them on publicity photographs, personalizing each one.

A chap reached the front of the queue.

'Who to?' I asked, without looking up.

'Willie Nelson,' said an American accent.

'Oh yeah!' I laughed, looking up with a mixture of slight sarcasm and good humour. I wrote 'To W. N. from Rolf' on the photo. As I watched him leave, I thought, 'Fancy someone going to all that trouble to dress up like Willie Nelson, with the trademark hat and beard, the accent and everything. Aren't people strange?'

Later that day, my musical director Bernard O'Neill came up to me and said, 'Wasn't it great that Willie Nelson took the time to come and see your set and stand in line for your autograph?'

I died inside. I still go hot and cold just thinking about it. I hadn't even known he was headlining at Glastonbury.

Afterwards, I got in touch with Willie's manager in New York and sent a letter and fax apologizing for my rudeness. Although I never heard back from Willie, I hope he got my message.

My comeback was now so complete that newspapers had labelled me 'Rock's Renaissance Man'. How ironic. I'd missed rock 'n' roll the first time round and had somehow come back for a second bite at the cherry.

I had to laugh at some of the things that were written about me. In a survey asking people to name a famous artist, I came out on top with 38 per cent of the vote, ahead of Van Gogh, Constable and Turner. When newspapers rang me for a comment, I said, 'It's only because Rembrandt and these other blokes didn't have their own TV shows where they painted a picture from start to finish each week.'

In the midst of this surge in popularity, I was trying to master a new instrument – the bagpipes. I'd been invited to lead a parade of 3,000 pipers and drummers from all over the world into the city of Edinburgh for the Festival. The parade was to raise money for Marie Curie Cancer Care.

Pipe Major Jim Banks had been giving me lessons twice a week. We'd walk up and down the garden in Bray, with me trying to make all these sounds, but mainly scaring the swans. I had to learn four tunes and I was desperate to look and sound like the real McCoy.

A week before the parade, word came through that the organizers had cut the number of tunes to two. What a relief! It halved my workload. Even so, I was worried sick about messing up on the big day.

Admitting defeat, I got Jim Banks to block off my pipes with corks before the march on the big day, so that no air would go through. They often do this with novice pipers on their first parade.

More than 300,000 people lined Princes Street in Edinburgh to see the parade in August 1995. The massed pipes sounded amazing as we marched down the long mile. I did all the right finger movements and puffed out my cheeks. I was fine until they started playing the two tunes they'd told me weren't going to be included. The television cameras were on me and I had to pretend that I knew what I was doing.

We reached the end of Princes Street and the cameras were all around me. I noticed Michael Aspel walking towards me.

'What are you doing up here?'

'Well, Rolf Harris, star of stage, screen and radio, this is your life.'

'What?' I should have added, 'Again?'

They whisked me off to the airport and flew me to London. Family and friends were waiting in the studio.

Counting my appearance in the Australian version of the show, it was my third *This Is Your Life*. It just goes to show that if you live long enough history *does* repeat itself.

Just as a postscript, five years later I was surprised all over again when Channel 9 in Australia did another *This Is Your Life*. That made it *four*! Surely it has to be the last.

Michael Parkinson is a neighbour of mine in Bray. We've known each other for years. I've always admired his skill as an interviewer – particularly when I think back to my efforts with the Beatles.

Our local cricket club, Maidenhead and Bray, holds a charity game every year against a showbiz XI. I turn up and sign autographs or draw cartoons. Parky wields the willow, while I wield a pen.

For my seventieth birthday in 2000, Alwen arranged to take me down to the club for a quiet dinner with a couple of friends. I thought it was a pretty strange venue, since they normally didn't do meals. Alwen convinced me otherwise.

When we arrived there were cars parked everywhere. A guy on the gate said, 'I'm sorry, the car park is full. Oh, it's you, Mr Harris. Go straight ahead and park near the clubhouse.'

'Strange?' I thought.

A huge marquee had been erected and lights were hanging from the surrounding trees. As we stepped out of the car I heard someone start singing 'Happy Birthday'.

'Shhhhhhhh,' someone else whispered.

There were more voices. 'No. No, it's too early.'

'He's here! He's here!'

'Be quiet.'

Hello, hello, I thought. I glanced at Alwen who looked very sheepish.

As I walked through the entrance a cheer went up. There must have been 200 people singing 'Happy Birthday'. I blinked into the spotlight and then started recognizing faces . . . Alex Haussmann and his wife, Kate Bush, Phil Cool, Tony Hart, Gloria Hunniford, Esther Rantzen, Paul Elliott, Sir George Martin and all the BBC people I had worked with down the years, including the guys and girls from *Animal Hospital*.

Lonnie Donegan and his band turned up to do the cabaret. They were marvellous!

I was called up on stage during the speeches and some of my band joined me as we did 'Kangaroo'. Barry Booth, still a very dear friend, slipped behind the piano and accompanied me for old times' sake.

The marquee had been transformed into an African landscape

with huge model animals, and the ceiling glittered with thousands of stars. The Noah's Ark birthday cake had seventy candles.

There were some lovely speeches which made me feel very humble and embarrassed. Lorraine Heggessey had even written a poem about me which she called 'Ode to Rolf Harris on the Occasion of his 70th Birthday'.

> *When I was a child he filled me with awe,*
> *I'd turn on the telly just to see him draw.*
> *He had a big brush and a great hairy beard,*
> *With his glasses and his accent he seemed a little weird.*
> *'Can you guess what it is yet?' he'd ask like a friend,*
> *But I never could, until the very end.*
> *He held me spellbound with every stroke,*
> *He made it look easy, this smiling Aussie bloke.*
>
> *But he wasn't just an artist, he was a singer, too,*
> *And he played a funny pipe called the didgeridoo.*
> *He tied down kangaroos and he made the sun arise.*
> *With two little boys he brought tears to my eyes.*
> *He did a funny walk with an extra leg,*
> *Everybody in Britain knows Jake the Peg!*
> *He held us spellbound with every note,*
> *He made it look easy, this crooning Aussie bloke.*

There were verses about *Animal Hospital* and the risk Lorraine took in choosing me as the presenter. Alan Yentob, the BBC controller, had told her afterwards that if she'd been wrong she would have lost her job.

The poem ended:

> *And the rest is history, as they say.*
> *The show's going strong to this very day.*
> *It became an overnight ratings sensation,*
> *And Rolf was the talk of this pet-loving nation.*

Every kind of beast came through the surgery door,
Rolf got bitten and scratched but came back for more.
Our rivals tried to copy, but it was never the same,
'Cos they didn't have that man with a four-letter name.
He still holds me spellbound with every animal he strokes,
He makes it look so easy, this amazing Aussie bloke.

The party didn't finish until 3 a.m. Not surprisingly, I felt every one of my seventy years the next day.

I had a lot of phone calls from newspapers and magazines with every journalist wanting to know if I was contemplating retirement.

'It's such a dreadful word,' I said. 'When I think of the word retiring, I think of going to bed, or to sleep, or dying. I can't do that. There's still too much to do. I have programmes to make, books to write, paintings to finish and songs to record. I can't imagine ever retiring.'

My career has been amazing. Every time one door closes another opens. Every successful record I had was a complete U-turn from the last.

Everything that has happened to me has seemed to conspire to bring these things into reach. I have no regrets about choosing a show business career. If I'd become a society portrait painter, as I planned, I don't think I could have handled all the sucking up to people required to get commissions.

I sometimes wonder what I might have achieved if I had concentrated on one particular discipline rather than doing lots of different things. But I think maybe I was meant to be a jack of all trades. Perhaps that's why I survived all those near misses. I was supposed to finish up here, showing people compassion and spreading a bit of happiness and love.

The last ten years have been a wonderful time for me. It isn't just because of *Animal Hospital* or the live concerts. It's about family. Alwen has started doing her art again after a break of twenty-five years.

Last year she won an art prize. It was only worth £500, but she was thrilled to bits. This might seem unimportant to most people, but you have to remember that this had been Alwen's dream until she sacrificed her career for mine.

I am so lucky to have found someone like her. I have often wondered how she has put up with me for all these years – spending months on her own while I was touring and then having me work long hours when I was home.

I have never been a perfect husband. I'm a perfectionist and a stick in the mud and I'm always telling people how to do things. In short I'm a real pain in the neck, which is probably why it has taken me so long to write my autobiography. I discovered that I wasn't the charming guy I originally thought I was.

Entertaining is like a drug – the greatest drug in the world. The public adulation, the applause . . . it's hard to give up these things if you're born to be a show-off. Trying to please everyone all the time can also be addictive. I hate the thought of hurting anyone's feelings by not having time for them. Yet the truth is that I can't possibly give everybody my undivided attention. Alwen and Bindi have to come first. It has only been in the last five years that I have realized this. Late, but better than never.

I became a grandfather in 1996. Bindi had a little boy, Marlon, who has drawn us closer together. We adore him. Whenever he sees me, his arms immediately reach up. He loves me unconditionally and I keep marvelling at how such a tiny new person can accept me so completely.

Bindi knows exactly who she is now. She has become a successful artist and no longer feels as though she is living in my shadow. Her first exhibition in 1995 at the Candid Gallery in London was a stunning success. Sadly, she once said that her childhood had taught her not to become too dependent on a man. She had seen me disappear for months at a time. I had no idea my absences had marked her so dreadfully. I hope she finds someone she can share her life with.

Bindi has started teaching me things about painting that I

dismissed as unimportant at art college because I couldn't do them very well. I'm also giving Marlon some of the time that I couldn't give his mother.

When I started this book, I didn't really know what I was going to say. I thought I'd just tell my story and let other people draw conclusions. I thought it might strike a chord. We all chase dreams and wonder, 'What if it happened to us?'

When I look at the walls around me – at the paintings, photographs and awards collected over a lifetime – I still see a young man, with dark curly hair, lugging an accordion case off the train at Waterloo Station. He is full of mad, youthful optimism and self-belief. But I'll tell you the strangest thing. I still feel exactly the same. I have greyish hair and a white beard, and now and again I use a walking stick because of my dodgy knees, but given half a chance, I'd do it all over again tomorrow.

Did I hear some of you groaning?

20 JANUARY 2001
BASSENDEAN, WESTERN
AUSTRALIA

T HE BOY FROM BASSENDEAN HAS COME HOME.
According to the radio it's 34°C and it's only eight thirty in
the morning. I remember days like this. The sealed roads would
get so hot they'd start to melt and bubble. As a kid I used to go out
and pop the bubbles with my bare toes. You had to be quick or a
molten blob of tar would stick to your skin.

Back then I had grazes on my knees and a sunburnt nose and I
didn't know the colour of my feet until it rained and I ran through
the wet grass. It seems like only yesterday.

This year is the centenary of Australian Federation – a hundred
years since we became a nation. Coincidentally, it also just happens
to be a hundred years since Bassendean was founded. There are
centenary celebrations up and down the country in towns and
suburbs. The big event in Bassendean is a free open-air concert.
'Rolf is coming home' is how they've labelled it. I'm very
flattered.

The taxi has air-conditioning, but I can still feel the heat outside. We're on Guildford Road, just leaving Bayswater and running parallel to the railway line. It's a straight run down the 'mad mile' to Bassendean. There is a new suburb called Ashfield on the right. When I was growing up it was just scrub and bike tracks. Now there are sprinklers revolving on lawns and Hill's clothes hoists spinning in the breeze.

About three-quarters of the way along the mad mile, if you turn right and head towards the river, you'll see where I grew up, although it doesn't look the same. The house has gone and the block has been subdivided.

One of the plots was bought by a farmer who had come down from the bush. He brought in a bulldozer and flattened every living thing – the famous fig tree and the multitude of trees that grew almonds, grapefruit, oranges, lemons and pomegranates. Then he cut down all the gums along the riverbank and covered the whole block with about six inches of sand. Having done all this, he decided that he didn't think he wanted to build after all. He destroyed the wonderful oasis that Mum and Dad had made and then cleared off. I cried when I saw what he had done.

A young bloke called Bob Manning now owns that half of the block. He's a friend and I remember teaching him to swim from our jetty. He built a nice modern place taking up most of the land. Even so, I can still visualize all the trees and where they used to be.

Harry Butler told me a few years ago that he wished I'd told him we were selling the old place. 'I'd have bought both blocks,' he said. 'I loved that place.' I could have kicked myself for not asking him.

Bassendean hasn't changed that much. It's still a bit of a backwater, although it's no longer an outer suburb. Perth has grown so big that seven miles is no distance at all. The roads are all paved and guttered; the trams are in transport museums; and the night carts are no more.

Bassendean Primary is still there. They were going to knock it down a few years ago and send the kids up the road to Ashfield.

There was a big public outcry and the Education Department changed its mind.

The picture theatre has gone. That's where the local council has its offices now. I don't know about the convent and the nuns. All the roads I used to ride my bike along, usually with no hands, are now covered in blue metal.

The Point Reserve is still a lovely oasis on hot days, with families picnicking in the shade. The twin jetties jut out into the river, fifty-five yards apart, but the Bassendean Swimming Club has moved on. Nowadays the swimming pools are in-ground and chlorinated.

The ABC has arranged to broadcast my concert. The producer wants to film an introduction for the show as I wander through my old haunts. The problem is that I can't walk more than twenty feet without people stopping and shaking my hand. 'G'day, Rolf. Welcome home,' they call out. I wave back and give a thumbs up. It's nice to feel so welcome.

Of all the criticisms that have been levelled at me – and I've been lucky to have had so few – the one that hurts the most is being called a 'professional Australian'. I'd like to think this referred to my professional attitude, but I know the truth. They're accusing me of cashing in, of milking my Australian-ness. 'You're an expat,' they say, using the term to whip me.

It's true. I don't live in Australia. England is my home. Britain is where I became a professional entertainer. Rightly or wrongly, I know how things work there. But why should it matter where I live? It didn't stop me getting misty-eyed over the Olympic Games in Sydney, or cheering Australia to victory in the Rugby World Cup in Cardiff. I sing songs about Australia, play the didgeridoo, tell Australian stories and paint bush scenes from memory.

I count myself very lucky to have discovered my real identity at the age of thirty. That's when I had the hit with 'Kangaroo' and realized that I didn't have to pretend to be someone else. I could *be* Australian and speak like an Australian and still be successful.

I wish more people in show business would realize that they don't have to go through this crisis of pretending to be someone else. It's awful having to constantly think, 'What would the person I am pretending to be do in this situation?'

I feel at ease living in the UK. Maybe because I'm everyone's favourite Aussie. Over the years I've noticed a change in attitude towards Australians. I think the British have come to realize that we're not all beer-drinking, carousing cricket fans, or bronzed surf lifesavers. The nation has grown up and Australians have made their mark in every field. We showed the world during the Olympics that we have come of age.

I have to remind myself sometimes that Bindi doesn't share my background. Although we've spent long periods in Australia, she has grown up and been educated in Britain. When she was about sixteen years old, we were on a holiday near Harvey in Western Australia. We all went for a bush walk, but after a few miles Bindi began to panic because she thought we were lost. Every tree looked the same.

'We'll never find our way back.'

'Yes we will. We came all the way down the hill from the road. At the bottom we turned left and followed this creek along. All we have to do is turn left, walk for about a mile and we'll cut across the road we came in on.'

'No, we're lost. We'll be stuck out here. We'll die.' She started crying.

Up until then I had just assumed Bindi felt at ease in the bush, as I did. In reality she found it hostile and frightening. It made me quite sad to realize that she would never have the same affinity with Australia as I do.

Since Mum died, I haven't been back to Perth very often. The local university, which incorporates my old teachers' college, gave me an honorary doctorate last year, which was wonderful. I still have a lot of friends in the west. Hazel lives not far from my old home, on the other side of the river; and Harry Butler has a house near Fremantle and a holiday home in Busselton, down past Bunbury.

I gave up touring two years ago. It had become a terrible slog – up early, driving hundreds of miles, doing Bundaberg one night, Tweed Heads the next, then flying to Sydney to do a show the night after. Crazy! I hated having to rehearse with new musicians for each State we went to. It meant having four guys around me who couldn't relax and have fun. They didn't know the material well enough and had their heads down reading music. I also began to wonder if I was still relevant any more in Australia. I'd rarely been off TV screens in Britain, but my profile in Australia had almost disappeared. So much so that people would hear my name and say, 'Is he still around?' or 'Whatever happened to him?'

Bruce had been good at feeding information to the media but unless you're on television regularly, people start to forget. That's why I'm a bit worried about the homecoming concert. I've been doing radio interviews all over the place, rushing from one studio to the next. Wouldn't it be terrible if nobody turned up?

The ABC film crew is still getting material for the opening sequence. I suggest the Bassendean pub. It's a wonderful old building, with sixteen foot high ceilings and a polished wooden staircase.

'They've got a Rolf Harris bar,' I say, 'and there's a really nice painting that I did for them on the wall. It shows our old boat down by the river.'

We all troop inside.

'Where's the painting I did of the river?' I ask.

The girl behind the bar shrugs. 'I don't know.'

'It was in the Rolf Harris bar.'

'Yeah, there used to be a bar called that.'

'Any idea what happened to the painting?'

'Well, it might be upstairs in the manager's office. I'll get the key.' She went looking.

Just then an old bloke clears his throat at the end of the bar. 'I remember that painting,' he says, with a cigarette dangling from the corner of his mouth. 'One of the chefs got the sack a few years back and he must of took it with him. They didn't notice it'd gone for a couple of days.'

'He stole it?'

'Yeah, I s'pose he did. Probably reckoned 'e was owed back wages.'

'But that's stealing.'

He shrugs. 'Yeah, I s'pose it is.'

Apparently, nobody had cared enough to call the police. It was all very casual.

I try not to let it bother me, but I know it's just another example of my decreasing profile in Australia. That's why I'm worried about tonight's concert.

We did two rehearsals yesterday, three hours in the morning and another session in the afternoon. The West Australian Youth Jazz Orchestra (WAYJO) is supporting me. There's also a five-piece band that Clive Lendich, my NSW musical director, has pulled together.

The orchestra is made up of kids in their teens and early twenties. Most of them vaguely know some of my songs. It's a really nice feeling to catch them smiling during rehearsals and to work with people who haven't been exposed to my routines before.

'Five minutes, Rolf.' The knock on the door echoes through the old changing rooms.

Bassendean Oval is home to the Swan Districts Football Club. They were my local Aussie Rules side when I was growing up. I didn't go and watch them play, I was more interested in swimming, but I supported them just like every other kid in the neighbourhood.

I remember going to a dance at the football club when I was about eighteen. I saw a bunch of kids from the swimming club, drinking bottles of beer around the back of the lavatories. They were only fifteen or so.

'What are you *doing*?' I asked in disbelief.

They said, 'We got to get drunk to give us the courage to ask these girls to dance.'

What a terrible commentary on life, I thought at the time. Then again, I knew what it was like to be nervous around girls.

The ABC producer pokes his head round the door and wishes me luck. I give him a big smile, trying to look relaxed. At the same time, I can hear the orchestra tuning up outside. The youngsters must be nervous and excited. It's a big night for all of us.

OK, it's showtime! I say a little prayer and take one last glance at the running order for the songs. Then it's out the door, along the corridor, past the banks of speaker boxes and scaffolding. Coloured lights are slung from the gantry above the stage and cables snake across the grass below. I have to make my way in darkness across the seats of the grandstand, which is now the backdrop of the stage. People are wishing me luck. The MC has started his introduction.

'Ladies and gentlemen, he's travelled a long way to be here. The boy from Bassendean has come home. Will you give him a huge welcome . . . Here he is . . . our very own . . . ROLF HARRIS!'

The cheer lifts me six inches off the stage and I float there all night. Bassendean Oval has never seen a crowd like it. More than 22,000 people have turned up. The place is so packed that police round the barriers debate whether to close the gates to stop anyone else coming in. In the end Bassendean Council decides to keep the gates open a little longer.

People of all ages have come to see us. Hundreds of children sit at the front, below the stage. I can see their faces shining up at me. They've never heard my songs before and they don't know me, but that doesn't matter. Mum and Dad have brought them along, or Grandma and Grandpa.

Nothing about the show has split-second timing or flashy costumes or a star who burns so brightly that no one in the crowd can touch him. Instead they see a lucky amateur, good old Rolf, who used to live down the road there, by the river.

I start off by giving them a heartfelt thank you for passing the hat round all those years ago and sending me to Melbourne for the swimming championships. Then for two and a half hours I sing all my old favourites and the new stuff too. They don't want me to go and I don't want to disappoint them. So I start another song and I get to the chorus and shout, 'All together now!'

We'll just have to keep on singing . . .

INDEX

NOTE: this index is arranged in alphabetical order except for the entries under the author's name, which are in chronological order.